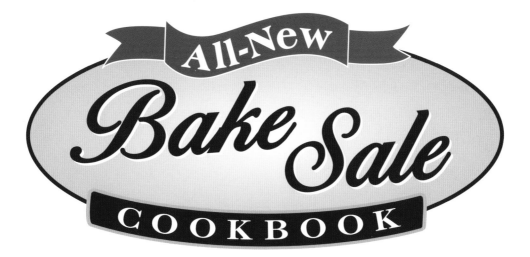

All-New Bake Sale COOKBOOK

Publications International, Ltd.

Favorite Brand Name Recipes at www.fbnr.com

Pictured on the front cover *(clockwise from top right):* Chocolate Banana Walnut Drops *(page 56)*, Pinwheel Cookies *(page 38)*, Peanut Butter Surprise *(page 176)*, Banana Split Cupcakes *(page 178)*, Philadelphia® Cheesecake Brownies *(page 136)*, Peanutty Cranberry Bars *(page 74)* and Wellesley Fudge Cake *(page 330)*.

Pictured on the back cover *(left to right):* Oreo® Cheesecake *(page 254)* and Cranberry Orange Ring *(page 236)*.

Microwave Cooking: Microwave ovens vary in wattage. Use the cooking times as guidelines and check for doneness before adding more time.

Preparation/Cooking Times: Preparation times are based on the approximate amount of time required to assemble the recipe before cooking, baking, chilling or serving. These times include preparation steps such as measuring, chopping and mixing. The fact that some preparations and cooking can be done simultaneously is taken into account. Preparation of optional ingredients and serving suggestions is not included.

Contents

Bake Sale Basics

There's no doubt about it—bake sales are an American icon. They're not about sophistication or finesse, just simple homemade goodness and tables heaped with every kind of cookie, brownie, pie, cake and muffin imaginable. The best part? Bake sales are happy events: Friends and neighbors baking and sharing their favorite treats, coming together for a good cause.

Bake Sale Savvy

• Bring plenty of price stickers or tags and marking pens.

• Make the math easy (for adding and making change): Price baked goods in increments of 25 cents.

• Increase the bottom line: Offer large bags or containers to encourage customers to buy several items. Auction off whole desserts to raise more money.

• People like to help a worthy cause—be sure the name of your organization is prominently displayed, and let customers know how the proceeds will be used.

• Draw attention to the merchandise. Stack brownies and bar cookies high on colorful platters, pile muffins into baskets lined with bright-colored napkins, and use decorative boxes or tins to display cookies.

• For single slices of pies and cakes, use plastic deli containers, available at restaurant supply and many party goods stores.

• Include storage directions for any perishable items that should be held in the refrigerator.

• Bake and sell your treats in disposable pans, so you don't have to worry about finding or cleaning your pans after the sale.

Dress to Impress

• Wrap stacks of cookies in cellophane or clear bags and tie with ribbon or raffia.

• Cut bar cookies to fit into decorative cupcake liners—they will look beautiful and be easier to handle.

• Keep a supply of decorator frosting and candies on hand to offer personalized cookies during the bake sale.

• Cut bar cookies into triangles and diamonds for variety.

• Make cookies stand out by dipping them partially or completely in chocolate. Simply dip cookies in melted chocolate (milk, dark, white or some of each) and place them on waxed paper until the chocolate has set.

• For any baked goods that are sold whole, such as breads, cakes or pies, use colored plastic wrap, cellophane, ribbons and raffia to package them attractively.

Advance Planning

Since bake sales don't always happen when you have time to bake, it's a good idea to plan ahead. Many items can be baked and frozen; some unbaked doughs can also be frozen to be baked up fresh in a few minutes. Not all items freeze well, however, so choose carefully before baking.

• In general, crisp cookies freeze better than soft, moist cookies. Rich, buttery bar cookies are an exception since they freeze extremely well.

• Meringue-based cookies do not freeze well, and chocolate-dipped cookies will discolor if frozen.

• Cakes with whipped cream frostings or cream fillings should be stored in the refrigerator.

• Cakes with fruit or custard fillings do not freeze well, as they become soggy when thawed.

• Custard, cream and meringue-topped pies should be stored in the refrigerator; they do not freeze well.

• Quick breads should be wrapped well in plastic wrap and stored at room temperature for up to one week, or wrapped in heavy-duty foil and frozen for up to three months.

• Muffins should be stored in a sealed plastic food storage bag for up to three days, or wrapped in heavy-duty foil and frozen for up to one month.

Great American Cookies

Easy Lemon Pudding Cookies

Prep Time: 10 minutes
Bake Time: 10 minutes

> 1 cup BISQUICK® Original Baking Mix
> 1 package (4-serving size) JELL-O® Lemon Flavor Instant Pudding
>   & Pie Filling
> ½ teaspoon ground ginger (optional)
> 1 egg, lightly beaten
> ¼ cup vegetable oil
>   Sugar
> 3 squares BAKER'S® Premium White Baking Chocolate, melted

HEAT oven to 350°F.

STIR baking mix, pudding mix and ginger in medium bowl. Mix in egg and oil until well blended. (Mixture will be stiff.) With hands, roll cookie dough into 1-inch diameter balls. Place balls 2 inches apart on lightly greased cookie sheets. Dip flat-bottom glass into sugar. Press glass onto each dough ball and flatten into ¼-inch-thick cookie.

BAKE 10 minutes or until edges are golden brown. Immediately remove from cookie sheets. Cool on wire racks. Drizzle cookies with melted white chocolate.

Makes about 20 cookies

How To Melt Chocolate: Microwave 3 squares BAKER'S® Premium White Baking Chocolate in heavy zipper-style plastic sandwich bag on HIGH 1 to 1½ minutes or until chocolate is almost melted. Gently knead bag until chocolate is completely melted. Fold down top of bag; snip tiny piece off 1 corner from bottom. Holding top of bag tightly, drizzle chocolate through opening across tops of cookies.

Easy Lemon Pudding Cookies

Spicy Ginger Molasses Cookies

2 cups all-purpose flour
1½ teaspoons ground ginger
1 teaspoon baking soda
½ teaspoon ground cloves
¼ teaspoon salt
¾ cup butter, softened
1 cup sugar
¼ cup molasses
1 egg
   Additional sugar
½ cup yogurt-covered raisins

1. Preheat oven to 375°F.

2. Combine flour, ginger, baking soda, cloves and salt in small bowl; set aside.

3. Beat butter and 1 cup sugar in large bowl of electric mixer at medium speed until light and fluffy. Add molasses and egg; beat until well blended. Gradually beat in flour mixture on low speed just until blended.

4. Drop dough by level ¼ cupfuls onto parchment-lined cookie sheets, spacing 3 inches apart. Flatten each ball of dough until 2 inches in diameter with bottom of glass that has been dipped in additional sugar. Press 7 to 8 yogurt-covered raisins into dough of each cookie.

5. Bake 11 to 12 minutes or until cookies are set. Cool cookies 2 minutes on cookie sheets; slide parchment paper and cookies onto countertop. Cool completely.

Makes about 1 dozen (4-inch) cookies

Hermits

¾ Butter Flavor CRISCO® Stick or ¾ cup
   Butter Flavor CRISCO® all-vegetable
   shortening
1½ cups firmly packed brown sugar
2 tablespoons milk
3 eggs
2½ cups all-purpose flour
1 teaspoon salt
1 teaspoon cinnamon
¾ teaspoon baking soda
¼ teaspoon nutmeg
⅛ teaspoon ground cloves
1 cup raisins
¾ cup chopped walnuts
   Powdered sugar

1. Heat oven to 400°F. Place sheets of foil on countertop for cooling cookies.

2. Combine ¾ cup shortening, sugar and milk in large bowl. Beat at medium speed of electric mixer until well blended. Add eggs one at a time. Beat well after each addition.

3. Combine flour, salt, cinnamon, baking soda, nutmeg and cloves. Mix into creamed mixture at low speed just until blended. Stir in raisins and nuts.

4. Drop level tablespoonfuls of dough 2 inches apart onto ungreased baking sheet.

5. Bake at 400°F for 7 to 8 minutes, or until set. *Do not overbake.* Remove cookies to foil to cool completely. Sift powdered sugar over cooled cookies.

Makes about 5 dozen cookies

Spicy Ginger Molasses Cookies

Chocolate Cherry Treats

½ cup (1 stick) butter, softened
¾ cup firmly packed light brown sugar
¼ cup granulated sugar
½ cup sour cream
1 large egg
1 tablespoon maraschino cherry juice
1 teaspoon vanilla extract
2 cups all-purpose flour
½ teaspoon baking soda
¼ teaspoon salt
1¼ cups "M&M's"® Milk Chocolate Mini
   Baking Bits
½ cup chopped walnuts
⅓ cup well-drained chopped maraschino
   cherries

Preheat oven to 350°F. In large bowl cream butter and sugars until light and fluffy; beat in sour cream, egg, maraschino cherry juice and vanilla. In medium bowl combine flour, baking soda and salt; add to creamed mixture. Stir in "M&M's"® Milk Chocolate Mini Baking Bits, walnuts and maraschino cherries. Drop by heaping tablespoonfuls about 2 inches apart onto ungreased cookie sheets. Bake about 15 minutes. Cool 1 minute on cookie sheets; cool completely on wire racks. Store in tightly covered container.   *Makes 3 dozen cookies*

Chocolate Oatmeal Raisin Cookies

1⅓ cups sugar
1 Butter Flavor CRISCO® Stick or 1 cup
   Butter Flavor CRISCO® all-vegetable
   shortening plus additional for greasing
2 eggs
2 cups all-purpose flour
⅓ cup cocoa
1 teaspoon baking soda
1 teaspoon salt
1 teaspoon ground cinnamon
½ cup milk
2 cups oats (quick, uncooked)
1 cup raisins
1 cup chopped pecans or walnuts

1. Heat oven to 350°F. Grease baking sheet with shortening. Place sheets of foil on countertop for cooling cookies.

2. Combine sugar and 1 cup shortening in large bowl. Beat at medium speed of electric mixer until well blended. Beat in eggs.

3. Combine flour, cocoa, baking soda, salt and cinnamon. Add alternately with milk to creamed mixture at low speed, beating well after each addition. Stir in oats, raisins and nuts with spoon. Drop by teaspoonfuls 2 inches apart onto greased baking sheet.

4. Bake at 350°F for 10 to 12 minutes. *Do not overbake.* Cool 2 minutes on baking sheet. Remove cookies to foil to cool completely.
                    Makes about 5 dozen cookies

Chocolate Cherry Treats

Nutty Footballs

1 cup butter, softened
½ cup sugar
1 egg
½ teaspoon vanilla
2 cups all-purpose flour
¼ cup unsweetened cocoa powder
1 cup finely chopped almonds
  Colored icings (optional)
  White icing

1. Beat butter and sugar in large bowl until creamy. Add egg and vanilla; mix until well blended. Stir together flour and cocoa; gradually add to butter mixture, beating until well blended. Add almonds; beat until well blended. Shape dough into disc. Wrap dough in plastic wrap and refrigerate 30 minutes.

2. Preheat oven to 350°F. Lightly grease cookie sheets. Roll out dough on floured surface to ¼-inch thickness. Cut dough with 2½- to 3-inch football-shaped cookie cutter*. Place 2 inches apart on prepared cookie sheets.

3. Bake 10 to 12 minutes or until set. Cool on cookie sheets 1 to 2 minutes. Remove to wire racks; cool completely. Decorate with colored icings, if desired. Pipe white icing onto footballs to make laces.

Makes 2 dozen cookies

If you do not have a football-shaped cookie cutter, shape 3 tablespoonfuls of dough into ovals. Place 3 inches apart on prepared cookie sheets. Flatten ovals to ¼-inch thickness; taper ends. Bake as directed.

White Chip Apricot Oatmeal Cookies

¾ cup (1½ sticks) butter or margarine, softened
½ cup granulated sugar
½ cup packed light brown sugar
1 egg
1 cup all-purpose flour
1 teaspoon baking soda
2½ cups rolled oats
1⅔ cups (10-ounce package) HERSHEY'S Premier White Chips
¾ cup chopped dried apricots

1. Heat oven to 375°F.

2. Beat butter, granulated sugar and brown sugar in large bowl until fluffy. Add egg; beat well. Add flour and baking soda; beat until well blended. Stir in oats, white chips and apricots. Loosely form rounded teaspoonfuls dough into balls; place on ungreased cookie sheet.

3. Bake 7 to 9 minutes or just until lightly browned; do not overbake. Cool slightly; remove from cookie sheet to wire rack. Cool completely.

Makes about 3½ dozen cookies

Nutty Footballs

Cinnamon Roll Cookies

Cinnamon Mixture
- 4 tablespoons granulated sugar
- 1 tablespoons ground cinnamon

Cookie Dough
- 1 cup Butter Flavor CRISCO® all-vegetable shortening or 1 Butter Flavor CRISCO® Stick
- 1 cup firmly packed light brown sugar
- 2 large eggs
- 1 teaspoon vanilla
- 3 cups all-purpose flour
- 2 teaspoons baking powder
- ½ teaspoon salt
- 1 teaspoon ground cinnamon

1. For cinnamon mixture, combine granulated sugar and 1 tablespoon cinnamon in small bowl; mix well. Set aside.

2. For cookie dough, combine 1 cup shortening and brown sugar in large bowl. Beat at medium speed with electric mixer until well blended. Beat in eggs and vanilla until well blended.

3. Combine flour, baking powder, salt and 1 teaspoon cinnamon in small bowl. Add to creamed mixture; mix well.

4. Turn dough onto sheet of waxed paper. Spread dough into 9×6-inch rectangle using rubber spatula. Sprinkle with 4 tablespoons cinnamon mixture to within 1 inch from edge. Roll up jelly-roll style into log. Dust log with remaining cinnamon mixture. Wrap tightly in plastic wrap; refrigerate 4 hours or overnight.

5. Heat oven to 375°F. Spray cookie sheets with CRISCO® No-Stick Cooking Spray.

6. Slice dough ¼ inch thick. Place on prepared cookie sheets. Bake at 350°F for 8 minutes or until lightly browned on top. Cool on cookie sheets 4 minutes; transfer to cooling racks.

Makes about 5 dozen cookies

Kitchen Hint: Be careful when working with this dough. It is a stiff dough and can crack easily when rolling. Roll the dough slowly and smooth any cracks with your finger as you go.

Chunky Chocolate Nut Cookies

- 1 cup margarine or butter, softened
- 1½ cups sugar
- 2 eggs
- 2 teaspoons vanilla extract
- 2½ cups all-purpose flour
- 1 teaspoon baking soda
- 1 teaspoon salt
- 8 ounces semisweet chocolate, coarsely chopped
- 1½ cups PLANTERS® Walnuts or Pecans, toasted and coarsely chopped
- 1 cup flaked coconut

1. Beat margarine or butter and sugar with mixer until creamy. Blend in eggs and vanilla until smooth. Stir in flour, baking soda and salt; mix in chocolate, walnuts and coconut.

2. Spoon by rounded tablespoonfuls onto lightly greased baking sheet. Bake at 375°F for 10 to 12 minutes or until lightly golden around edges. Remove from baking sheet; cool completely on wire rack. Store in airtight container. *Makes 4 dozen*

Cinnamon Roll Cookies

Giant Peanut Butter Cup Cookies

½ cup (1 stick) butter or margarine, softened
¾ cup sugar
⅓ cup REESE'S® Creamy or Crunchy Peanut Butter
1 egg
½ teaspoon vanilla extract
1¼ cups all-purpose flour
½ teaspoon baking soda
¼ teaspoon salt
16 REESE'S® Peanut Butter Cup Miniatures, cut into fourths

1. Heat oven to 350°F.

2. Beat butter, sugar and peanut butter in medium bowl until creamy. Add egg and vanilla; beat well. Stir together flour, baking soda and salt. Add to butter mixture; blend well. Drop dough by level ¼ cup measurements onto ungreased cookie sheets, three cookies per sheet. (Cookies will spread while baking.) Push about seven pieces of peanut butter cup into each cookie, flattening cookie slightly.

3. Bake 15 to 17 minutes or until light golden brown around the edges. Centers will be pale and slightly soft. Cool 1 minute on cookie sheet. Remove to wire rack; cool completely.   *Makes 9 cookies*

Philadelphia® Sugar Cookies

Prep Time: 10 minutes plus refrigerating
Bake Time: 15 minutes

1 package (8 ounces) PHILADELPHIA® Cream Cheese, softened
1 cup (2 sticks) butter *or* margarine, softened
⅔ cup sugar
¼ teaspoon vanilla
2 cups flour
Colored sugar, sprinkles and colored gels

BEAT cream cheese, butter, ⅔ cup sugar and vanilla with electric mixer on medium speed until well blended. Mix in flour. Refrigerate several hours or overnight.

ROLL dough to ¼-inch thickness on lightly floured surface. Cut into desired shapes; sprinkle with colored sugar. Place on ungreased cookie sheets.

BAKE at 350°F for 12 to 15 minutes or until edges are lightly browned. Cool on wire racks. Decorate as desired with colored sugar, sprinkles and colored gels.
Makes 3½ dozen

Giant Peanut Butter Cup Cookies

Ali's Oatmeal Cookies

1 Butter Flavor CRISCO® Stick or 1 cup
    Butter Flavor CRISCO® all-vegetable
    shortening
1 cup granulated sugar
1 cup firmly packed light brown sugar
2 eggs
1 teaspoon vanilla
1½ cups plus 1 tablespoon all-purpose flour,
    divided
1 teaspoon baking soda
¾ teaspoon salt
2½ cups oats (quick or old-fashioned,
    uncooked)
1 cup finely chopped hazelnuts
1 cup finely diced dried apricots
1 cup chopped vanilla milk chips

1. Heat oven to 350°F. Place sheets of foil on
countertop for cooling cookies.

2. Combine 1 cup shortening, granulated sugar,
brown sugar, eggs and vanilla in large bowl. Beat at
medium speed of electric mixer until well blended.

3. Combine 1½ cups flour, baking soda and salt. Add
gradually to creamed mixture at low speed. Beat
until well blended. Stir in oats and nuts with spoon.

4. Toss apricots with remaining 1 tablespoon flour.
Stir into dough. Stir in vanilla milk chips. Shape
into 1½-inch balls. Flatten slightly. Place 2 inches
apart on ungreased baking sheet.

5. Bake at 350°F for 11 to 13 minutes or until just
beginning to brown around edges and slightly moist
in center. *Do not overbake.* Cool 2 minutes on baking
sheet. Remove cookies to foil to cool completely.
    Makes about 3 dozen cookies

Apple Sauce Gingerbread Cookies

4 cups all-purpose flour
2 teaspoons ground ginger
2 teaspoons ground cinnamon
1 teaspoon baking soda
½ teaspoon salt
¼ teaspoon ground nutmeg
½ cup butter, softened
1 cup sugar
⅓ cup GRANDMA'S® Molasses
1 cup MOTT'S® Natural Apple Sauce
    Decorator Icing (recipe follows)

Heat oven to 350°F. In large bowl, sift together
flour, ginger, cinnamon, baking soda, salt and
nutmeg; set aside. In bowl of electric mixer, fitted
with paddle, beat butter, sugar and molasses until
creamy. Alternately blend in dry ingredients and
apple sauce. Cover and chill dough for several hours
or overnight.

On floured surface, roll dough out to ⅛-inch
thickness with lightly floured rolling pin. Cut with
floured cookie cutter. Place on greased baking sheet.
Bake 12 minutes or until done. Remove from sheet;
cool on wire rack. Frost with Decorator Icing as
desired. After icing dries, store in airtight container.
    Makes 2½ dozen (5½-inch) cookies

Decorator Icing: Mix 2 cups confectioners' sugar
and 1 tablespoon water. Add more water, 1 teaspoon
at a time, until icing holds its shape and can be
piped through decorating tube.

Ali's Oatmeal Cookies

Chocolate-Dipped Coconut Macaroons

Prep Time: 15 minutes
Bake Time: 20 minutes

> 1 package (14 ounces) BAKER'S® ANGEL
>   FLAKE® Coconut (5⅓ cups)
> ⅔ cup sugar
> 6 tablespoons flour
> ¼ teaspoon salt
> 4 egg whites
> 1 teaspoon almond extract
> 1 package (8 squares) BAKER'S®
>   Semi-Sweet Baking Chocolate, melted

HEAT oven to 325°F.

MIX coconut, sugar, flour and salt in large bowl. Stir in egg whites and almond extract until well blended. Drop by teaspoonfuls onto greased and floured cookie sheets.

BAKE 20 minutes or until edges of cookies are golden brown. Immediately remove from cookie sheets to wire racks and cool completely. Dip cookies halfway into melted chocolate. Let stand at room temperature or refrigerate on wax paper-lined tray 30 minutes or until chocolate is firm.

Makes about 3 dozen cookies

Storage Know-How: Store in tightly covered container up to 1 week.

Chocolate Toffee Chip Popcorn Cookies

> 6 tablespoons margarine or butter, softened
> ½ cup packed light brown sugar
> ⅓ cup granulated sugar
> 2 large egg whites
> 1 teaspoon vanilla extract
> 1⅓ cups all-purpose flour
> 1 teaspoon baking soda
> 2 cups popped NEWMAN'S OWN® Butter
>   Flavored Microwave Popcorn, chopped
>   in food processor
> 1 cup semisweet chocolate chips
> 1 (3½-ounce) jar macadamia nuts, chopped
>   (optional)
> ½ cup uncooked quick-cooking oats
> ½ cup toffee bits

Preheat oven to 375°F. In large bowl, with mixer at high speed, beat margarine and sugars until light and creamy. Add egg whites and vanilla; beat until smooth. Add flour and baking soda; beat on low speed just until blended. Stir in popcorn, chocolate chips, macadamia nuts, oats and toffee bits. Drop by rounded tablespoonfuls onto *ungreased* cookie sheet. Bake 12 to 15 minutes or until lightly browned. Transfer to wire rack to cool.

Makes about 2½ dozen cookies

Chocolate-Dipped Coconut Macaroons

Ultimate Chocolate Chip Cookies

1¼ cups firmly packed brown sugar
¾ Butter Flavor CRISCO® Stick or ¾ cup
    Butter Flavor CRISCO® all-vegetable
    shortening
2 tablespoons milk
1 tablespoon vanilla
1 egg
1¾ cups all-purpose flour
1 teaspoon salt
¾ teaspoon baking soda
1 cup semisweet chocolate chips
1 cup coarsely chopped pecans*

You may substitute an additional ½ cup semisweet chocolate chips for pecans.

1. Heat oven to 375°F. Place sheets of foil on countertop for cooling cookies.

2. Combine sugar, ¾ cup shortening, milk and vanilla in large bowl. Beat at medium speed of electric mixer until well blended. Beat in egg.

3. Combine flour, salt and baking soda. Mix into shortening mixture at low speed just until blended. Stir in chocolate chips and nuts.

4. Drop by rounded tablespoonfuls 3 inches apart onto ungreased baking sheets.

5. Bake at 375°F for 8 to 10 minutes for chewy cookies or 11 to 13 minutes for crisp cookies. *Do not overbake.* Cool 2 minutes on baking sheets. Remove to foil to cool completely.

Makes about 3 dozen cookies

Drizzle: Combine 1 teaspoon BUTTER FLAVOR CRISCO® and 1 cup semisweet chocolate chips or

1 cup white melting chocolate, cut into small pieces, in microwave-safe measuring cup. Microwave at 50% (MEDIUM). Stir after 1 minute. Repeat until smooth (or melt on rangetop in small saucepan on very low heat). To thin, add more Butter Flavor Crisco®. Drizzle back and forth over cookies. Sprinkle with nuts before chocolate hardens, if desired. To quickly harden chocolate, place cookies in refrigerator to set.

Chocolate Dipped: Melt chocolate as directed for Drizzle. Dip half of cooled cookies in chocolate. Sprinkle with finely chopped nuts before chocolate hardens. Place on waxed paper until chocolate is firm. To quickly harden chocolate, place cookies in refrigerator to set.

Snowballs

½ cup DOMINO® Confectioners 10-X Sugar
¼ teaspoon salt
1 cup butter or margarine, softened
1 teaspoon vanilla extract
2¼ cups all-purpose flour
½ cup chopped pecans
    DOMINO® Confectioners 10-X Sugar

In large bowl, combine ½ cup confectioners sugar, salt and butter; mix well. Add extract. Gradually stir in flour. Work nuts into dough. Chill well. Form into 1-inch balls. Place on ungreased cookie sheets. Bake at 400°F for 8 to 10 minutes or until set but not brown. Roll in confectioners sugar immediately. Cool on rack. Roll in sugar again. Store in airtight container.

Makes 5 dozen cookies

Ultimate Chocolate Chip Cookies

Stained Glass Cookies

½ cup margarine or butter, softened
½ cup sugar
½ cup honey
1 egg
1 teaspoon vanilla extract
3 cups all-purpose flour
1 teaspoon CALUMET® Baking Powder
½ teaspoon baking soda
½ teaspoon salt
5 (1.14-ounce) rolls LIFE SAVERS®
  Five Flavor Roll Candy

1. Beat margarine or butter, sugar, honey, egg and vanilla in large bowl with electric mixer until creamy. Mix in flour, baking powder, baking soda and salt. Cover; refrigerate at least 2 hours.

2. Roll dough on lightly floured surface to ¼-inch thickness. Cut dough into desired shapes with 2½- to 3-inch floured cookie cutters. Trace smaller version of cookie shape on dough leaving ½- to ¾-inch border of dough. Cut out and remove dough from center of cookies; set aside. Place cut-out shapes on baking sheets lined with foil. Repeat with reserved dough, re-rolling scraps as necessary.

3. Crush each color of candy separately between two layers of wax paper with a mallet. Spoon crushed candy inside centers of cut-out cookie shapes (about ½ teaspoon for each cookie).

4. Bake at 350°F for 6 to 8 minutes or until candy is melted and cookies are lightly browned. Cool cookies completely before removing from foil.

Makes 3½ dozen

Buttery Almond Cookies

1¼ cups all-purpose flour
½ teaspoon baking powder
⅛ teaspoon salt
10 tablespoons butter, softened
¾ cup sugar
1 egg
1 teaspoon vanilla
¾ cup slivered almonds, finely chopped
½ cup slivered almonds, for garnish

Preheat oven to 350°F. Grease cookie sheets. Combine flour, baking powder and salt in small bowl.

Beat butter in large bowl with electric mixer at medium speed until smooth. Gradually beat in sugar until blended; increase speed to high and beat until light and fluffy. Beat in egg until fluffy. Beat in vanilla until blended. Stir in flour mixture until blended. Stir in chopped almonds just until combined.

Drop rounded teaspoonfuls of dough about 2 inches apart onto prepared cookie sheets. Top each cookie with several slivered almonds, pressing into dough.

Bake 12 minutes or until edges are golden brown. Let cookies stand on cookie sheets 5 minutes; transfer to wire racks to cool completely. Store in airtight container. *Makes about 42 cookies*

Stained Glass Cookies

Peanut Butter Crunchies

1 cup granulated sugar
1 cup firmly packed light brown sugar
1 cup JIF® Creamy Peanut Butter
½ Butter Flavor CRISCO® Stick or ½ cup
    Butter Flavor CRISCO® all-vegetable
    shortening
2 eggs
1½ cups all-purpose flour
½ teaspoon baking soda
1 cup peanut butter chips
⅔ cup almond brickle chips

1. Heat oven to 350°F. Place sheets of foil on countertop for cooling cookies.

2. Combine granulated sugar, brown sugar, peanut butter and ½ cup shortening in large bowl. Beat at medium-high speed of electric mixer until well blended. Beat in eggs.

3. Combine flour and baking soda. Add gradually to creamed mixture at low speed. Stir in peanut butter chips and almond brickle chips with spoon. Shape into 1½-inch balls. Place 2 inches apart on ungreased baking sheet. Dip fork in flour; flatten dough slightly in crisscross pattern.

4. Bake at 350°F for 9 to 11 minutes or until bottoms are light brown and set. *Do not overbake.* Cool 5 minutes on baking sheet. Remove cookies to foil to cool completely.

Makes about 3 dozen cookies

Coconut Chocolate Jumbles

Prep Time: 15 minutes
Bake Time: 12 minutes

½ cup (1 stick) butter *or* margarine
½ cup granulated sugar
¼ cup firmly packed brown sugar
1 egg
½ teaspoon vanilla
1 cup flour
1 teaspoon baking soda
¼ teaspoon salt
6 squares BAKER'S® Semi-Sweet Baking
    Chocolate *or* BAKER'S® Premium
    White Baking Chocolate, chopped
1 package (7 ounces) BAKER'S® ANGEL
    FLAKE® Coconut (2⅔ cups)
1 cup *each* chopped, toasted walnuts and
    raisins

HEAT oven to 350°F.

BEAT butter and sugars in large bowl with electric mixer on medium speed until light and fluffy. Beat in egg and vanilla. Mix in flour, baking soda and salt. Stir in chocolate, coconut, walnuts and raisins.

DROP by rounded tablespoonfuls, 1½ inches apart, onto ungreased cookie sheets.

BAKE 10 to 12 minutes or until golden brown. Cool 2 to 3 minutes; remove from cookie sheets. Cool completely on wire racks. Store in tightly covered container. *Makes about 3 dozen cookies*

Storage Know-How: Store in tightly covered container up to 1 week.

Peanut Butter Crunchies

Chocolate Malted Cookies

½ cup butter, softened
½ cup shortening
1¾ cups powdered sugar, divided
1 teaspoon vanilla
2 cups all-purpose flour
1 cup malted milk powder, divided
¼ cup unsweetened cocoa powder

1. Beat butter, shortening, ¾ cup powdered sugar and vanilla in large bowl. Add flour, ½ cup malted milk powder and cocoa until well blended. Refrigerate several hours or overnight.

2. Preheat oven to 350°F. Shape slightly mounded teaspoonfuls of dough into balls. Place dough balls about 2 inches apart on ungreased cookie sheets. Bake 14 to 16 minutes or until lightly browned.

3. Meanwhile, combine remaining 1 cup powdered sugar and ½ cup malted milk powder in medium bowl. Remove cookies to wire racks; cool 5 minutes. Roll cookies in powdered sugar mixture.

Makes about 4 dozen cookies

Tip: Substitute 6 ounces melted semisweet chocolate for the 1 cup powdered sugar and ½ cup malted milk powder used to roll the cookies. Instead, dip cookies in melted chocolate and let dry on wire racks until coating is set.

Pineapple Oatmeal Crunchies

Prep Time: 20 minutes
Bake Time: 30 minutes per batch

2 cans (8 ounces each) DOLE® Crushed Pineapple
1½ cups margarine
1½ cups packed brown sugar
2 eggs
3 cups all-purpose flour
3 cups old-fashioned rolled oats
1 teaspoon baking powder
1 teaspoon ground cinnamon
½ teaspoon salt
5 bags (1.4 ounces each) chocolate covered toffee nuggets

• Drain crushed pineapple well, reserving ½ cup juice.

• Beat margarine and sugar until light and fluffy. Beat in eggs. Stir in pineapple and reserved juice.

• Combine flour, oats, baking powder, cinnamon and salt. Add to pineapple mixture and mix well. Stir in candy.

• Drop by ¼ cup scoopfuls 1 inch apart onto cookie sheets coated with cooking spray. Flatten slightly. Bake at 375°F 30 minutes.

Makes 24 large cookies

Chocolate Malted Cookies

Peanut Butter and Jelly Cookies

1 Butter Flavor CRISCO® Stick or 1 cup
  Butter Flavor CRISCO® all-vegetable
  shortening
1 cup JIF® Creamy Peanut Butter
1 teaspoon vanilla
⅔ cup firmly packed light brown sugar
⅓ cup granulated sugar
2 large eggs
2 cups all-purpose flour
1 cup SMUCKER'S® Strawberry Preserves
  or any flavor

1. Heat oven to 350°F.

2. Combine 1 cup shortening, peanut butter and
vanilla in food processor fitted with metal blade.
Process until well blended and smooth. Add sugars;
process until incorporated completely. Add eggs;
beat just until blended. Add flour; pulse until dough
begins to form ball. *Do not overprocess.*

3. Place dough in medium bowl. Roll ½ tablespoon
dough into ball for each cookie. Place 1½ inches
apart on ungreased cookie sheets. Press thumb into
center of each ball to create deep well. Fill each well
with about ½ teaspoon preserves. Bake at 350°F for
10 minutes or until lightly browned and firm. Cool
on cookie sheets 4 minutes; transfer to cooling racks.
Leave on racks about 30 minutes or until completely
cool. *Makes about 5 dozen cookies*

Chewy Chocolate-Cinnamon Cookies

6 tablespoons butter or margarine, softened
⅔ cup packed light brown sugar
3 tablespoons plus ¼ cup granulated sugar,
  divided
1 egg
1 teaspoon baking soda
½ cup light corn syrup
1 teaspoon vanilla extract
1½ cups all-purpose flour
⅓ cup HERSHEY'S Cocoa
¼ to ½ teaspoon ground cinnamon

1. Heat oven to 350°F. Spray cookie sheet with
nonstick cooking spray.

2. Beat butter until creamy. Add brown sugar and
3 tablespoons granulated sugar; beat until blended.
Add egg, baking soda, corn syrup and vanilla; beat
well.

3. Stir together flour and cocoa; beat into butter
mixture. If batter becomes to stiff, use wooden
spoon to stir in remaining flour. Cover; refrigerate
about 30 minutes, if necessary, until batter is firm
enough to shape. Shape dough into 1-inch balls.
Combine remaining ¼ cup granulated sugar and
cinnamon; roll balls in mixture. Place balls 2 inches
apart on prepared cookie sheet.

4. Bake 9 to 10 minutes or until cookies are set and
tops are cracked. Cool slightly; remove from cookie
sheet to wire rack. Cool completely.

Makes about 40 cookies

Peanut Butter and Jelly Cookies

Kate's Chocolate Chip Cookies

1 Butter Flavor CRISCO® Stick or 1 cup
   Butter Flavor CRISCO® all-vegetable
   shortening plus additional for greasing
1 cup granulated sugar
1 cup firmly packed brown sugar
3 eggs
2 teaspoons vanilla
3½ cups all-purpose flour
1 teaspoon baking soda
1 teaspoon salt
1 cup uncooked quick oats
1 package (12 ounces) semisweet chocolate
   chips (2 cups)
1 cup chopped pecans, walnuts or peanuts

1. Heat oven to 375°F. Grease baking sheet with shortening. Place sheets of foil on countertop for cooling cookies.

2. Combine 1 cup shortening, granulated sugar, brown sugar, eggs and vanilla in large bowl. Beat at high speed with electric mixer until fluffy (about 5 minutes).

3. Combine flour, baking soda and salt. Add gradually to creamed mixture at low speed. Mix until well blended. Add oats. Mix until well blended. Stir in chocolate chips and pecans. Drop by rounded teaspoonfuls 2 inches apart onto prepared sheet.

4. Bake for 10 to 12 minutes or until light golden brown. *Do not overbake.* Cool 2 minutes on baking sheet. Remove cookies to foil to cool completely.

Makes 3½ dozen cookies

Choc-Oat-Chip Cookies

1 cup (2 sticks) butter or margarine,
   softened
1 cup firmly packed brown sugar
½ cup granulated sugar
2 eggs
2 tablespoons milk
2 teaspoons vanilla
1¾ cups all-purpose flour
1 teaspoon baking soda
½ teaspoon salt (optional)
2½ cups QUAKER® Oats (quick or old
   fashioned, uncooked)
2 cups semisweet chocolate pieces
1 cup coarsely chopped nuts (optional)

Preheat oven to 375°F. Beat together butter and sugars until creamy. Add eggs, milk and vanilla; beat well. Add combined flour, baking soda and salt; mix well. Stir in oats, chocolate pieces and nuts; mix well. Drop by rounded tablespoonfuls onto ungreased cookie sheets.* Bake at 375°F for 9 to 10 minutes for a chewy cookie or 12 to 13 minutes for a crisp cookie. Cool 1 minute on cookie sheets; remove to wire racks. Cool completely. Store in tightly covered container. *Makes about 5 dozen*

*For Bar Cookies: Press dough into bottom of ungreased 13×9-inch metal baking pan. Bake 30 to 35 minutes or until light golden brown. Cool completely; cut into bars. Store tightly covered.

High altitude adjustment: Increase flour to 2 cups

Variations: Prepare cookies as recipe directs, except substitute 1 cup of any of the following for 1 cup chocolate: raisins, chopped dried apricots, dried cherries, crushed toffee pieces, candy-coated chocolate pieces or white chocolate baking pieces.

Kate's Chocolate Chip Cookies

Pinwheel Cookies

½ cup shortening plus additional for
   greasing
⅓ cup plus 1 tablespoon butter, softened and
   divided
2 egg yolks
½ teaspoon vanilla
1 package DUNCAN HINES® Moist Deluxe®
   Fudge Marble Cake Mix

1. Combine ½ cup shortening, ⅓ cup butter, egg
yolks and vanilla in large bowl. Mix at low speed of
electric mixer until blended. Set aside cocoa packet
from cake mix. Gradually add cake mix. Blend well.

2. Divide dough in half. Add cocoa packet and
remaining 1 tablespoon butter to one half of dough.
Knead until well blended and chocolate colored.

3. Roll out yellow dough between two pieces of
waxed paper into 18×12×⅛-inch rectangle. Repeat
for chocolate dough. Remove top pieces of waxed
paper from chocolate and yellow doughs. Place
yellow dough directly on top of chocolate dough.
Remove remaining layers of waxed paper. Roll up
jelly-roll fashion, beginning at wide side. Refrigerate
2 hours.

4. Preheat oven to 350°F. Grease cookie sheets.

5. Cut dough into ⅛-inch slices. Place sliced dough
1 inch apart on prepared cookie sheets. Bake 9 to
11 minutes or until lightly browned. Cool 5 minutes
on cookie sheets. Remove to cooling racks.

Makes about 3½ dozen cookies

Choco Peanut Butter Dreams

1½ cups firmly packed brown sugar
1 cup creamy or chunk-style peanut butter
¾ cup (1½ sticks) margarine, softened
⅓ cup water
1 egg
1 teaspoon vanilla
3 cups QUAKER® Oats (quick or
   old fashioned, uncooked)
1½ cups all-purpose flour
½ teaspoon baking soda
1½ cups semisweet chocolate pieces
4 teaspoons vegetable shortening
⅓ cup chopped peanuts (optional)

Preheat oven to 350°F. Beat brown sugar, peanut
butter and margarine until fluffy. Blend in water,
egg and vanilla. Add combined oats, flour and
baking soda; mix well. Shape into 1-inch balls. Place
on ungreased cookie sheets. Using bottom of glass
dipped in sugar, press into ¼-inch thick circles. Bake
8 to 10 minutes or until edges are golden brown.
Remove to wire rack; cool completely.

In saucepan over low heat, melt chocolate pieces
and shortening, stirring until smooth.* Top each
cookie with ½ teaspoon melted chocolate; sprinkle
with chopped peanuts. Chill until set. Store tightly
covered.   *Makes about 6 dozen cookies*

**Microwave Directions: Place chocolate pieces and
shortening in microwavable bowl. Microwave at HIGH
1 to 2 minutes, stirring after 1 minute and then every
30 seconds until smooth.*

Pinwheel Cookies

Sun Dried Cranberry-Walnut Oatmeal Cookies

¾ Butter Flavor CRISCO® Stick or ¾ cup
  Butter Flavor CRISCO® all-vegetable
  shortening
¾ cup firmly packed light brown sugar
¾ cup granulated sugar
2 large eggs
1 teaspoon vanilla
1 cup all-purpose flour
1 teaspoon baking soda
¼ teaspoon salt
2¾ cups rolled oats
1 cup sun dried cranberries
1 cup walnut pieces

1. Heat oven to 375°F.

2. Combine ¾ cup shortening and sugars in large bowl. Beat at medium speed with electric mixer until well blended. Beat in eggs and vanilla until well blended.

3. Combine flour, baking soda and salt in small bowl. Stir into creamed mixture; mix well. Add oats, sun dried cranberries and walnuts. Spray cookie sheets with CRISCO® No-Stick Cooking Spray. Dust with flour. Drop dough by teaspoonfuls about 2 inches apart onto prepared cookie sheets. Bake at 375°F for 8 minutes or until firm and brown. Cool on cookie sheets 4 minutes; transfer to cooling rack.

Makes about 6 dozen cookies

Mini Chip Slice and Bake Cookies

⅓ cup butter or margarine, softened
¾ cup granulated sugar
½ cup packed light brown sugar
1 egg
1 teaspoon vanilla extract
2½ cups all-purpose flour
1 teaspoon baking soda
½ teaspoon baking powder
½ teaspoon salt
2 to 3 tablespoons milk
1 cup HERSHEY'S MINI CHIPS™
  Semi-Sweet Chocolate Chips

1. Beat butter, granulated sugar and brown sugar in large bowl on medium speed of mixer until creamy. Add egg and vanilla; beat well. Stir together flour, baking soda, baking powder and salt; gradually add to butter mixture, beating until well blended. Add milk, 1 tablespoon at a time, until dough holds together. Stir in small chocolate chips.

2. Divide dough in half. Shape each half into 1½-inch-thick roll. Wrap tightly in wax paper; refrigerate 5 to 24 hours.

3. Heat oven to 350°F. Lightly grease cookie sheet.

4. Using a sharp knife and a sawing motion, cut rolls into ¼-inch slices. Place on prepared cookie sheet.

5. Bake 8 to 10 minutes or until set. Remove from cookie sheet to wire rack. Cool completely.

Makes about 6 dozen cookies

Sun Dried Cranberry-Walnut Oatmeal Cookies

Lollipop Sugar Cookies

1¼ cups granulated sugar
 1 cup Butter Flavor CRISCO® all-vegetable shortening or 1 Butter Flavor CRISCO® Stick
 2 eggs
 ¼ cup light corn syrup or regular pancake syrup
 1 tablespoon vanilla
 3 cups all-purpose flour
 ¾ teaspoon baking powder
 ½ teaspoon baking soda
 ½ teaspoon salt
36 flat ice cream sticks
   Any of the following: miniature baking chips, raisins, red hots, nonpareils, colored sugar or nuts

1. Combine sugar and 1 cup shortening in large bowl. Beat at medium speed of electric mixer until well blended. Add eggs, syrup and vanilla; beat until well blended and fluffy.

2. Combine flour, baking powder, baking soda and salt. Add gradually to creamed mixture at low speed until well blended. Wrap dough in plastic wrap. Refrigerate at least 1 hour.

3. Heat oven to 375°F. Place foil on countertop for cooling cookies.

4. Shape dough into 1½-inch balls. Push ice cream stick into center of each ball. Place balls 3 inches apart on ungreased baking sheet. Flatten balls to ½-inch thickness with bottom of greased and floured glass. Decorate as desired; press decorations gently into dough.*

5. Bake at 375°F for 8 to 10 minutes. *Do not overbake.* Cool on baking sheet 2 minutes. Remove cookies to foil to cool completely.

Makes about 3 dozen cookies

Cookies can also be painted before baking. Mix 1 egg yolk and ¼ teaspoon water. Divide into 3 small cups. Add 2 to 3 drops food color to each. Stir. Use clean water color brushes to paint designs on cookies.

Old-Fashioned Molasses Cookies

4 cups sifted all-purpose flour
2 teaspoons ARM & HAMMER® Baking Soda
2 teaspoons ground ginger
1 teaspoon ground cinnamon
⅛ teaspoon salt
1½ cups molasses
½ cup butter flavored shortenting
¼ cup butter or margarine, melted
⅓ cup boiling water
  Sugar

In medium bowl, combine flour, Baking Soda, spices and salt. In large bowl, mix molasses, shortening, butter and water. Add dry ingredients to molasses mixture; blend well. Cover; refrigerate until firm, about 2 hours. Roll out dough ¼ inch thick on well-floured surface. Cut out with 3½-inch cookie cutters; sprinkle with sugar. Place 2 inches apart on ungreased cookie sheets. Bake in preheated 375°F oven about 12 minutes. Remove to wire racks to cool.

Makes about 3 dozen cookies

Lollipop Sugar Cookies

Dandy Candy Oatmeal Cookies

½ Butter Flavor CRISCO® Stick or ½ cup
    Butter Flavor CRISCO® all-vegetable
    shortening plus additional for greasing
1 jar (12 ounces) JIF® Creamy Peanut
    Butter
1 cup granulated sugar
1 cup firmly packed brown sugar
3 eggs
¾ teaspoon vanilla
¾ teaspoon maple (or maple-blend) syrup
2 teaspoons baking soda
4½ cups quick oats, uncooked, divided
1 package (8 ounces) candy-coated
    chocolate pieces

1. Heat oven to 350°F. Grease baking sheet with shortening. Place sheets of foil on countertop for cooling cookies.

2. Combine peanut butter, granulated sugar, brown sugar and ½ cup shortening in large bowl. Beat at medium speed with electric mixer until well blended and fluffy. Add eggs, vanilla and maple syrup. Beat at high speed 3 to 4 minutes. Add baking soda and 2¼ cups oats; stir. Stir in candy. Stir in remaining 2¼ cups oats. Shape dough into 1½-inch balls. Flatten slightly. Place 2 inches apart on prepared baking sheet.

3. Bake for 9 to 10 minutes for chewy cookies or 11 to 12 minutes for crispy cookies. Cool 2 minutes. Remove cookies to foil to cool completely.

Makes 3½ dozen cookies

Honey Chocolate Chippers

1 cup honey
1 cup butter or margarine, softened
1 egg yolk
1 teaspoon vanilla extract
2 cups all-purpose flour
1 cup rolled oats
½ teaspoon baking soda
½ teaspoon salt
1 cup chopped toasted pecans
1 cup (6 ounces) semi-sweet chocolate
    chips

In medium bowl, beat honey and butter until creamy but not fluffy. Beat in egg yolk and vanilla. In separate bowl, combine flour, oats, baking soda and salt. Stir dry ingredients into wet mixture until thoroughly blended. Mix in pecans and chocolate chips. Chill dough for 30 minutes. Drop dough by rounded tablespoons onto ungreased cookie sheets. Flatten each cookie with a spoon. Bake at 350°F for 15 to 20 minutes, or until tops are dry. Cool on wire racks.

Makes 2 dozen

Favorite recipe from **National Honey Board**

Dandy Candy Oatmeal Cookies

Sensational Cinnamon Chip Biscotti

½ cup (1 stick) butter, softened
1 cup sugar
2 eggs
1 teaspoon vanilla extract
2½ cups all-purpose flour
1½ teaspoons baking powder
¼ teaspoon salt
1⅔ cups (10-ounce package) HERSHEY'S
    Cinnamon Chips (divided)
1 cup very finely chopped walnuts
2 teaspoons shortening (do not use butter,
    margarine, spread or oil)
White Chip Drizzle (recipe follows)

1. Heat oven 325°F. Lightly grease cookie sheet.

2. Beat butter and sugar in large bowl until blended. Add eggs and vanilla; beat well. Stir together flour, baking powder and salt; gradually add to butter mixture, beating until smooth. (Dough will be stiff.) Using spoon or with hands, work 1 cup cinnamon chips and walnuts into dough.

3. Divide dough into four equal parts. Shape each part into a log about 8 inches long. Place on prepared cookie sheet, at least 2 inches apart; flatten slightly.

4. Bake 25 to 30 minutes or until logs are set and wooden pick inserted in center comes out clean. Remove from oven; let cool on cookie sheet 30 minutes. Transfer to cutting board. Using serrated knife and sawing motion, cut logs diagonally into ½-inch-wide slices. Place slices close together, cut side down on ungreased cookie sheet. Return to oven; bake 5 to 6 minutes. Turn each slice; bake an additional 5 to 8 minutes. Remove from oven; cool slightly. Remove from cookie sheet to wire rack. Cool completely. Melt remaining cinnamon chips with shortening; drizzle over each cookie. Drizzle White Chip Drizzle over top.
Makes about 5 dozen cookies

White Chip Drizzle: Place ¼ cup HERSHEY'S Premier White Chips and 1 teaspoon shortening (do not use butter, margarine, spread or oil) in small microwave-safe bowl. Microwave at HIGH (100%) 30 to 45 seconds or until smooth when stirred.

Brown Sugar Shortbread

1 cup (2 sticks) I CAN'T BELIEVE IT'S
    NOT BUTTER!® Spread
¾ cup firmly packed light brown sugar
2 cups all-purpose flour
⅓ cup semisweet chocolate chips, melted

Preheat oven to 325°F. Grease 9-inch round cake pan; set aside.

In large bowl, with electric mixer, beat I Can't Believe It's Not Butter! Spread and brown sugar until light and fluffy, about 5 minutes. Gradually add flour and beat on low until blended. Spread mixture into prepared pan and press into even layer. With knife, score surface into 8 pie-shaped wedges.

Bake 30 minutes or until lightly golden. On wire rack, cool 20 minutes; remove from pan and cool completely. To serve, pour melted chocolate into small plastic storage bag. Snip corner and drizzle chocolate over shortbread. Cut into wedges.
Makes 8 servings

Sensational Cinnamon Chip Biscotti

Baker's® Premium Chocolate Chunk Cookies

Prep Time: 15 minutes
Bake Time: 11 to 13 minutes

1¾ cups flour
¾ teaspoon baking soda
¼ teaspoon salt
¾ cup (1½ sticks) butter *or* margarine, softened
½ cup granulated sugar
½ cup firmly packed brown sugar
1 egg
1 teaspoon vanilla
1 package (12 ounces) BAKER'S® Semi-Sweet Chocolate Chunks
1 cup chopped nuts (optional)

HEAT oven to 375°F.

MIX flour, baking soda and salt in medium bowl; set aside.

BEAT butter and sugars in large bowl with electric mixer on medium speed until light and fluffy. Add egg and vanilla; beat well. Gradually beat in flour mixture. Stir in chocolate chunks and nuts. Drop by heaping tablespoonfuls onto ungreased cookie sheets.

BAKE 11 to 13 minutes or just until golden brown. Cool on cookie sheets 1 minute. Remove to wire racks and cool completely.

Makes about 3 dozen cookies

Bar Cookies: Spread dough in greased foil-lined 15×10×1-inch baking pan. Bake at 375°F for 18 to 20 minutes or until golden brown. (Or, bake in 13×9-inch pan for 20 to 22 minutes.) Cool completely in pan on wire rack. Makes 3 dozen.

Chocolate Chunkoholic Cookies: Omit nuts. Stir in 2 packages (12 ounces each) BAKER'S® Semi-Sweet Chocolate Chunks. Drop by scant ¼ cupfuls onto cookie sheets. Bake at 375°F for 12 to 14 minutes. Makes about 22 large cookies.

Freezing Cookie Dough: Freeze heaping tablespoonfuls of cookie dough on cookie sheet 1 hour. Transfer to airtight plastic container or freezer zipper-style plastic bag. Freeze dough up to 1 month. Bake frozen cookie dough at 375°F for 15 to 16 minutes or just until golden brown.

Gold Mine Nuggets

½ cup margarine
¾ cup brown sugar, packed
½ teaspoon vanilla extract
1 egg
1 can (8 ounces) DOLE® Crushed Pineapple
1 cup rolled oats
1 cup all-purpose flour
1 teaspoon baking soda
1 teaspoon salt
½ teaspoon ground cinnamon
½ cup chopped walnuts
1 package (6 ounces) chocolate chips

Preheat oven to 350°F. Beat margarine, sugar and vanilla until fluffy. Beat in egg and undrained crushed pineapple. Combine oats, flour, soda, salt and cinnamon; stir into pineapple mixture with nuts and chocolate chips. Drop by teaspoonfuls onto ungreased cookie sheets. Bake at 350°F 12 to 15 minutes. *Makes about 3 dozen cookies*

Baker's® Premium Chocolate Chunk Cookies

Cookie Pizza

Prep Time: 15 minutes
Bake Time: 14 minutes

1 (18-ounce) package refrigerated sugar
    cookie dough
2 cups (12 ounces) semi-sweet chocolate
    chips
1 (14-ounce) can EAGLE® BRAND
    Sweetened Condensed Milk
    (NOT evaporated milk)
2 cups candy-coated milk chocolate candies
2 cups miniature marshmallows
½ cup peanuts

1. Preheat oven 375°F. Press cookie dough into
2 ungreased 12-inch pizza pans. Bake 10 minutes
or until golden. Remove from oven.

2. In medium-sized saucepan, melt chips with Eagle
Brand. Spread over crusts. Sprinkle with milk
chocolate candies, marshmallows and peanuts.

3. Bake 4 minutes or until marshmallows are lightly
toasted. Cool. Cut into wedges.

Makes 2 pizzas (24 servings)

Brown Sugar Granola Cookies

¾ cup (1½ sticks) butter or margarine,
    softened
1 cup firmly packed light brown sugar
1 large egg
1 teaspoon vanilla extract
2 cups all-purpose flour
1 teaspoon baking soda
1¾ cups "M&M's"® Chocolate Mini Baking
    Bits
6 KUDOS® Milk Chocolate Granola Bars
    Fudge, chopped

Preheat oven to 350°F. Lightly grease cookie sheets.
In large bowl cream butter and sugar until light and
fluffy; beat in egg and vanilla. In medium bowl
combine flour and baking soda; blend into creamed
mixture. Stir in "M&M's"® Chocolate Mini Baking
Bits and chopped KUDOS® Milk Chocolate Granola
Bars Fudge. Drop dough by tablespoonfuls onto
prepared cookie sheets. Bake 11 to 13 minutes. Cool
2 to 3 minutes on cookie sheets; cool completely on
wire racks. *Makes about 3½ dozen cookies*

Cookie Pizza

Tropical Chunk Cookies

Prep Time: 15 minutes
Bake Time: 11 to 13 minutes

> 1 package (12 ounces) BAKER'S® White
> Chocolate Chunks, divided
> 1¾ cups flour
> 1½ cups BAKER'S® ANGEL FLAKE®
> Coconut, toasted
> ¾ teaspoon baking soda
> ¼ teaspoon salt
> ½ cup (1 stick) butter *or* margarine,
> softened
> ⅓ cup firmly packed brown sugar
> 1 egg
> 1 teaspoon vanilla
> 1 cup chopped macadamia nuts

HEAT oven to 375°F.

MICROWAVE 1 cup of the chocolate chunks in microwavable bowl on HIGH 2 minutes until almost melted. Stir until chocolate is completely melted; cool slightly. Mix flour, coconut, baking soda and salt in medium bowl; set aside.

BEAT butter and sugar in large bowl with electric mixer on medium speed until light and fluffy. Add egg and vanilla; beat well. Stir in melted chocolate. Gradually beat in flour mixture. Stir in remaining chocolate chunks and nuts. Drop by heaping tablespoonfuls onto ungreased cookie sheets.

BAKE 11 to 13 minutes or just until golden brown. Cool on cookie sheets 1 minute. Remove to wire racks and cool completely. *Makes about 3 dozen*

Great Substitute: Substitute toasted, slivered almonds for the macadamia nuts.

Tip: Store in airtight container up to 1 week.

Party Peanut Butter Cookies

> 1½ cups all-purpose flour
> ½ cup sugar
> ½ teaspoon baking soda
> ¾ cup JIF® Creamy Peanut Butter, divided
> ½ Butter Flavor CRISCO® Stick or ½ cup
> Butter Flavor CRISCO® all-vegetable
> shortening
> ¼ cup light corn syrup
> 1 teaspoon vanilla

1. Combine flour, sugar and baking soda in medium bowl. Cut in ½ cup peanut butter and ½ cup shortening until mixture resembles coarse meal. Stir in syrup and vanilla until blended.

2. Form dough into 2-inch roll. Wrap in waxed paper. Refrigerate 1 hour.

3. Heat oven to 350°F. Place sheets of foil on countertop for cooling cookies.

4. Cut dough into ¼-inch slices. Place ½ of slices 2 inches apart on ungreased baking sheet. Spread ½ teaspoon peanut butter on each slice. Top with remaining slices. Seal edges with fork.

5. Bake at 350°F for 10 minutes, or until lightly browned. *Do not overbake.* Cool 2 minutes on baking sheet. Remove to foil to cool completely.
Makes about 2 dozen cookies

Tropical Chunk Cookies

Black & White Hearts

¾ cup sugar
1 cup butter, softened
1 package (3 ounces) cream cheese, softened
1 egg
1½ teaspoons vanilla
3 cups all-purpose flour
1 cup semisweet chocolate chips
2 tablespoons shortening

1. Combine sugar, butter, cream cheese, egg and vanilla in large bowl. Beat at medium speed of electric mixer, scraping bowl often, until light and fluffy. Add flour; beat until well mixed. Divide dough in half; wrap each half in waxed paper. Refrigerate 2 hours or until firm.

2. Preheat oven to 375°F. Roll out dough to 1¼-inch thickness on lightly floured surface. Cut out with lightly floured heart-shaped cookie cutters. Place 1 inch apart on ungreased cookie sheets. Bake 7 to 10 minutes or until edges are very lightly browned. Remove immediately to wire racks to cool completely.

3. Melt chocolate chips and shortening in small saucepan over low heat 4 to 6 minutes or until melted. Dip half of each heart into melted chocolate. Refrigerate on cookie sheets or trays lined with waxed paper until chocolate is firm. Store, covered, in refrigerator.

Makes about 3½ dozen

Choco-Peanut Butter-Brickle Cookies

Prep Time: 15 minutes

1 (14-ounce) can EAGLE® BRAND Sweetened Condensed Milk (NOT evaporated milk)
1 cup chunky peanut butter
2 eggs
1 teaspoon vanilla extract
1½ cups all-purpose flour
1 teaspoon baking soda
½ teaspoon baking powder
½ teaspoon salt
1 cup (6 ounces) semi-sweet chocolate morsels
1 cup almond brickle chips

1. Preheat oven to 350°F. In large mixing bowl, beat Eagle Brand, peanut butter, eggs and vanilla until well blended.

2. In medium mixing bowl, combine flour, baking soda, baking powder and salt; add to peanut butter mixture, beating until blended. Stir in chocolate chips and brickle chips. Drop by heaping tablespoonfuls onto lightly greased baking sheets.

3. Bake 12 minutes or until lightly browned. Cool slightly on baking sheets; remove to wire racks to cool.

Makes 3 dozen cookies

Chocolate Banana Walnut Drops

½ cup (1 stick) butter or margarine, softened
½ cup solid vegetable shortening
1¼ cups firmly packed light brown sugar
1 large egg
1 medium banana, mashed (about ½ cup)
2¼ cups all-purpose flour
1 teaspoon baking soda
1 teaspoon ground cinnamon
½ teaspoon ground nutmeg
¼ teaspoon salt
2 cups quick-cooking or old-fashioned oats, uncooked
1 cup coarsely chopped walnuts
1¾ cups "M&M's"® Chocolate Mini Baking Bits

Preheat oven to 350°F. In large bowl cream butter, shortening and sugar until light and fluffy; beat in egg and banana. In medium bowl combine flour, baking soda, cinnamon, nutmeg and salt; blend into creamed mixture. Blend in oats and nuts. Stir in "M&M's"® Chocolate Mini Baking Bits. Drop by tablespoonfuls about 2 inches apart onto ungreased cookie sheets. Bake 8 to 10 minutes just until set. Do not overbake. Cool 1 minute on cookie sheets; cool completely on wire racks. Store in tightly covered container.   *Makes about 3 dozen cookies*

Lemonade Cookies

1¼ cups granulated sugar
¾ Butter Flavor CRISCO® Stick or ¾ cup Butter Flavor CRISCO® all-vegetable shortening
2 tablespoons freshly squeezed lemon juice
1 tablespoon grated lemon peel
1 teaspoon vanilla
1 teaspoon lemon extract
1 egg
1¾ cups all-purpose flour
¾ teaspoon baking soda
½ teaspoon salt
½ cup flaked coconut (optional)

1. Heat oven to 375°F. Place sheets of foil on countertop for cooling cookies.

2. Place sugar, ¾ cup shortening, lemon juice, lemon peel, vanilla and lemon extract in large bowl. Beat at medium speed of electric mixer until well blended. Add egg; beat well.

3. Combine flour, baking soda and salt. Add to shortening mixture; beat at low speed just until blended.

4. Drop dough by rounded measuring tablespoonfuls 3 inches apart onto ungreased baking sheets. Sprinkle tops with coconut, if desired.

5. Bake one baking sheet at a time at 375°F for 8 to 10 minutes or until cookies are set and edges are lightly browned. (Watch closely; do not allow coconut to burn.) *Do not overbake.* Cool 2 minutes on baking sheet. Remove cookies to foil to cool completely.   *Makes about 3 dozen cookies*

Chocolate Banana Walnut Drops

Double Lemon Delights

2¼ cups all-purpose flour
½ teaspoon baking powder
½ teaspoon salt
1 cup butter, softened
¾ cup granulated sugar
1 egg
2 tablespoons grated lemon peel, divided
1 teaspoon vanilla
    Additional sugar
1 cup powdered sugar
4 to 5 teaspoons lemon juice

1. Preheat oven to 375°F.

2. Combine flour, baking powder and salt in small bowl; set aside. Beat butter and granulated sugar in large bowl of electric mixer at medium speed until light and fluffy. Beat in egg, 1 tablespoon lemon peel and vanilla until well blended. Gradually beat in flour mixture on low speed until blended.

3. Drop dough by level ¼ cupfuls onto ungreased cookie sheets, spacing 3 inches apart. Flatten dough until 3 inches in diameter with bottom of glass that has been dipped in additional sugar.

4. Bake 12 to 14 minutes or until cookies are just set and edges are golden brown. Cool on cookie sheets 2 minutes; transfer to wire racks. Cool completely.

5. Combine powdered sugar, lemon juice and remaining 1 tablespoon lemon peel in small bowl; drizzle mixture over cookies. Let stand until icing is set.   *Makes about 1 dozen (4-inch) cookies*

Ranger Cookies

1 cup (2 sticks) margarine or butter, softened
1 cup granulated sugar
1 cup firmly packed brown sugar
2 eggs
1 teaspoon vanilla
2 cups all-purpose flour
1 teaspoon baking soda
½ teaspoon baking powder
½ teaspoon salt (optional)
2 cups QUAKER® Oats (quick or old fashioned, uncooked)
2 cups cornflakes
½ cup flaked or shredded coconut
½ cup chopped nuts

Heat oven to 350°F. Beat margarine and sugars until creamy. Add eggs and vanilla; beat well. Add combined flour, baking soda, baking powder and salt; mix well. Stir in oats, cornflakes, coconut and nuts; mix well. Drop dough by heaping tablespoonfuls onto ungreased cookie sheets. Bake 10 to 12 minutes or until light golden brown. Cool 1 minute on cookie sheets; remove to wire rack. Cool completely. Store tightly covered.

Makes 2 dozen large cookies

Double Lemon Delights

Oatmeal Toffee Cookies

1 cup (2 sticks) butter or margarine,
    softened
2 eggs
2 cups packed light brown sugar
2 teaspoons vanilla extract
1¾ cups all-purpose flour
1 teaspoon baking soda
1 teaspoon ground cinnamon
½ teaspoon salt
3 cups quick-cooking oats
1¾ cups (10-ounce package) HEATH®
    Almond Toffee Bits or SKOR® English
    Toffee Bits
1 cup MOUNDS® Coconut Flakes (optional)

1. Heat oven to 375°F. Lightly grease cookie sheet. Beat butter, eggs, brown sugar and vanilla until well blended. Add flour, baking soda, cinnamon and salt; beat until blended.

2. Stir in oats, toffee and coconut, if desired, with spoon. Drop dough by rounded teaspoons about 2 inches apart onto prepared sheet.

3. Bake 8 to 10 minutes or until edges are lightly browned. Cool 1 minute; remove to wire rack.

Makes about 4 dozen cookies

Lone Star Peanut Butter Cutouts

¼ cup smooth peanut butter
¼ cup granulated sugar
3 tablespoons softened butter or margarine
1¼ cups buttermilk baking mix
2 tablespoons water
½ teaspoon ground cinnamon
⅔ cup dry-roasted peanut halves
½ cup semisweet chocolate chips

In large bowl, stir together peanut butter, sugar and butter until smooth. Stir in baking mix, water and cinnamon until well-blended. Shape mixture into ball. Wrap dough with plastic wrap and chill about 1 hour or until firm. Cut dough in half. Roll each piece ⅛ inch thick on lightly floured board. Cut dough into shapes with cookie cutter; transfer cutouts to *ungreased* cookie sheets. Press several roasted peanut halves into top of each cookie. Bake in preheated 375°F oven 8 to 10 minutes or until golden brown around edges. With spatula, transfer cookies to cooling rack.

Melt chocolate chips in microwave on HIGH 2 minutes; stir until smooth. Drizzle chocolate glaze over each cookie. Refrigerate until glaze is set. Store cookies in airtight container.

Makes about 2 dozen cookies

Favorite recipe from **Texas Peanut Producers Board**

Oatmeal Toffee Cookies

Lemony Butter Cookies

½ cup butter, softened
½ cup sugar
1 egg
1½ cups all-purpose flour
2 tablespoons fresh lemon juice
1 teaspoon grated lemon peel
½ teaspoon baking powder
⅛ teaspoon salt
Additional sugar

Beat butter and sugar in large bowl with electric mixer at medium speed until creamy. Beat in egg until light and fluffy. Mix in flour, lemon juice and peel, baking powder and salt. Cover; refrigerate about 2 hours or until firm.

Preheat oven to 350°F. Roll out dough, a small portion at a time, on well-floured surface to ¼-inch thickness. (Keep remaining dough in refrigerator.) Cut with 3-inch round or fluted cookie cutter. Transfer to ungreased cookie sheets. Sprinkle with sugar.

Bake 8 to 10 minutes or until edges are lightly browned. Cool 1 minute on cookie sheets. Remove to wire racks; cool completely. Store in airtight container. *Makes about 2½ dozen cookies*

Reese's® Cookies

2 cups all-purpose flour
1 teaspoon baking soda
1 cup shortening or ¾ cup (1½ sticks) butter or margarine, softened
1 cup granulated sugar
½ cup packed light brown sugar
1 teaspoon vanilla extract
2 eggs
1⅔ cups (10-ounce package) REESE'S® Peanut Butter Chips
⅔ cup HERSHEY'S Semi-Sweet Chocolate Chips or Milk Chocolate Chips

1. Heat oven to 350°F. Stir together flour and baking soda.

2. Beat shortening, granulated sugar, brown sugar and vanilla in large bowl until creamy. Add eggs; beat well. Gradually add flour mixture, beating well. Stir in chips. Drop by rounded teaspoons onto ungreased cookie sheet.

3. Bake 8 to 10 minutes or until lightly browned. Cool slightly; remove from cookie sheet to wire rack. Cool completely. *Makes about 5 dozen cookies*

Lemony Butter Cookies

Peanut Butter Surprise Cookies

24 miniature peanut butter cups
1 can (14 ounces) sweetened condensed milk (not evaporated milk)
¾ cup JIF® Creamy Peanut Butter
¼ Butter Flavor CRISCO® Stick or ¼ cup Butter Flavor CRISCO® all-vegetable shortening
1 egg
1 teaspoon vanilla
2 cups regular all-purpose baking mix

1. Remove wrappers from peanut butter cups. Cut candy into quarters.

2. Combine condensed milk, peanut butter, ¼ cup shortening, egg and vanilla in large bowl. Beat at medium speed of electric mixer until smooth. Add baking mix. Beat until well blended. Stir in candy pieces with spoon. Cover. Refrigerate 1 hour.

3. Heat oven to 350°F. Place sheets of foil on countertop for cooling cookies.

4. Drop dough by slightly rounded teaspoonfuls 2 inches apart onto ungreased baking sheet. Shape into balls with spoon.

5. Bake at 350°F for 7 to 9 minutes or until light brown around edges and center is just set. *Do not overbake.* Cool 2 minutes on baking sheet. Remove cookies to foil to cool completely.

Makes about 4 dozen cookies

Variation: Shape dough into 1¼-inch balls. Place 2 inches apart onto ungreased baking sheet. Dip fork in flour; flatten dough slightly in crisscross pattern.

Crunchy Chocolate Chip Cookies

2¼ cups unsifted all-purpose flour
1 teaspoon ARM & HAMMER® Baking Soda
1 teaspoon salt
1 cup softened margarine or butter
¾ cup granulated sugar
¾ cup packed brown sugar
1 teaspoon vanilla extract
2 eggs
2 cups (12 ounces) semi-sweet chocolate chips
1 cup chopped nuts (peanuts, walnuts or pecans)

Preheat oven to 375°F. Sift together flour, Baking Soda and salt in small bowl. Beat margarine, sugars and vanilla in large bowl with electric mixer until creamy. Beat in eggs. Gradually add flour mixture; mix well. Stir in chocolate chips and nuts. Drop by rounded teaspoons onto ungreased cookie sheets. Bake 8 minutes or until lightly browned.

Makes about 8 dozen 2-inch cookies

Peanut Butter Surprise Cookies

Quick-Fix Gingersnaps

1 package (1 pound 1.5 ounces) sugar
    cookie mix
½ cup (1 stick) butter or margarine, melted
1 egg
1 tablespoon light molasses
1 teaspoon ground ginger
½ teaspoon ground cinnamon
¼ cup sugar
½ cup finely chopped pecans

Preheat oven to 375°F.

Combine cookie mix, butter, egg, molasses, ginger and cinnamon in large bowl; mix well. Form dough into 1-inch balls. (Dampen hands when handling dough to prevent sticking.)

Place sugar in shallow bowl. Roll balls of dough in sugar to coat completely. Arrange 2 inches apart on ungreased cookie sheets; flatten slightly with back of metal spatula. Sprinkle with pecans.

Bake 8 to 10 minutes or until lightly browned. Cool 1 minute on cookie sheets. Transfer to wire racks and cool completely. Store in airtight container.

Makes about 4 dozen cookies

Lemon Pecan Cookies

1 Butter Flavor CRISCO® Stick or 1 cup
    Butter Flavor CRISCO® all-vegetable
    shortening
1½ cups granulated sugar
2 large eggs
3 tablespoons fresh lemon juice
3 cups all-purpose flour
2 teaspoons baking powder
¼ teaspoon salt
1 cup chopped pecans

1. Heat oven to 350°F.

2. Combine 1 cup shortening and sugar in large bowl. Beat at medium speed with electric mixer until well blended. Beat in eggs and lemon juice until well blended.

3. Combine flour, baking powder and salt in medium bowl. Add to creamed mixture; mix well. Stir in pecans. Spray cookie sheets lightly with CRISCO® No-Stick Cooking Spray. Drop dough by teaspoonfuls about 2 inches apart onto prepared cookie sheets. Bake at 350°F for 10 fo 12 minutes or until lightly browned. Cool on cookie sheets 4 minutes; transfer to cooling rack.

Makes about 6 dozen cookies

Quick-Fix Gingersnaps

Chocolate-Peanut Butter Checkerboards

½ cup (1 stick) butter or margarine, softened
1 cup sugar
1 egg
1 teaspoon vanilla extract
1 cup plus 3 tablespoons all-purpose flour, divided
½ teaspoon baking soda
¼ cup HERSHEY'S Cocoa
½ cup REESE'S® Peanut Butter Chips, melted

1. Beat butter, sugar, egg and vanilla in large bowl until fluffy. Add 1 cup flour and baking soda; beat until blended. Remove ¾ cup batter to small bowl; set aside. Add cocoa and remaining 3 tablespoons flour to remaining batter in large bowl; blend well.

2. Place peanut butter chips in small microwave-safe bowl. Microwave at HIGH (100%) 30 seconds or until melted and smooth when stirred. Immediately add to batter in small bowl, stirring until smooth. Divide chocolate dough into four equal parts. Roll each part between plastic wrap or waxed paper into a log 7 inches long about 1 inch in diameter. Repeat with peanut butter dough. Wrap the eight rolls individually in waxed paper or plastic wrap. Refrigerate several hours until very firm.

3. Heat oven to 350°F. Remove rolls from waxed paper. Place 1 chocolate roll and 1 peanut butter roll side by side on a cutting board. Top each roll with another roll of the opposite flavor to make checkerboard pattern. Lightly press rolls together; repeat with remaining four rolls. Working with one checkerboard at a time (keep remaining checkerboard covered and refrigerated), cut into ¼-inch slices. Place on ungreased cookie sheet.

4. Bake 8 to 9 minutes or until peanut butter portion is lightly browned. Cool 1 minute; remove from cookie sheet to wire rack. Cool completely.

Makes about 4½ dozen cookies

Oatmeal Pecan Scotchies

½ cup margarine or butter, softened
½ cup packed light brown sugar
1 egg
1¼ cups all-purpose flour
1 cup old-fashioned rolled oats
1 teaspoon CALUMET® Baking Powder
¼ cup milk
½ cup PLANTERS® Pecan Pieces
½ cup butterscotch chips

1. Beat margarine or butter and sugar in large bowl with mixer at medium speed until creamy. Blend in egg.

2. Mix flour, oats and baking powder in small bowl. Alternately stir flour mixture and milk into egg mixture. Stir in pecans and butterscotch chips.

3. Drop batter by rounded teaspoonfuls onto ungreased baking sheets. Bake at 350°F for 12 to 15 minutes or until lightly golden. Remove from pan; cool on wire rack. Store in airtight container.

Makes 4 dozen cookies

Chocolate-Peanut Butter Checkerboards

Dreamy Chocolate Chip Cookies

1¼ cups firmly packed brown sugar
¾ Butter Flavor CRISCO® Stick or ¾ cup Butter Flavor CRISCO® all-vegetable shortening
3 eggs, lightly beaten
2 teaspoons vanilla
1 (4-ounce) package German sweet chocolate, melted, cooled
3 cups all-purpose flour
1 teaspoon baking soda
½ teaspoon salt
1 (11½-ounce) package milk chocolate chips
1 (10-ounce) package premium semisweet chocolate pieces
1 cup coarsely chopped macadamia nuts

1. Heat oven to 375°F. Place sheets of foil on countertop for cooling cookies.

2. Combine brown sugar, ¾ cup shortening, eggs and vanilla in large bowl. Beat at low speed of electric mixer until blended. Increase speed to high. Beat 2 minutes. Add melted chocolate. Mix until well blended.

3. Combine flour, baking soda and salt. Add gradually to shortening mixture at low speed.

4. Stir in chocolate chips, chocolate pieces and nuts with spoon. Drop by rounded tablespoonfuls 3 inches apart onto ungreased baking sheets.

5. Bake at 375°F for 9 to 11 minutes or until set. *Do not overbake.* Cool 2 minutes on baking sheet. Remove cookies to foil to cool completely.

Makes about 3 dozen cookies

Cranberry Brown Sugar Cookies

Prep Time: 30 minutes
Bake Time: 10 minutes
Cooling Time: 30 minutes

2 cups firmly packed DOMINO® Dark Brown Sugar
1 cup butter or margarine, softened
2 eggs
½ cup sour cream
3½ cups all-purpose flour
1 teaspoon baking soda
1 teaspoon salt
1 teaspoon ground cinnamon
½ teaspoon ground nutmeg
¼ teaspoon ground cloves
1 cup dried cranberries (5 ounces)
1 cup golden raisins

Heat oven to 400°F. Lightly grease cookie sheets. Beat sugar and butter in large bowl until light and fluffy. Add eggs and sour cream; beat until creamy. Stir together flour, baking soda, salt, cinnamon, nutmeg and cloves in small bowl; gradually add to sugar mixture, beating until well mixed. Stir in cranberries and raisins. Drop by rounded teaspoonfuls onto cookie sheets. Bake 8 to 10 minutes or until lightly browned. Remove from cookie sheets to cooling racks. Cool.

Makes about 5 dozen cookies

Tips: 1 cup chopped dried cherries may be substituted for 1 cup dried cranberries. If cranberries are exceptionally large, chop before adding to cookie dough.

Dreamy Chocolate Chip Cookies

Best-Selling Bar Cookies

White Chocolate Squares

Prep Time: 15 minutes
Bake Time: 20 to 25 minutes

- 1 (12-ounce) package white chocolate chips, divided
- ¼ cup (½ stick) butter or margarine
- 1 (14-ounce) can EAGLE® BRAND Sweetened Condensed Milk
  (NOT evaporated milk)
- 1 egg
- 1 teaspoon vanilla extract
- 2 cups all-purpose flour
- ½ teaspoon baking powder
- 1 cup chopped pecans, toasted
- Powdered sugar

1. Preheat oven to 350°F. Grease 13×9-inch baking pan. In large saucepan over low heat, melt 1 cup chips and butter. Stir in Eagle Brand, egg and vanilla. Stir in flour and baking powder until blended. Stir in pecans and remaining chips. Spoon mixture into prepared pan.

2. Bake 20 to 25 minutes. Cool. Sprinkle with powdered sugar; cut into squares. Store covered at room temperature.

Makes 24 squares

White Chocolate Squares

Peanutty Cranberry Bars

½ cup (1 stick) butter or margarine,
    softened
½ cup granulated sugar
¼ cup packed light brown sugar
1 cup all-purpose flour
1 cup quick-cooking rolled oats
¼ teaspoon baking soda
¼ teaspoon salt
1 cup REESE'S® Peanut Butter Chips
1½ cups fresh or frozen whole cranberries
⅔ cup light corn syrup
½ cup water
1 teaspoon vanilla extract

1. Heat oven to 350°F. Grease 8-inch square
baking pan.

2. Beat butter, granulated sugar and brown sugar in
medium bowl until fluffy. Stir together flour, oats,
baking soda and salt; gradually add to butter
mixture, mixing until mixture is consistency of
coarse crumbs. Stir in peanut butter chips.

3. Reserve 1½ cups mixture for crumb topping.
Firmly press remaining mixture evenly into
prepared pan. Bake 15 minutes or until set.
Meanwhile, in medium saucepan, combine
cranberries, corn syrup and water. Cook over
medium heat, stirring occasionally, until mixture
boils. Reduce heat; simmer 15 minutes, stirring
occasionally. Remove from heat. Stir in vanilla.
Spread evenly over baked layer. Sprinkle reserved
1½ cups crumbs evenly over top.

4. Return to oven. Bake 15 to 20 minutes or until
set. Cool completely in pan on wire rack. Cut into
bars. *Makes about 16 bars*

Chocolate & Almond Bars

1½ cups unsifted all-purpose flour
⅔ cup sugar
¾ cup (1½ sticks) cold butter or margarine
1½ cups semi-sweet chocolate chips, divided
1 (14-ounce) can EAGLE® BRAND
    Sweetened Condensed Milk
    (NOT evaporated milk)
1 egg
2 cups almonds, toasted and chopped
½ teaspoon almond extract
1 teaspoon solid shortening

1. Preheat oven to 350°F. In large mixing bowl,
combine flour and sugar; cut in butter until
crumbly. Press firmly on bottom of ungreased
13×9-inch baking pan. Bake 20 minutes or until
lightly browned.

2. In medium saucepan over low heat, melt 1 cup
chips with Eagle Brand. Remove from heat; cool
slightly. Beat in egg. Stir in almonds and extract.
Spread over prepared crust. Bake 25 minutes or
until set. Cool.

3. Melt remaining ½ cup chips with shortening;
drizzle over bars. Chill 10 minutes or until set.
Cut into bars. Store covered at room temperature.
Makes about 24 bars

Outlandish Oatmeal Bars

¾ Butter Flavor CRISCO® Stick or ¾ cup
   Butter Flavor CRISCO® all-vegetable
   shortening plus additional for greasing
¾ cup firmly packed brown sugar
½ cup granulated sugar
1 egg
¼ cup apple butter
2 tablespoons milk
1¼ cups all-purpose flour
½ teaspoon baking soda
½ teaspoon salt
2½ cups quick oats (not instant or old
   fashioned)
1 cup SMUCKER'S® Raspberry Preserves,
   stirred
¾ cup white chocolate baking chips

1. Heat oven to 350°F. Grease 13×9×2-inch pan with shortening.

2. Combine ¾ cup shortening, brown sugar, granulated sugar, egg, apple butter and milk in large bowl. Beat at medium speed of electric mixer until well blended.

3. Combine flour, baking soda and salt. Mix into creamed mixture at low speed until just blended. Stir in oats, 1 cup at a time, until well blended.

4. Spread ½ of the dough in bottom of pan. Spread raspberry preserves over dough to within ¼ inch of sides. Mix white chocolate chips in remaining dough. Drop by spoonfuls over preserves. Spread evenly.

5. Bake at 350°F for 30 to 35 minutes, or until golden brown. (Center will be soft.) *Do not overbake.* Run spatula around edge of pan to loosen before cooling. Cool in pan on cooling rack. Cut into 2×1½-inch bars.
Makes 3 dozen bars

Cinnamony Apple Streusel Bars

1¼ cups graham cracker crumbs
1¼ cups all-purpose flour
¾ cup packed brown sugar, divided
¼ cup granulated sugar
1 teaspoon ground cinnamon
¾ cup butter, melted
2 cups chopped apples (2 medium apples,
   cored and peeled)
Glaze (recipe follows)

Preheat oven to 350°F. Grease 13×9-inch baking pan. Combine graham cracker crumbs, flour, ½ cup brown sugar, granulated sugar, cinnamon and melted butter in large bowl until well blended; reserve 1 cup. Press remaining crumb mixture into bottom of prepared pan. Bake 8 minutes. Remove from oven; set aside.

Toss remaining ¼ cup brown sugar with apples in medium bowl until dissolved; arrange apples over baked crust. Sprinkle reserved 1 cup crumb mixture over filling. Bake 30 to 35 minutes or until apples are tender. Remove pan to wire rack; cool completely. Drizzle with Glaze. Cut into bars.
Makes 3 dozen bars

Glaze: Combine ½ cup powdered sugar and 1 tablespoon milk in small bowl until well blended.

Cinnamony Apple Streusel Bars

Chocolate Chip Candy Cookie Bars

1⅔ cups all-purpose flour
2 tablespoons plus 1½ cups sugar, divided
¾ teaspoon baking powder
1 cup (2 sticks) cold butter or margarine, divided
1 egg, slightly beaten
½ cup plus 2 tablespoons (5-ounce can) evaporated milk, divided
2 cups (12-ounce package) HERSHEY'S Semi-Sweet Chocolate Chips, divided
½ cup light corn syrup
1½ cups sliced almonds

1. Heat oven to 375°F.

2. Stir together flour, 2 tablespoons sugar and baking powder in medium bowl; using pastry blender, cut in ½ cup butter until mixture forms coarse crumbs. Stir in egg and 2 tablespoons evaporated milk; stir until mixture holds together in ball shape. Press onto bottom and ¼-inch up sides of 15½×10½×1-inch jelly-roll pan.

3. Bake 8 to 10 minutes or until lightly browned; remove from oven, leaving oven on. Sprinkle 1½ cups chocolate chips evenly over crust; do not disturb chips.

4. Place remaining 1½ cups sugar, remaining ½ cup butter, remaining ½ cup evaporated milk and corn syrup in 3-quart saucepan. Cook over medium heat, stirring constantly, until mixture boils; stir in almonds. Continue cooking and stirring to 240°F on candy thermometer (soft-ball stage) or until small amount of mixture, when dropped into very cold water, forms a soft ball which flattens when removed from water. (Bulb of candy thermometer should not rest on bottom of saucepan.) Remove from heat. Immediately spoon almond mixture evenly over chips and crust; do not spread.

5. Bake 10 to 15 minutes or just until almond mixture is golden brown. Remove from oven; cool 5 minutes. Sprinkle remaining ½ cup chips over top; cool completely. Cut into bars.

Makes about 48 bars

Tip

Candy thermometers are inexpensive and easy to find at kitchenware stores. Most look like long glass tubes with a small bulb at the end, and they should have an adjustable clip to secure them to a pan. When using a candy thermometer, make sure the bulb is completely immersed in the candy syrup (but not touching the bottom of the pan), and read the temperature at eye level.

Chocolate Chip Candy Cookie Bars

Cranberry Cheese Bars

2 cups all-purpose flour
1½ cups quick-cooking or old-fashioned oats, uncooked
¾ cup plus 1 tablespoon firmly packed light brown sugar, divided
1 cup (2 sticks) butter or margarine, softened
1¾ cups "M&M's"® Chocolate Mini Baking Bits, divided
1 (8-ounce) package cream cheese
1 (14-ounce) can sweetened condensed milk
¼ cup lemon juice
1 teaspoon vanilla extract
2 tablespoons cornstarch
1 16-ounce can whole berry cranberry sauce

Preheat oven to 350°F. Lightly grease 13×9×2-inch baking pan; set aside. In large bowl combine flour, oats, ¾ cup sugar and butter; mix until crumbly. Reserve 1½ cups crumb mixture for topping. Stir ½ cup "M&M's"® Chocolate Mini Baking Bits into remaining crumb mixture; press into prepared pan. Bake 15 minutes. Cool completely. In large bowl beat cream cheese until light and fluffy; gradually mix in condensed milk, lemon juice and vanilla until smooth. Pour evenly over crust. In small bowl combine remaining 1 tablespoon sugar, cornstarch and cranberry sauce. Spoon over cream cheese mixture. Stir remaining 1¼ cups "M&M's"® Chocolate Mini Baking Bits into reserved crumb mixture. Sprinkle over cranberry mixture. Bake 40 minutes. Cool at room temperature; refrigerate before cutting. Store in refrigerator in tightly covered container.

Makes 32 bars

Golden Peanut Butter Bars

Prep Time: 20 minutes
Bake Time: 40 minutes

2 cups all-purpose flour
¾ cup firmly packed light brown sugar
1 egg, beaten
½ cup (1 stick) cold butter or margarine
1 cup finely chopped peanuts
1 (14-ounce) can EAGLE® BRAND Sweetened Condensed Milk (NOT evaporated milk)
½ cup peanut butter
1 teaspoon vanilla extract

1. Preheat oven to 350°F. In large mixing bowl, combine flour, brown sugar and egg; cut in cold butter until crumbly. Stir in peanuts. Reserve 2 cups crumb mixture. Press remaining mixture on bottom of 13×9-inch baking pan.

2. Bake 15 minutes or until lightly browned.

3. Meanwhile, in another large mixing bowl, beat Eagle Brand, peanut butter and vanilla. Spread over prepared crust; top with reserved crumb mixture.

4. Bake an additional 25 minutes or until lightly browned. Cool. Cut into bars. Store covered at room temperature.

Makes 24 to 36 bars

Cranberry Cheese Bars

Awesome Apricot Oatmeal Bars

⅔ cup chopped dried apricots
⅔ cup water
½ cup SMUCKER'S® Apricot Preserves
1 tablespoon granulated sugar
½ teaspoon almond extract
1 Butter Flavor CRISCO® Stick or 1 cup
    Butter Flavor CRISCO® all-vegetable
    shortening
1½ cups firmly packed brown sugar
1½ cups all-purpose flour
1½ cups quick oats (not instant or old
    fashioned)
1 teaspoon baking powder
½ teaspoon salt

1. Combine apricots and water in small covered saucepan. Cook on medium heat about 10 minutes. Remove lid. Cook until apricots are tender and water has evaporated. Add preserves, granulated sugar and almond extract. Stir until preserves melt. Cool to room temperature.

2. Heat oven to 350°F. Place cooling rack on counter top.

3. Combine 1 cup shortening, brown sugar, flour, oats, baking powder and salt in large bowl. Mix at low speed of electric mixer until well blended and crumbly.

4. Press ½ of the mixture in bottom of ungreased 13×9×2-inch pan. Spread filling evenly over crust. Sprinkle remaining mixture over filling. Press down gently.

5. Bake at 350°F for 30 minutes, or until crust is golden brown. *Do not overbake.* Remove pan to rack. Cool slightly. Run spatula around edge of pan to loosen. Cut into 2×1½-inch bars. Cool in pan on cooling rack.   *Makes 3 dozen bars*

Easy Turtle Squares

1 package (about 18 ounces) chocolate cake
    mix
½ cup butter, melted
¼ cup milk
1 cup (6-ounce package) semisweet
    chocolate chips
1 cup chopped pecans, divided
1 jar (12 ounces) caramel ice cream topping

1. Preheat oven to 350°F. Spray 13×9-inch pan with nonstick cooking spray.

2. Combine cake mix, butter and milk in large bowl. Press half of mixture into prepared pan.

3. Bake 7 to 8 minutes or until batter begins to form crust. Carefully remove from oven. Sprinkle chocolate chips and ½ cup pecans over partially baked crust. Drizzle caramel topping over chips and pecans. Drop spoonfuls of remaining cake batter over caramel mixture; sprinkle with remaining ½ cup pecans.   *Makes 24 bar cookies*

Easy Turtle Squares

Fruit and Nut Bars

1 cup unsifted all-purpose flour
1 cup quick oats
⅔ cup brown sugar
2 teaspoons baking soda
½ teaspoon salt
½ teaspoon cinnamon
⅔ cup buttermilk
3 tablespoons vegetable oil
2 egg whites, lightly beaten
1 Washington Golden Delicious apple, cored and chopped
½ cup dried cranberries or raisins, chopped
¼ cup chopped nuts
2 tablespoons flaked coconut (optional)

1. Heat oven to 375°F. Lightly grease 9-inch square baking pan. In large mixing bowl, combine flour, oats, brown sugar, baking soda, salt and cinnamon; stir to blend.

2. Add buttermilk, oil and egg whites; beat with electric mixer just until mixed. Stir in apple, dried fruit and nuts; spread evenly in pan and top with coconut, if desired. Bake 20 to 25 minutes or until cake tester inserted in center comes out clean. Cool and cut into 10 bars. *Makes 10 bars*

Favorite recipe from **Washington Apple Commission**

Chewy Toffee Almond Bars

1 cup (2 sticks) butter, softened
½ cup sugar
2 cups all-purpose flour
1¾ cups (10-ounce package) SKOR® English Toffee Bits or HEATH® BITS 'O BRICKLE™
¾ cup light corn syrup
1 cup sliced almonds, divided
¾ cup MOUNDS® Sweetened Coconut Flakes, divided

1. Heat oven to 350°F. Grease sides of 13×9×2-inch baking pan.

2. Beat butter and sugar until fluffy. Gradually add flour, beating until well blended. Press dough evenly into prepared pan.

3. Bake 15 to 20 minutes or until edges are lightly browned. Meanwhile, combine toffee bits and corn syrup in medium saucepan. Cook over medium heat, stirring constantly, until toffee is melted (about 10 to 12 minutes). Stir in ½ cup almonds and ½ cup coconut. Spread toffee mixture to within ¼ inch of edges of crust. Sprinkle remaining ½ cup almonds and remaining ¼ cup coconut over top.

4. Bake an additional 15 minutes or until bubbly. Cool completely in pan on wire rack. Cut into bars. *Makes about 36 bars*

Double Delicious Cookie Bars

Prep Time: 10 minutes
Bake Time: 25 to 30 minutes

  ½ cup (1 stick) butter or margarine
1½ cups graham cracker crumbs
  1 (14-ounce) can EAGLE® BRAND
     Sweetened Condensed Milk
     (NOT evaporated milk)
  2 cups (12 ounces) semi-sweet chocolate
     chips*
  1 cup (6 ounces) peanut butter-flavored
     chips*

Butterscotch-flavored chips or white chocolate chips can be substituted for the semi-sweet chocolate chips and/or peanut butter-flavored chips.

1. Preheat oven to 350°F (325°F for glass dish). In 13×9-inch baking pan, melt butter in oven.

2. Sprinkle crumbs evenly over butter; pour Eagle Brand evenly over crumbs. Top with remaining ingredients; press down firmly.

3. Bake 25 to 30 minutes or until lightly browned. Cool. Cut into bars. Store covered at room temperature.　　*Makes 2 to 3 dozen bars*

Chewy Chocolate No-Bakes

  1 cup (6 ounces) semisweet chocolate pieces
16 large marshmallows
  ⅓ cup (5 tablespoons plus 1 teaspoon)
     margarine or butter
  2 cups QUAKER® Oats (quick or
     old fashioned, uncooked)
  1 cup (any combination of) raisins, diced
     dried mixed fruit, flaked coconut,
     miniature marshmallows or chopped
     nuts
  1 teaspoon vanilla

In large saucepan over low heat, melt chocolate pieces, marshmallows and margarine, stirring until smooth. Remove from heat; cool slightly. Stir in remaining ingredients. Drop by rounded teaspoonfuls onto waxed paper. Chill 2 to 3 hours. Let stand at room temperature about 15 minutes before serving. Store in tightly covered container in refrigerator.　　*Makes 3 dozen cookies*

Microwave Directions: Place chocolate pieces, margarine and marshmallows in large microwavable bowl. Microwave on HIGH 1 to 2 minutes or until mixture is melted and smooth, stirring every 30 seconds. Proceed as recipe directs.

Double Delicious Cookie Bars

Praline Bars

Prep Time: 30 minutes
Bake Time: 53 minutes

   ¾ cup butter or margarine, softened
   1 cup sugar, divided
   1 teaspoon vanilla, divided
   1½ cups flour
   2 packages (8 ounces each)
       PHILADELPHIA® Cream Cheese,
       softened
   2 eggs
   ½ cup almond brickle chips
   3 tablespoons caramel ice cream topping

MIX butter, ½ cup of the sugar and ½ teaspoon of
the vanilla with electric mixer on medium speed
until light and fluffy. Gradually add flour, mixing
on low speed until blended. Press onto bottom of
13×9-inch pan. Bake at 350°F for 20 to 23 minutes
or until lightly browned.

MIX cream cheese, remaining ½ cup sugar and
½ teaspoon vanilla with electric mixer on medium
speed until well blended. Add eggs; mix well. Blend
in chips. Pour over crust. Dot top of cream cheese
mixture with topping. Cut through batter with knife
several times for marble effect.

BAKE at 350°F for 30 minutes. Cool in pan on wire
rack. Cut into bars.   *Makes 2 dozen bars*

Fruit and Chocolate Dream Bars

Crust
   1¼ cups all-purpose flour
   ½ cup granulated sugar
   ½ cup (1 stick) butter or margarine

Topping
   ⅔ cup all-purpose flour
   ½ cup chopped pecans
   ⅓ cup packed brown sugar
   6 tablespoons butter or margarine, softened
   ½ cup raspberry or strawberry jam
   1¾ cups (11.5-ounce package) NESTLÉ®
       TOLL HOUSE® Milk Chocolate Morsels

PREHEAT oven to 375°F. Grease 9-inch-square pan.

For Crust
COMBINE flour and granulated sugar in medium
bowl. Cut in butter with pastry blender or two
knives until mixture resembles coarse crumbs.
Press onto bottom of prepared baking pan.

BAKE for 18 to 22 minutes or until set but not
brown.

For Topping
COMBINE flour, nuts and brown sugar in small
bowl. Cut in butter with pastry blender or two
knives until mixture resembles coarse crumbs.

SPREAD jam over hot crust. Sprinkle with morsels
and topping.

BAKE for 15 to 20 minutes or until golden brown.
Cool completely in pan on wire rack.
                              Makes 2½ dozen bars

Praline Bars

Emily's Dream Bars

½ Butter Flavor CRISCO® Stick or ½ cup
    Butter Flavor CRISCO® all-vegetable
    shortening plus additional for greasing
1 cup JIF® Crunchy Peanut Butter
½ cup firmly packed brown sugar
½ cup light corn syrup
1 egg
1 teaspoon vanilla
1 cup all-purpose flour
½ teaspoon baking powder
¼ cup milk
2 cups 100% natural oats, honey and raisins
    cereal
1 package (12 ounces) miniature semi-sweet
    chocolate chips (2 cups), divided
1 cup almond brickle chips
1 cup milk chocolate covered peanuts
1 package (2 ounces) nut topping (⅓ cup)

1. Heat oven to 350°F. Grease 13×9×2-inch pan with shortening. Place cooling rack on top of countertop.

2. Combine ½ cup shortening, peanut butter, brown sugar and corn syrup in large bowl. Beat at medium speed of electric mixer until creamy. Add egg and vanilla. Beat well.

3. Combine flour and baking powder. Add alternately with milk to creamed mixture at medium speed. Stir in cereal, 1 cup chocolate chips, almond brickle chips and chocolate covered nuts with spoon. Spread in prepared pan.

4. Bake at 350°F for 20 to 26 minutes or until golden brown and toothpick inserted in center comes out clean. *Do not overbake.* Sprinkle remaining 1 cup chocolate chips over top immediately after removing from oven. Remove pan to cooling rack. Let stand about 3 minutes or until chips become shiny and soft. Spread over top. Sprinkle with nut topping. Cool completely. Cut into 2×1- inch bars.

Makes 4½ dozen bars

Tip

When measuring sticky liquids such as corn syrup or molasses, lightly coat the measuring cup or spoon with oil or nonstick cooking spray before measuring. The liquids will slide right out and make cleanup much easier.

Emily's Dream Bars

Peanut Butter Chips and Jelly Bars

1½ cups all-purpose flour
½ cup sugar
¾ teaspoon baking powder
½ cup (1 stick) cold butter or margarine
1 egg, beaten
¾ cup grape jelly
1⅔ cups (10-ounce package) REESE'S®
    Peanut Butter Chips, divided

1. Heat oven to 375°F. Grease 9-inch square baking pan.

2. Stir together flour, sugar and baking powder in large bowl. With pastry blender or two knives, cut in butter until mixture resembles coarse crumbs. Add egg; blend well. Reserve half of mixture; press remaining mixture onto bottom of prepared pan. Spread jelly over crust. Sprinkle 1 cup peanut butter chips over jelly. Stir together reserved crumb mixture with remaining ⅔ cup chips; sprinkle over top.

3. Bake 25 to 30 minutes or until lightly browned. Cool completely in pan on wire rack. Cut into bars.

Makes about 16 bars

Tip: For a whimsical twist on this tried-and-true classic, use cookie cutters to cut out shapes for added fun.

Pumpkin Snack Bars

Prep Time: 20 minutes
Bake Time: 20 minutes

Cake
  1 package (2-layer size) spice cake mix
  1 can (16 ounces) pumpkin
  ¾ cup MIRACLE WHIP® or MIRACLE
    WHIP® LIGHT Dressing
  3 eggs

Frosting
  3½ cups powdered sugar
  ½ cup (1 stick) butter *or* margarine,
    softened
  2 tablespoons milk
  1 teaspoon vanilla

Cake
BLEND cake mix, pumpkin, dressing and eggs with electric mixer on medium speed until well blended. Pour into greased 15×10×1-inch baking pan.

BAKE at 350°F for 18 to 20 minutes or until toothpick inserted in center comes out clean. Cool completely on wire rack.

Frosting
BLEND all ingredients with electric mixer on low speed until moistened. Beat on high speed until light and fluffy. Spread over cake. Cut into bars.

Makes about 3 dozen bars

Note: Bars can be baked in greased 13×9-inch baking pan. Bake at 350°F for 32 to 35 minutes or until toothpick inserted in center comes out clean. Cool and frost as directed.

Peanut Butter Chips and Jelly Bars

Caramel Apple Bars

Crust

¾ **Butter Flavor CRISCO® Stick or ¾ cup Butter Flavor CRISCO® all-vegetable shortening plus additional for greasing**
1 **cup firmly packed light brown sugar**
1 **egg**
1½ **cups all-purpose flour**
½ **teaspoon salt**
½ **teaspoon baking soda**
1¾ **cups quick oats, uncooked**

Filling

3 to 4 **Granny Smith or Golden Delicious apples, peeled and cut into ½-inch dice (about 4 cups)**
2 **tablespoons all-purpose flour**
1 **teaspoon lemon juice**
1 **bag (14 ounces) caramel candy, unwrapped**

1. Heat oven to 350°F. Grease 13×9×2-inch baking pan with shortening.

2. For crust, combine ¾ cup shortening and brown sugar in large bowl. Beat at medium speed of electric mixer. Add egg to creamed mixture. Beat until well blended.

3. Combine 1½ cups flour, salt and baking soda. Add to creamed mixture gradually. Add in oats. Mix until blended. Reserve 1¼ cups of mixture for topping. Press remaining mixture into prepared pan.

4. Bake at 350°F for 10 minutes.

5. For filling, toss apples with 2 tablespoons flour and lemon juice. Distribute apple mixture evenly over partially baked crust. Press in lightly.

6. Place caramels in microwave-safe bowl. Microwave at HIGH (100%) for 1 minute. Stir. Repeat until caramels are melted. Drizzle melted caramel evenly over apples. Crumble reserved topping evenly over caramel.

7. Bake at 350°F for 30 to 40 minutes, or until apples are tender and top is golden brown. *Do not overbake.* Loosen caramel from sides of pan with knife. Cool completely. Cut into 1½-inch bars. Cover tightly with plastic wrap to store.

Makes about 4 dozen bars

Raspberry Crisp Bars

Crust
>   ½ Butter Flavor CRISCO® Stick or ½ cup
>   Butter Flavor CRISCO® all-vegetable
>   shortening
>   ⅓ cup confectioners' sugar
>   1 cup all-purpose flour

Topping
>   ½ cup all-purpose flour
>   3 tablespoons firmly packed light brown
>   sugar
>   ¼ teaspoon baking powder
>   ¼ teaspoon ground cinnamon
>   4 tablespoons Butter Flavor CRISCO®
>   all-vegetable shortening
>   1 egg yolk
>   ½ teaspoon vanilla
>   ¾ cup SMUCKER'S® Raspberry Preserves
>   or favorite flavor

1. Heat oven to 350°F.

2. For crust, combine ½ cup shortening and confectioners' sugar in large bowl. Beat at medium speed with electric mixer until well blended. Stir in 1 cup flour until mixture is just crumbly. Press into bottom of ungreased 8-inch square baking pan. Bake at 350°F for 10 to 12 minutes or until crust is set but not browned. Remove from oven and place on cooling rack.

3. For topping, combine ½ cup flour, brown sugar, baking powder and cinnamon in medium bowl; mix well. Cut in shortening with fork until mixture forms even crumbs. Add egg yolk and vanilla; mix well.

4. Spread preserves evenly over crust. Sprinkle topping evenly over preserves. Bake at 350°F for 30 minutes or until topping is golden. Place on cooling rack and allow to cool completely. Cut into bars. *Makes 1 dozen bars*

Tip

Always use the pan size called for in bar cookie recipes. If your pan is too small, the cookies will turn out thick and gummy. A pan that is too large will cause the cookies to be thin and dry.

Peanut Butter Chip Triangles

Prep Time: 20 minutes
Bake Time: 40 minutes
Cool Time: 2 hours

>   1½ cups all-purpose flour
>   ½ cup packed light brown sugar
>   ½ cup (1 stick) cold butter or margarine
>   1⅔ cups (10-ounce package) REESE'S®
>   Peanut Butter Chips, divided
>   1 can (14 ounces) sweetened condensed
>   milk (not evaporated milk)
>   1 egg, slightly beaten
>   1 teaspoon vanilla extract
>   ¾ cup chopped walnuts
>   Powdered sugar (optional)

1. Heat oven to 350°F. Stir together flour and brown sugar in medium bowl. Cut in butter with pastry blender or fork until mixture resembles coarse crumbs. Stir in ½ cup peanut butter chips. Press mixture into bottom of ungreased 13×9×2-inch baking pan. Bake 15 minutes.

2. Meanwhile, combine sweetened condensed milk, egg and vanilla in large bowl. Stir in remaining chips and walnuts. Spread evenly over hot baked crust.

3. Bake 25 minutes or until golden brown. Cool completely in pan on wire rack. Cut into 2- or 2½-inch squares; cut squares diagonally into triangles. Sift powdered sugar over top, if desired.

Makes 24 or 40 triangles

Tip: To sprinkle powdered sugar over brownies, bars, cupcakes or other desserts, place sugar in a wire mesh strainer. Hold over top of desserts and gently tap sides of strainer.

Buttery Black Raspberry Bars

>   1 cup butter or margarine
>   1 cup sugar
>   2 egg yolks
>   2 cups all-purpose flour
>   1 cup chopped walnuts
>   ½ cup SMUCKER'S® Seedless Black
>   Raspberry Jam

Beat butter until soft and creamy. Gradually add sugar, beating until mixture is light and fluffy. Add egg yolks; blend well. Gradually add flour; mix thoroughly. Fold in walnuts.

Spoon half of batter into greased 8-inch square pan; spread evenly. Top with jam; cover with remaining batter.

Bake at 325°F for 1 hour or until lightly browned. Cool and cut into 2×1-inch bars. *Makes 32 bars*

Peanut Butter Chip Triangles

Candy Bar Bars

Prep Time: 20 minutes
Bake Time: 40 minutes

¾ cup (1½ sticks) butter or margarine, softened
¼ cup peanut butter
1 cup firmly packed light brown sugar
1 teaspoon baking soda
2 cups quick-cooking oats
1½ cups all-purpose flour
1 egg
1 (14-ounce) can **EAGLE® BRAND Sweetened Condensed Milk (NOT evaporated milk)**
4 cups chopped candy bars (such as chocolate-coated caramel-topped nougat bars with peanuts, chocolate-covered crisp wafers, chocolate-covered caramel-topped cookie bars, or chocolate-covered peanut butter cups)

1. Preheat oven to 350°F. In large mixing bowl, combine butter and peanut butter. Add brown sugar and baking soda; beat well. Stir in oats and flour. Reserve 1¾ cups crumb mixture.

2. Stir egg into remaining crumb mixture; press firmly on bottom of ungreased 15×10×1-inch baking pan. Bake 15 minutes.

3. Pour Eagle Brand evenly over baked crust. Stir together reserved crumb mixture and candy bar pieces; sprinkle evenly over top. Bake 25 minutes or until golden. Cool. Cut into bars. Store covered at room temperature. *Makes 4 dozen bars*

Double Decker Bars

Prep Time: 20 minutes
Bake Time: 35 minutes

3 ripe DOLE® Bananas, divided
½ cup margarine
1 cup granulated sugar
1 cup packed brown sugar
2 eggs
¼ cup plus 3 tablespoons peanut butter, divided
1 teaspoon vanilla extract
2 cups all-purpose flour
2 teaspoons baking powder
¼ teaspoon salt
2 tablespoons milk
2½ cups powdered sugar

• Blend 1 banana in blender (½ cup). Beat margarine and sugars in large bowl. Beat in puréed banana, eggs, 3 tablespoons peanut butter and vanilla.

• Combine flour, baking powder and salt in medium bowl. Gradually beat dry ingredients into banana mixture.

• Spread half of batter in greased 13×9-inch baking pan. Finely chop 1 banana; sprinkle over batter in pan. Cover with remaining batter.

• Bake at 350°F, 30 to 35 minutes. Cool completely.

• For Peanut Butter Frosting, blend remaining banana in blender (¼ cup). Combine banana, remaining peanut butter and milk. Slowly beat in powdered sugar until thick and smooth. Frost bars. *Makes 24 bars*

Candy Bar Bars

Fabulous Fruit Bars

1½ cups all-purpose flour, divided
1½ cups sugar, divided
½ cup MOTT'S® Apple Sauce, divided
½ teaspoon baking powder
2 tablespoons margarine
½ cup chopped peeled apple
½ cup chopped dried apricots
½ cup chopped cranberries
1 whole egg
1 egg white
1 teaspoon lemon juice
½ teaspoon vanilla extract
1 teaspoon ground cinnamon

1. Preheat oven to 350°F. Spray 13×9-inch baking pan with nonstick cooking spray.

2. In medium bowl, combine 1¼ cups flour, ½ cup sugar, ⅓ cup apple sauce and baking powder. Cut in margarine with pastry blender or fork until mixture resembles coarse crumbs.

3. In large bowl, combine apple, apricots, cranberries, remaining apple sauce, whole egg, egg white, lemon juice and vanilla.

4. In small bowl, combine remaining 1 cup sugar, ¼ cup flour and cinnamon. Add to fruit mixture, stirring just until mixed.

5. Press half of crumb mixture evenly into bottom of prepared pan. Top with fruit mixture. Sprinkle with remaining crumb mixture.

6. Bake 40 minutes or until lightly browned. Broil, 4 inches from heat, 1 to 2 minutes or until golden brown. Cool on wire rack 15 minutes; cut into 16 bars.   *Makes 16 servings*

Chocolate Cranberry Bars

Prep Time: 15 minutes
Bake Time: 25 to 30 minutes

2 cups vanilla wafer crumbs
½ cup unsweetened cocoa
3 tablespoons sugar
⅔ cup (1⅓ sticks) cold butter, cut into pieces
1 (14-ounce) can EAGLE® BRAND
    Sweetened Condensed Milk
    (NOT evaporated milk)
1⅓ cups (6-ounce package) sweetened dried
    cranberries or raisins
1 cup peanut butter-flavored chips
1 cup finely chopped walnuts

1. Preheat oven to 350°F. In medium mixing bowl, combine wafer crumbs, cocoa and sugar; cut in butter until crumbly.

2. Press mixture evenly on bottom and ½ inch up sides of ungreased 13×9-inch baking pan. Pour Eagle Brand evenly over crumb mixture. Sprinkle evenly with dried cranberries, peanut butter chips and nuts; press down firmly.

3. Bake 25 to 30 minutes or until lightly browned. Cool completely in pan on wire rack. Cover with foil; let stand several hours. Cut into bars. Store covered at room temperature.   *Makes about 36 bars*

Fabulous Fruit Bars

Chocolate Cream Cheese Sugar Cookie Bars

1 package (22.3 ounces) golden sugar cookie mix
3 eggs, divided
⅓ cup plus 6 tablespoons butter or margarine, softened and divided
1 teaspoon water
1 package (8 ounces) cream cheese, softened
1 package (3 ounces) cream cheese, softened
¾ cup granulated sugar
⅓ cup HERSHEY'S Cocoa
1½ teaspoons vanilla extract
Powdered sugar

1. Heat oven to 350°F.

2. Empty cookie mix into large bowl. Break up any lumps. Add 2 eggs, ⅓ cup butter and water; stir with spoon or fork until well blended. Spread into ungreased 13×9×2-inch baking pan.

3. Beat cream cheese and remaining 6 tablespoons butter in medium bowl on medium speed of mixer until fluffy. Stir together granulated sugar and cocoa; gradually add to cream cheese mixture, beating until smooth and well blended. Add remaining egg and vanilla; beat well. Spread cream cheese mixture evenly over cookie batter.

4. Bake 35 to 40 minutes or until no imprint remains when touched lightly in center. Cool completely in pan on wire rack. Sprinkle powdered sugar over top. Cut into bars. Cover; store leftover bars in refrigerator. *Makes about 24 to 30 bars*

Peanut Butter & Jelly Streusel Bars

1¼ cups firmly packed light brown sugar
¾ cup JIF® Creamy Peanut Butter
½ CRISCO® Stick or ½ cup CRISCO® all-vegetable shortening plus additional for greasing
3 tablespoons milk
1 tablespoon vanilla
1 egg
1¾ cups all-purpose flour
¾ teaspoon baking soda
¾ teaspoon salt
1 cup SMUCKER'S® Strawberry Jam, stirred
½ cup quick oats, uncooked

1. Heat oven to 350°F. Grease 13×9-inch baking pan. Place cooling rack on countertop.

2. Place brown sugar, peanut butter, ½ cup shortening, milk and vanilla in large bowl. Beat at medium speed of electric mixer until well blended. Add egg; beat just until blended.

3. Combine flour, baking soda and salt. Add to shortening mixture; beat at low speed just until blended.

4. Press ⅔ of dough onto bottom of prepared pan. Spread jam over dough to within ¼ inch of edges.

5. Add oats to remaining dough. Drop dough by spoonfuls onto jam.

6. Bake at 350°F for 20 to 25 minutes or until edges and streusel topping are lightly browned. *Do not overbake.* Cool completely on cooling rack. Cut into 2×1½-inch bars. *Makes about 3 dozen bars*

Chocolate Cream Cheese Sugar Cookie Bars

Coconut Pecan Bars

¾ cup (1½ sticks) butter or margarine, softened, divided
1¼ cups granulated sugar, divided
½ cup plus 3 tablespoons all-purpose flour, divided
1½ cups finely chopped pecans, divided
2 large eggs
1 tablespoon vanilla extract
1¾ cups "M&M's"® Chocolate Mini Baking Bits, divided
1 cup shredded coconut

Preheat oven to 350°F. Lightly grease 13×9×2-inch baking pan; set aside. Melt ¼ cup butter. In large bowl combine ¾ cup sugar, ½ cup flour and ½ cup nuts; add melted butter and mix well. Press mixture onto bottom of prepared pan. Bake 10 minutes or until set; cool slightly. In large bowl cream remaining ½ cup butter and ½ cup sugar; beat in eggs and vanilla. Combine 1 cup "M&M's"® Chocolate Mini Baking Bits and remaining 3 tablespoons flour; stir into creamed mixture. Spread mixture over cooled crust. Combine coconut and remaining 1 cup nuts; sprinkle over batter. Sprinkle remaining ¾ cup "M&M's"® Chocolate Mini Baking Bits over coconut and nuts; pat down lightly. Bake 25 to 30 minutes or until set. Cool completely. Cut into bars. Store in tightly covered container.

Makes 24 bars

Apricot Honey Oat Bar Cookies

1½ cups old-fashioned rolled oats, uncooked
½ cup finely chopped dried apricots
½ cup honey
¼ cup nonfat plain yogurt
2 egg whites
3 tablespoons butter or margarine, melted
2 tablespoons wheat germ
2 tablespoons all-purpose flour
½ teaspoon ground cinnamon
½ teaspoon vanilla
¼ teaspoon salt

Spray 8-inch square baking pan with nonstick cooking spray. Combine all ingredients in large bowl; mix well. Spread mixture evenly into prepared pan. Bake at 325°F about 25 minutes or until center is firm and edges are lightly browned. Cool and cut into 2-inch squares.

Makes 8 servings

Favorite recipe from **National Honey Board**

Coconut Pecan Bars

Rocky Road Bars

2 cups (12-ounce package) NESTLÉ®
    TOLL HOUSE® Semi-Sweet Chocolate
    Morsels, *divided*
1½ cups all-purpose flour
1½ teaspoons baking powder
  1 cup granulated sugar
  6 tablespoons (¾ stick) butter or
    margarine, softened
1½ teaspoons vanilla extract
  2 large eggs
  2 cups miniature marshmallows
1½ cups coarsely chopped walnuts

PREHEAT oven to 375°F. Grease 13×9-inch baking pan.

MICROWAVE *1 cup* morsels in medium, microwave-safe bowl on HIGH (100%) power for 1 minute; stir. Microwave at additional 10- to 20-second intervals; stir until smooth. Cool to room temperature. Combine flour and baking powder in small bowl.

BEAT sugar, butter and vanilla in large mixer bowl until crumbly. Beat in eggs. Add melted chocolate; beat until smooth. Gradually beat in flour mixture. Spread batter into prepared baking pan.

BAKE for 16 to 20 minutes or until wooden pick inserted in center comes out still slightly sticky.

REMOVE from oven; sprinkle immediately with marshmallows, nuts and *remaining* morsels. Return to oven for 2 minutes or just until marshmallows begin to melt. Cool in pan on wire rack for 20 to 30 minutes. Cut into bars with wet knife. Serve warm.

Makes 2½ dozen bars

Magic Apple Cookie Bars

¼ Butter Flavor CRISCO® Stick or ¼ cup
    Butter Flavor CRISCO® all-vegetable
    shortening plus additional for greasing
  1 cup uncooked oats
  ¾ cup graham cracker crumbs
1½ cups very finely chopped peeled Granny
    Smith or other firm, tart cooking
    apples
  ½ cup butterscotch chips (optional)
  ½ cup flaked coconut
  ½ cup finely chopped nuts
  1 can (14 ounces) sweetened condensed
    milk (not evaporated milk)

1. Heat oven to 350°F. Grease 11×7×2-inch glass baking dish with shortening. Place cooling rack on countertop.

2. Combine oats, graham cracker crumbs and ¼ cup shortening. Stir well. Press firmly on bottom of greased baking dish. Top with apples, butterscotch chips, coconut and nuts. Pour condensed milk evenly over top.

3. Bake for 30 to 35 minutes or until lightly browned. *Do not overbake.* Loosen from sides of dish while still warm. Cool completely. Cut into bars about 2×1½ inches. Serve immediately or refrigerate.

Makes 3 dozen bars

Rocky Road Bars

Frosted Pumpkin Squares

Prep Time: 20 minutes
Bake Time: 35 minutes

Cake

- ¾ cup (1½ sticks) butter *or* margarine
- 2 cups granulated sugar
- 1 can (16 ounces) pumpkin
- 4 eggs
- 2 cups flour
- 2 teaspoons CALUMET® Baking Powder
- 1 teaspoon ground cinnamon
- ½ teaspoon baking soda
- ½ teaspoon salt
- ¼ teaspoon ground nutmeg
- 1 cup chopped PLANTERS® Walnuts

Frosting

- 1 package (8 ounces) PHILADELPHIA® Cream Cheese, softened
- ⅓ cup butter *or* margarine
- 1 teaspoon vanilla
- 3 cups sifted powdered sugar

Cake

MIX butter and sugar with electric mixer on medium speed until light and fluffy. Blend in pumpkin and eggs. Mix in combined dry ingredients. Stir in walnuts.

SPREAD into greased and floured 15×10×1-inch baking pan.

BAKE at 350°F for 30 to 35 minutes or until wooden pick inserted in center comes out clean; cool.

Frosting

MIX cream cheese, butter and vanilla in large bowl with electric mixer until creamy. Gradually add sugar, mixing well after each addition. Spread onto cake. Cut into squares.   *Makes 2 dozen squares*

Make-Ahead: Prepare recipe as directed, omitting frosting. Wrap securely; freeze. When ready to serve, thaw at room temperature. Frost, if desired.

Tip

When a recipe calls for sifted powdered sugar or sifted flour, it's important to sift before measuring. Sifting after measuring can result in a different amount of sugar or flour, and this may affect the final product. (However, if a recipe calls for sugar or flour, sifted, then the sifting should be done after measuring.)

Frosted Pumpkin Square

Chocolate Nut Bars

Prep Time: 10 minutes
Bake Time: 33 to 38 minutes

1¾ cups graham cracker crumbs
½ cup (1 stick) butter or margarine, melted
1 (14-ounce) can EAGLE® BRAND Sweetened Condensed Milk (NOT evaporated milk)
2 cups (12 ounces) semi-sweet chocolate chips, divided
1 teaspoon vanilla extract
1 cup chopped nuts

1. Preheat oven to 375°F. In medium mixing bowl, combine crumbs and butter; press firmly on bottom of ungreased 13×9-inch baking pan. Bake 8 minutes. Reduce oven temperature to 350°F.

2. In small saucepan, melt Eagle Brand with 1 cup chips and vanilla. Spread chocolate mixture over prepared crust. Top with remaining 1 cup chips and nuts; press down firmly.

3. Bake 25 to 30 minutes. Cool. Chill, if desired. Cut into bars. Store loosely covered at room temperature.

Makes 24 to 36 bars

Chocolate Scotcheroos

1 cup light corn syrup
1 cup sugar
1 cup peanut butter
6 cups KELLOGG'S® RICE KRISPIES® cereal
1 package (6 ounces, 1 cup) semi-sweet chocolate morsels
1 package (6 ounces, 1 cup) butterscotch morsels

1. Place corn syrup and sugar in large saucepan. Cook over medium heat, stirring frequently, until sugar dissolves and mixture begins to boil. Remove from heat. Stir in peanut butter; mix well. Add Kellogg's® Rice Krispies® cereal. Stir until well coated. Press mixture into 13×9×2-inch pan coated with cooking spray. Set aside.

2. Melt chocolate and butterscotch morsels together in small saucepan over low heat, stirring constantly. Spread evenly over cereal mixture. Let stand until firm. Cut into bars when cool.

Makes about 48 bars

Chocolate Nut Bars

Toffee-Top Cheesecake Bars

Prep Time: 20 minutes
Bake Time: 40 minutes
Cool Time: 15 minutes

1¼ cups all-purpose flour
1 cup powdered sugar
½ cup unsweetened cocoa
¼ teaspoon baking soda
¾ cup (1½ sticks) butter or margarine
1 (8-ounce) package cream cheese, softened
1 (14-ounce) can EAGLE® BRAND Sweetened Condensed Milk (NOT evaporated milk)
2 eggs
1 teaspoon vanilla extract
1½ cups (8-ounce package) English toffee bits, divided

1. Preheat oven to 350°F. In medium mixing bowl, combine flour, powdered sugar, cocoa and baking soda; cut in butter until mixture is crumbly. Press firmly on bottom of ungreased 13×9-inch baking pan. Bake 15 minutes.

2. In large mixing bowl, beat cream cheese until fluffy. Add Eagle Brand, eggs and vanilla; beat until smooth. Stir in 1 cup English toffee bits. Pour mixture over hot crust. Bake 25 minutes or until set and edges just begin to brown.

3. Remove from oven. Cool 15 minutes. Sprinkle remaining ½ cup English toffee bits evenly over top. Cool completely. Refrigerate several hours or until cold. Store leftovers covered in refrigerator.

Makes about 36 bars

Oreo® Shazam Bars

28 OREO® Chocolate Sandwich Cookies, divided
¼ cup margarine or butter, melted
1 cup shredded coconut
1 cup white chocolate chips
½ cup chopped nuts
1 (14-ounce) can sweetened condensed milk

1. Finely roll 20 cookies. Mix cookie crumbs and margarine or butter; spread over bottom of 9×9×2-inch baking pan, pressing lightly.

2. Chop remaining cookies. Layer coconut, chips, nuts and chopped cookies in prepared pan; drizzle evenly with condensed milk.

3. Bake at 350°F for 25 to 30 minutes or until golden and set. Cool completely. Cut into bars.

Makes 24 bars

Toffee-Top Cheesecake Bars

Apple Golden Raisin Cheesecake Bars

1½ cups rolled oats
¾ cup all-purpose flour
½ cup firmly packed light brown sugar
¾ cup plus 2 tablespoons granulated sugar, divided
¾ Butter Flavor CRISCO® Stick or ¾ cup Butter Flavor CRISCO® all-vegetable shortening
2 (8-ounce) packages cream cheese, softened
2 large eggs
1 teaspoon vanilla
1 cup chopped Granny Smith apples
½ cup golden raisins
1 teaspoon almond extract
½ teaspoon ground cinnamon
¼ teaspoon ground nutmeg
¼ teaspoon ground allspice

1. Heat oven to 350°F.

2. Combine oats, flour, brown sugar and ¼ cup granulated sugar in large bowl; mix well. Cut in ¾ cup shortening with fork until crumbs form. Reserve 1 cup mixture.

3. Spray 13×9-inch baking pan with CRISCO® No-Stick Cooking Spray. Press remaining mixture onto bottom of prepared pan. Bake at 350°F for 12 to 15 minutes or until mixture is set. *Do not brown.* Place on cooling rack.

4. Combine cream cheese, eggs, ½ cup granulated sugar and vanilla in large bowl. Beat at medium speed with electric mixer until well blended. Spread evenly over crust.

5. Combine apples and raisins in medium bowl. Add almond extract; stir. Add 2 tablespoons sugar, cinnamon, nutmeg and allspice; mix well. Top cream cheese mixture evenly with apple mixture; sprinkle reserved oat mixture evenly over top. Bake at 350°F for 20 to 25 minutes or until top is golden. Place on cooling rack; cool completely. Cut into bars.

Makes 18 bars

Kitchen Hint: Forgot to take the cream cheese out to soften? Don't worry, simply remove from wrapper and place in medium microwave-safe bowl. Microwave on MEDIUM (50% power) 15 to 20 seconds or until slightly softened.

Apple Golden Raisin Cheesecake Bars

Creamy Lemon Bars

Prep Time: 15 minutes
Bake Time: 35 minutes

1 package (2-layer size) lemon cake mix
3 large eggs, divided
½ cup oil
2 packages (8 ounces each)
    PHILADELPHIA® Cream Cheese,
    softened
1 container (8 ounces) BREAKSTONE'S®
    or KNUDSEN® Sour Cream
½ cup granulated sugar
1 teaspoon grated lemon peel
1 tablespoon lemon juice
    Powdered sugar

MIX cake mix, 1 egg and oil. Press mixture onto bottom and up sides of lightly greased 15×10×1-inch baking pan. Bake at 350°F for 10 minutes.

BEAT cream cheese with electric mixer on medium speed until smooth. Add remaining 2 eggs, sour cream, granulated sugar, peel and juice; mix until blended. Pour batter into crust.

BAKE at 350°F for 30 to 35 minutes or until filling is just set in center and edges are light golden brown. Cool. Sprinkle with powdered sugar. Cut into bars. Store leftover bars in refrigerator.

Makes 2 dozen bars

Use bigger cookie
sheet than 15 x 1

Buckeye Cookie Bars

Prep Time: 20 minutes
Bake Time: 25 to 30 minutes

1 (18.25-ounce) package chocolate cake mix
¼ cup vegetable oil
1 egg
1 cup chopped peanuts
1 (14-ounce) can EAGLE® BRAND
    Sweetened Condensed Milk
    (NOT evaporated milk)
½ cup peanut butter

1. Preheat oven to 350°F. In large mixing bowl, combine cake mix, oil and egg; beat at medium speed of electric mixer until crumbly. Stir in peanuts. Reserve 1½ cups crumb mixture; press remaining crumb mixture firmly on bottom of greased 13×9 inch baking pan.

2. In medium mixing bowl, beat Eagle Brand with peanut butter until smooth; spread over prepared crust. Sprinkle with reserved crumb mixture.

3. Bake 25 to 30 minutes or until set. Cool. Cut into bars. Store loosely covered at room temperature.

Makes 24 to 36 bars

Creamy Lemon Bars

Cherry Cheese Bars

Base

   1 cup walnut pieces, divided
   1¼ cups all-purpose flour
   ½ cup firmly packed brown sugar
   ½ Butter Flavor CRISCO® Stick or ½ cup
      Butter Flavor CRISCO® all-vegetable
      shortening
   ½ cup flake coconut

Filling

   2 packages (8 ounces each) cream cheese,
      softened
   ⅔ cup granulated sugar
   2 eggs
   2 teaspoons vanilla
   1 can (21 ounces) cherry pie filling*

You may substitute another fruit pie filling for the cherry pie filling.

1. Heat oven to 350°F. Grease 13×9×2-inch pan with shortening. Place cooling rack on countertop.

2. Chop ½ cup nuts coarsely. Reserve for topping. Chop remaining ½ cup nuts finely.

3. For base, combine flour and brown sugar in medium bowl. Cut in ½ cup shortening until fine crumbs form. Add ½ cup finely chopped nuts and coconut. Mix well. Reserve ½ cup crumbs for topping. Press remaining crumbs in bottom of pan. Bake at 350°F for 12 to 15 minutes, or until edges are lightly browned. *Do not overbake.*

4. For filling, combine cream cheese, granulated sugar, eggs and vanilla in small bowl. Beat at medium speed of electric mixer until well blended. Spread over hot baked base. Return to oven. Bake 15 minutes. *Do not overbake.*

5. Spread cherry pie filling over cheese layer.

6. Combine reserved coarsely chopped nuts and reserved crumbs. Sprinkle over pie filling. Return to oven. Bake for 15 minutes. *Do not overbake.* Cool in pan on cooling rack. Refrigerate several hours. Cut into 2×1½-inch bars.   *Makes 3 dozen bars*

Kitchen Hint: Store brown sugar in a sealed plastic bag. It stays moist, measures easily and can be packed into a cup through the bag—no more sticky hands.

Cherry Cheese Bars

Yellow's Nuts for Nutty Squares

1 cup (2 sticks) plus 2 tablespoons butter, softened and divided
½ cup powdered sugar
2¼ cups all-purpose flour
¼ teaspoon salt
¾ cup granulated sugar
½ cup light corn syrup
2 large eggs, beaten
½ teaspoon vanilla extract
2 cups coarsely chopped mixed nuts
1 cup "M&M's"® Semi-Sweet Chocolate Mini Baking Bits

Preheat oven to 325°F. Lightly grease 13×9-inch baking pan; set aside. In large bowl beat 1 cup (2 sticks) butter and powdered sugar; gradually add flour and salt until well blended. Press dough evenly onto bottom and ½ inch up sides of prepared pan. Bake 25 to 30 minutes or until very light golden brown. In small saucepan melt remaining 2 tablespoons butter; let cool slightly. In large bowl combine melted butter, granulated sugar, corn syrup, eggs and vanilla. Pour filling over partially baked crust; sprinkle with nuts and "M&M's"® Semi-Sweet Chocolate Mini Baking Bits. Return to oven; bake 30 to 35 minutes or until filling is set. Remove pan to wire rack; cool completely. Cut into bars. Store in tightly covered container.

Makes 2 dozen bars

Marbled Cheesecake Bars

Prep Time: 20 minutes
Bake Time: 45 to 50 minutes

2 cups finely crushed crème-filled chocolate sandwich cookie crumbs (about 24 cookies)
3 tablespoons butter or margarine, melted
3 (8-ounce) packages cream cheese, softened
1 (14-ounce) can EAGLE® BRAND Sweetened Condensed Milk (NOT evaporated milk)
3 eggs
2 teaspoons vanilla extract
2 (1-ounce) squares unsweetened chocolate, melted

1. Preheat oven to 300°F. Line 13×9-inch baking pan with heavy foil; set aside. In medium mixing bowl, combine crumbs and butter; press firmly on bottom of prepared pan.

2. In large mixing bowl, beat cream cheese until fluffy. Gradually beat in Eagle Brand until smooth. Add eggs and vanilla; mix well. Pour half the batter evenly over prepared crust.

3. Stir melted chocolate into remaining batter; spoon over vanilla batter. With table knife or metal spatula, gently swirl through batter to marble.

4. Bake 45 to 50 minutes or until set. Cool. Chill. Cut into bars. Store covered in refrigerator.

Makes 2 to 3 dozen bars

Helpful Hint: For even marbling, do not oversoften or overbeat the cream cheese.

Caramel Oatmeal Chewies

1¾ cups quick or old-fashioned oats
1¾ cups all-purpose flour, *divided*
¾ cup packed brown sugar
½ teaspoon baking soda
¼ teaspoon salt (optional)
¾ cup (1½ sticks) butter or margarine, melted
2 cups (12-ounce package) NESTLÉ® TOLL HOUSE® Semi-Sweet Chocolate Morsels
1 cup chopped nuts
1 cup caramel ice-cream topping

PREHEAT oven to 350°F. Grease bottom of 13×9-inch baking pan.

COMBINE oats, *1½ cups* flour, brown sugar, baking soda and salt in large bowl. Stir in butter; mix well. Reserve *1 cup* oat mixture; press *remaining* oat mixture onto bottom of prepared baking pan.

BAKE for 12 to 15 minutes or until golden brown. Sprinkle with morsels and nuts. Mix caramel topping with *remaining* flour in small bowl; drizzle over morsels to within ¼ inch of pan edges. Sprinkle with *reserved* oat mixture.

BAKE for 18 to 22 minutes or until golden brown. Cool in pan on wire rack; refrigerate until firm.

Makes about 2½ dozen bars

Magic Cookie Bars

Bake Time: 25 minutes

½ cup (1 stick) butter or margarine
1½ cups graham cracker crumbs
1 (14-ounce) can EAGLE® BRAND Sweetened Condensed Milk (NOT evaporated milk)
2 cups (12 ounces) semi-sweet chocolate chips
1⅓ cups flaked coconut
1 cup chopped nuts

1. Preheat oven to 350°F (325°F for glass dish). In 13×9-inch baking pan, melt butter in oven.

2. Sprinkle crumbs over butter; pour Eagle Brand evenly over crumbs. Layer evenly with remaining ingredients; press down firmly.

3. Bake 25 minutes or until lightly browned. Cool. Chill, if desired. Cut into bars. Store loosely covered at room temperature. *Makes 2 to 3 dozen bars*

7-Layer Magic Cookie Bars: Substitute 1 cup (6 ounces) butterscotch-flavored chips for 1 cup semi-sweet chocolate chips.

Magic Peanut Cookie Bars: Substitute 2 cups (about ¾ pound) chocolate-covered peanuts for semi-sweet chocolate chips and chopped nuts.

Magic Rainbow Cookie Bars: Substitute 2 cups plain candy-coated chocolate pieces for semi-sweet chocolate chips.

Caramel Oatmeal Chewies

Blue Ribbon Brownies

Rocky Road Brownies

1 cup HERSHEY'S Semi-Sweet Chocolate Chips
1¼ cups miniature marshmallows
1 cup chopped nuts
½ cup (1 stick) butter or margarine
1 cup sugar
1 teaspoon vanilla extract
2 eggs
½ cup all-purpose flour
⅓ cup HERSHEY'S Cocoa
½ teaspoon baking powder
½ teaspoon salt

1. Heat oven to 350°F. Grease 9-inch square baking pan.

2. Stir together chocolate chips, marshmallows and nuts; set aside. Place butter in large microwave-safe bowl. Microwave at HIGH (100% power) 1 to 1½ minutes or until melted. Add sugar, vanilla and eggs, beating with spoon until well blended. Add flour, cocoa, baking powder and salt; blend well. Spread batter in prepared pan.

3. Bake 22 minutes. Sprinkle chocolate chip mixture over top. Continue baking 5 minutes or until marshmallows have softened and puffed slightly. Cool completely. With wet knife, cut into squares. *Makes about 20 brownies*

Rocky Road Brownies

Cheesecake-Topped Brownies

Prep Time: 20 minutes
Bake Time: 40 to 45 minutes

- 1 (21.5- or 23.6-ounce) package fudge brownie mix
- 1 (8-ounce) package cream cheese, softened
- 2 tablespoons butter or margarine, softened
- 1 tablespoon cornstarch
- 1 (14-ounce) can EAGLE® BRAND Sweetened Condensed Milk (NOT evaporated milk)
- 1 egg
- 2 teaspoons vanilla extract
- Ready-to-spread chocolate frosting, if desired
- Orange peel, if desired

1. Preheat oven to 350°F. Prepare brownie mix as package directs. Spread into well-greased 13×9-inch baking pan.

2. In large mixing bowl, beat cream cheese, butter and cornstarch until fluffy.

3. Gradually beat in Eagle Brand. Add egg and vanilla; beat until smooth. Pour cheesecake mixture evenly over brownie batter.

4. Bake 40 to 45 minutes or until top is lightly browned. Cool. Spread with frosting or sprinkle with orange peel, if desired. Cut into bars. Store covered in refrigerator. *Makes 3 to 3½ dozen brownies*

Chocolate Mint Brownie Bars

- ⅔ cup butter or margarine
- 1⅔ cups (10-ounce package) HERSHEY'S Mint Chocolate Chips, divided
- 1½ cups sugar
- 1 cup all-purpose flour
- ⅓ cup HERSHEY'S Cocoa
- 1 teaspoon vanilla extract
- ½ teaspoon baking powder
- ½ teaspoon salt
- 3 eggs
- 1 cup coarsely chopped walnuts

1. Heat oven to 350°F. Grease 13×9×2-inch baking pan.

2. Place butter and 1 cup mint chocolate chips in large microwave-safe bowl. Microwave at HIGH (100%) 1 to 1½ minutes or until chips are melted when stirred. Add sugar, flour, cocoa, vanilla, baking powder, salt and eggs; stir with spoon until smooth. Stir in remaining ⅔ cup chips. Spread batter into prepared pan; sprinkle walnuts over top.

3. Bake 30 minutes or until center is set. Cool completely in pan on wire rack. Cut into bars.
Makes about 36 brownies

Cheesecake-Topped Brownies

Chocolate Chunk Caramel Pecan Brownies

Prep Time: 20 minutes
Bake Time: 55 minutes

> 4 squares BAKER'S® Unsweetened Baking
>   Chocolate
> ¾ cup (1½ sticks) butter *or* margarine
> 2 cups sugar
> 4 eggs
> 1 cup flour
> 1 package (14 ounces) KRAFT® Caramels,
>   unwrapped
> ⅓ cup whipping (heavy) cream
> 2 cups pecan *or* walnut halves, divided
> 1 package (12 ounces) BAKER'S® Semi-
>   Sweet Chocolate Chunks, divided

HEAT oven to 350°F. Line 13×9-inch baking pan with foil; grease foil.

MICROWAVE chocolate and butter in large microwavable bowl on HIGH 2 minutes or until butter is melted. Stir until chocolate is completely melted. Stir sugar into chocolate mixture until well blended. Mix in eggs. Stir in flour until well blended. Spread ½ of brownie batter in prepared pan.

BAKE 25 minutes or until brownie is firm to touch.

MEANWHILE, microwave caramels and cream in microwavable bowl on HIGH 2 minutes or until caramels begin to melt. Stir until smooth. Stir in 1 cup of pecan halves. Gently spread caramel mixture over baked brownie in pan. Sprinkle with ½ of chocolate chunks. Pour remaining unbaked brownie batter evenly over top; sprinkle with remaining chocolate chunks and 1 cup pecan halves. (Some caramel mixture may peak through.)

BAKE an additional 30 minutes or until brownie is firm to the touch. Cool in pan on wire rack. Lift out of pan onto cutting board. *Makes 2 dozen*

Tip: For 13×9-inch glass baking dish, bake at 325°F.

Tip

When making brownies and bar cookies, lining the pan with foil saves a lot of cleanup time. Removing the bars from the pan before cutting them also prevents your pan from getting scratched. Be sure to leave at least 3 inches of foil overhanging each end of the pan so it's easy to lift the bars out.

Chocolate Chunk Caramel Pecan Brownies

Decadent Blonde Brownies

1½ cups all-purpose flour
 1 teaspoon baking powder
 ½ teaspoon salt
 ¾ cup granulated sugar
 ¾ cup packed light brown sugar
 ½ cup butter, softened
 2 large eggs
 2 teaspoons vanilla
 1 package (10 ounces) semisweet chocolate chunks*
 1 jar (3½ ounces) macadamia nuts, coarsely chopped, to measure ¾ cup

If chocolate chunks are not available, cut 1 (10-ounce) thick chocolate candy bar into ½-inch pieces to equal 1½ cups.

Preheat oven to 350°F. Grease 13×9-inch baking pan. Combine flour, baking powder and salt in small bowl; set aside.

Beat granulated sugar, brown sugar and butter in large bowl with electric mixer at medium speed until light and fluffy. Beat in eggs and vanilla. Add flour mixture. Beat at low speed until well blended. Stir in chocolate chunks and macadamia nuts. Spread batter evenly into prepared pan. Bake 25 to 30 minutes or until golden brown. Remove pan to wire rack; cool completely. Cut into 3¼×1½-inch bars.

Makes 2 dozen brownies

Baker's® One Bowl White Chocolate Brownies

Prep Time: 10 minutes
Bake Time: 35 minutes

 1 package (6 squares) BAKER'S® Premium White Baking Chocolate
 ¼ cup (½ stick) butter *or* margarine
 ¾ cup sugar
 2 eggs
 1 cup flour
 ½ teaspoon *each* CALUMET® Baking Powder and salt
 1 cup coarsely chopped toasted walnuts, pecans *or* salted cashews (optional)

HEAT oven to 350°F (325°F for glass baking dish). Line 8-inch square baking pan with foil extending over edges to form handles. Grease foil.

MICROWAVE chocolate and butter in large microwavable bowl on HIGH 1 minute or until butter is melted. Stir until chocolate is completely melted.

STIR sugar into chocolate mixture until well blended. Mix in eggs. Stir in flour, baking powder, salt and nuts until well blended. Spread in prepared pan.

BAKE 30 to 35 minutes or until toothpick inserted in center comes out with fudgy crumbs. DO NOT OVERBAKE. Cool in pan. Lift out of pan onto cutting board. Cut into squares.

Makes 24 brownies

Note: Recipe may be doubled. Bake in 13×9-inch baking pan for 40 to 45 minutes.

Decadent Blonde Brownies

Chocolate Chip Brownies

¾ cup granulated sugar
½ cup butter
2 tablespoons water
2 cups semisweet chocolate chips or
    mini chocolate chips, divided
1½ teaspoons vanilla
1¼ cups all-purpose flour
½ teaspoon baking soda
½ teaspoon salt
2 eggs
    Powdered sugar (optional)

Preheat oven to 350°F. Grease 9-inch square baking pan.

Combine granulated sugar, butter and water in medium microwavable mixing bowl. Microwave at HIGH 2½ to 3 minutes or until butter is melted. Stir in 1 cup chocolate chips; stir gently until chips are melted and mixture is well blended. Stir in vanilla; let stand 5 minutes to cool.

Combine flour, baking soda and salt in small bowl. Beat eggs into chocolate mixture, 1 at a time. Add flour mixture; mix well. Stir in remaining 1 cup chocolate chips. Spread batter evenly into prepared pan.

Bake 25 minutes for fudgy brownies or 30 to 35 minutes for cakelike brownies. Remove pan to wire rack to cool completely. Cut into 2¼-inch squares. Place powdered sugar in fine-mesh strainer and sprinkle over brownies, if desired. Store tightly covered at room temperature or freeze up to 3 months. *Makes 16 brownies*

Chewy Butterscotch Brownies

2½ cups all-purpose flour
2 teaspoons baking powder
½ teaspoon salt
1 cup (2 sticks) butter or margarine,
    softened
1¾ cups packed brown sugar
1 tablespoons vanilla extract
2 large eggs
1⅔ cups (11-ounce package) NESTLÉ®
    TOLL HOUSE® Butterscotch Flavored
    Morsels, *divided*
1 cup chopped nuts

PREHEAT oven to 350°F.

COMBINE flour, baking powder and salt in medium bowl. Beat butter, sugar and vanilla extract in large mixer bowl until creamy. Beat in eggs. Gradually beat in flour mixture. Stir in *1 cup* morsels and nuts. Spread into ungreased 13×9-inch baking pan. Sprinkle with *remaining* morsels.

BAKE for 30 to 40 minutes or until wooden pick inserted in center comes out clean. Cool in pan on wire rack. *Makes about 4 dozen brownies*

Chocolate Chip Brownies

Fancy Frosted Fudge Brownies

Prep Time: 15 minutes plus refrigerating
Bake Time: 50 minutes

Brownie Layer
  6 squares BAKER'S® Unsweetened
     Baking Chocolate
  1 cup (2 sticks) butter *or* margarine
  2 cups sugar
  4 eggs
  1 teaspoon vanilla
  1 cup flour
  1½ cups chopped toasted pecans
  ¼ teaspoon salt

Frosting
  5 squares BAKER'S® Semi-Sweet Baking
     Chocolate
  ⅔ cup sweetened condensed milk
  ½ cup BAKER'S® ANGEL FLAKE® Coconut

HEAT oven to 350°F. Line 9-inch square baking pan with foil. Grease foil.

Brownie Layer
MICROWAVE unsweetened chocolate and butter in large microwavable bowl on HIGH 2 minutes or until butter is melted. Stir until chocolate is completely melted.

STIR sugar into chocolate mixture until well blended. Mix in eggs and vanilla. Stir in flour, pecans and salt until well blended. Spread in prepared pan.

BAKE 45 to 50 minutes or until toothpick inserted in center comes out with fudgy crumbs. Cool in pan.

Frosting
MICROWAVE semi-sweet chocolate and milk in medium microwavable bowl on HIGH 2 minutes or until chocolate is almost melted. Stir until chocolate is completely melted. Spread evenly on top of cooled brownies. Sprinkle with coconut.

REFRIGERATE 1 hour or until frosting is set. Lift out of pan onto cutting board. Cut into squares.
Makes 16 brownies

White Chocolate & Almond Brownies

  12 ounces white chocolate, broken into pieces
  1 cup unsalted butter
  3 eggs
  ¾ cup all-purpose flour
  1 teaspoon vanilla
  ½ cup slivered almonds

Preheat oven to 325°F. Grease and flour 9-inch square pan. Melt white chocolate and butter in large saucepan over low heat, stirring constantly. (Do not be concerned if the white chocolate separates.) Remove from heat when chocolate is just melted. With electric mixer, beat in eggs until mixture is smooth. Beat in flour and vanilla. Spread batter evenly in prepared pan. Sprinkle almonds evenly over top. Bake 30 to 35 minutes or just until set in center. Cool completely in pan on wire rack. Cut into 2-inch squares.

Makes about 16 brownies

Double Decadence Chocolate Chip Brownies

1 cup granulated sugar
1 stick plus 3 tablespoons margarine or
    butter, softened
2 eggs
1 teaspoon vanilla
2 cups (12-ounce package) semisweet
    chocolate pieces, divided
1¼ cups all-purpose flour
1 cup QUAKER® Oats (quick or old
    fashioned, uncooked)
1 teaspoon baking powder
½ cup chopped nuts (optional)
    Powdered sugar (optional)

Heat oven to 350°F. Lightly grease 13×9-inch
baking pan. Beat sugar, margarine, eggs and vanilla
until smooth. Add 1 cup chocolate, melted;* mix
well. Add flour, oats, baking powder, remaining
1 cup chocolate pieces and nuts, mixing well. Spread
into prepared pan. Bake 25 to 30 minutes or until
brownies just begin to pull away from sides of pan.
Cool completely. Sprinkle with powdered sugar, if
desired. Cut into bars.   *Makes 2 dozen brownies*

**To melt 1 cup chocolate pieces: Microwave at HIGH 1 to
2 minutes, stirring every 30 seconds until smooth. Or, heat
in heavy saucepan over low heat, stirring until smooth.*

Easy Minty Brownies

Prep Time: 20 minutes plus refrigerating
Bake Time: 35 minutes

¾ cup (1½ sticks) butter *or* margarine
4 squares BAKER'S® Unsweetened Baking
    Chocolate
2 cups sugar
4 eggs
1 cup flour
1 teaspoon peppermint extract, or to taste
1 can (16 ounces) ready-to-spread vanilla
    frosting
4 squares BAKER'S® Semi-Sweet Baking
    Chocolate
4 tablespoons *each* water and butter *or*
    margarine

PREPARE and bake Baker's® One Bowl Brownies
as directed inside box of BAKER'S® Unsweetened
Baking Chocolate Squares using ¾ cup butter,
unsweetened chocolate, sugar, eggs and flour listed
above. Cool completely.

STIR peppermint extract into frosting; spread
evenly over cooled brownies.

MICROWAVE semi-sweet chocolate, water and
4 tablespoons butter in medium bowl on HIGH
1½ minutes or until butter is melted. Stir until
chocolate is completely melted. Cool to room
temperature. Spread evenly over top of mint filling
on brownies. Refrigerate 1 hour or until ready to
serve. Cut into squares.   *Makes 24 brownies*

Philadelphia® Cheesecake Brownies

Prep Time: 20 minutes
Bake Time: 40 minutes

    1 package (19.8 ounces) brownie mix (do
       not use mix that includes syrup pouch)
    1 package (8 ounces) PHILADELPHIA®
       Cream Cheese, softened
    ⅓ cup sugar
    1 egg
    ½ teaspoon vanilla

PREPARE brownie mix as directed on package. Pour into greased 13×9-inch baking pan.

BEAT cream cheese with electric mixer on medium speed until smooth. Mix in sugar until blended. Add egg and vanilla; mix just until blended. Pour cream cheese mixture over brownie batter; cut through batter with knife several times for marble effect.

BAKE at 350°F for 35 to 40 minutes or until cream cheese mixture is lightly browned. Cool. Cut into squares.   *Makes 2 dozen*

Irresistible Peanut Butter Chip Brownies

    1 cup (2 sticks) butter or margarine,
       softened
    1 package (3 ounces) cream cheese,
       softened
    2 cups sugar
    3 eggs
    1 teaspoon vanilla extract
    1 cup all-purpose flour
    ¾ cup HERSHEY'S Cocoa
    ½ teaspoon salt
    ¼ teaspoon baking powder
    1⅔ cups (10-ounce package) REESE'S®
       Peanut Butter Chips
       Brownie Frosting (recipe follows,
       optional)

1. Heat oven to 325°F. Grease bottom of 13×9×2-inch baking pan.

2. Beat butter, cream cheese and sugar until fluffy. Beat in eggs and vanilla. Combine flour, cocoa, salt and baking powder; gradually add to butter mixture, beating well. Stir in chips. Spread batter into pan.

3. Bake 35 to 40 minutes or until brownies begin to pull away from sides of pan. Cool completely. Frost with Brownie Frosting, if desired. Cut into bars.
                    Makes about 36 bars

Brownie Frosting: Beat 3 tablespoons softened butter or margarine and 3 tablespoons HERSHEY'S Cocoa until blended. Gradually add 1⅓ cups powdered sugar and ¾ teaspoon vanilla extract alternately with 1 to 2 tablespoons milk, beating to spreading consistency. Makes about 1 cup.

Philadelphia® Cheesecake Brownies

Brownie Caramel Pecan Bars

½ cup sugar
2 tablespoons butter or margarine
2 tablespoons water
2 cups (12-ounce package) HERSHEY'S
    Semi-Sweet Chocolate Chips, divided
2 eggs
1 teaspoon vanilla extract
⅔ cup all-purpose flour
¼ teaspoon baking soda
¼ teaspoon salt
    Classic Caramel Topping (recipe follows)
1 cup pecan pieces

1. Heat oven to 350°F. Line 9-inch square baking pan with foil, extending foil over edges of pan. Grease and flour foil.

2. Combine sugar, butter and water in medium saucepan. Cook over low heat, stirring constantly, until mixture boils. Remove from heat. Immediately add 1 cup chocolate chips; stir until melted. Beat in eggs and vanilla until well blended. Stir together flour, baking soda and salt; stir into chocolate mixture. Spread batter into prepared pan.

3. Bake 15 to 20 minutes or until brownies begin to pull away from sides of pan. Meanwhile, prepare Classic Caramel Topping. Remove brownies from oven; immediately and carefully spread with prepared topping. Sprinkle remaining 1 cup chips and pecans over topping. Cool completely in pan on wire rack, being careful not to disturb chips while soft. Lift out of pan. Cut into bars.

Makes about 16 bars

Classic Caramel Topping: Remove wrappers from 25 HERSHEY'S Classic Caramels. Combine ¼ cup (½ stick) butter or margarine, caramels and 2 tablespoons milk in medium microwave-safe bowl. Microwave at HIGH (100%) 1 minute; stir. Microwave an additional 1 to 2 minutes, stirring every 30 seconds, or until caramels are melted and mixture is smooth when stirred. Use immediately.

Chocolate Syrup Brownies

1 egg
1 cup packed light brown sugar
¾ cup HERSHEY'S Syrup
1½ cups all-purpose flour
¼ teaspoon baking soda
    Dash salt
½ cup (1 stick) butter or margarine, melted
¾ cup chopped pecans or walnuts

1. Heat oven to 350°F. Grease 9-inch square baking pan.

2. Beat egg lightly in small bowl; add brown sugar and syrup, beating until well blended. Stir together flour, baking soda and salt; gradually add to egg mixture, beating until blended. Stir in butter and nuts. Spread batter into prepared pan.

3. Bake 35 to 40 minutes or until brownies begin to pull away from sides of pan. Cool completely in pan on wire rack. Cut into squares.

Makes about 16 brownies

Brownie Caramel Pecan Bars

White Chocolate Brownies

6 tablespoons butter
5 squares (1 ounce each) white chocolate, divided
1 large egg
½ cup granulated sugar
¾ cup all-purpose flour
¾ teaspoon vanilla extract
¼ teaspoon salt
1¼ cups "M&M's"® Semi-Sweet Chocolate Mini Baking Bits, divided
½ cup chopped walnuts

Preheat oven to 325°F. Lightly grease 8×8×2-inch baking pan; set aside. In small saucepan melt butter and 4 squares white chocolate over low heat; stir to blend. Remove from heat; let cool slightly. In medium bowl beat egg and sugar until light; stir in white chocolate mixture, flour, vanilla and salt. Spread batter evenly in prepared pan. Sprinkle with ¾ cup "M&M's"® Semi-Sweet Chocolate Mini Baking Bits and walnuts. Bake 35 to 37 minutes or until firm in center. Cool completely on wire rack. Place remaining 1 square white chocolate in small microwave-safe bowl. Microwave at HIGH 20 seconds; stir. Repeat as necessary until white chocolate is completely melted, stirring at 10-second intervals. Drizzle over brownies and sprinkle with remaining ½ cup "M&M's"® Semi-Sweet Chocolate Mini Baking Bits. Cut into bars. Store in tightly covered container. *Makes 16 brownies*

Peanut Butter and Jelly Brownies

Prep Time: 20 minutes
Bake Time: 40 minutes

1 cup firmly packed brown sugar
½ cup chunky peanut butter
¼ cup (½ stick) butter *or* margarine
2 eggs
1 teaspoon vanilla
½ cup flour
¼ teaspoon salt
6 squares BAKER'S® Semi-Sweet Baking Chocolate *or* 1 package (6 squares) BAKER'S® Premium White Baking Chocolate, chopped
½ cup strawberry jam

HEAT oven to 350°F. Line 9-inch square baking pan with foil. Grease foil.

BEAT sugar, peanut butter and butter in large bowl with electric mixer on medium speed until well mixed. Beat in eggs and vanilla. Mix in flour and salt. Stir in chocolate. Spread in prepared pan. Drop jam by spoonfuls over batter. Swirl with knife to marbleize.

BAKE 35 to 40 minutes or until toothpick inserted in center comes out almost clean. *Do not overbake.* Cool in pan. Cut into squares.

Makes 16 brownies

Double Chocolate Brownies

Prep Time: 15 minutes
Bake Time: 35 minutes

1¼ cups all-purpose flour, divided
¼ cup sugar
½ cup (1 stick) cold butter or margarine
1 (14-ounce) can EAGLE® BRAND
    Sweetened Condensed Milk
    (NOT evaporated milk)
¼ cup unsweetened cocoa
1 egg
1 teaspoon vanilla extract
½ teaspoon baking powder
1 (8-ounce) milk chocolate bar, broken into
    chunks
¾ cup chopped nuts, if desired

1. Preheat oven to 350°F. Line 13×9-inch baking pan with foil; set aside.

2. In medium mixing bowl, combine 1 cup flour and sugar; cut in butter until crumbly. Press firmly on bottom of prepared pan. Bake 15 minutes.

3. In large bowl, beat Eagle Brand, cocoa, egg, remaining ¼ cup flour, vanilla and baking powder. Stir in chocolate chunks and nuts, if desired. Spread over baked crust. Bake 20 minutes or until set.

4. Cool. Use foil to lift out of pan. Cut into bars. Store tightly covered at room temperature.

Makes 24 brownies

Divine Truffle Brownies

Prep Time: 15 minutes
Bake Time: 40 minutes

1 package (8 squares) BAKER'S® Semi-
    Sweet Baking Chocolate *or* 1 package
    (6 squares) BAKER'S® Bittersweet
    Baking Chocolate Squares, divided
¼ cup (½ stick) butter *or* margarine
¾ cup sugar, divided
3 eggs, divided
¾ cup flour
⅔ cup heavy (whipping) cream

HEAT oven to 350°F (325°F for glass baking dish). Line 8-inch baking pan with foil, extending over edges to form handles. Grease foil.

MICROWAVE 2 squares of the chocolate and butter in medium microwavable bowl on HIGH 1½ minutes or until butter is melted. Stir until chocolate is melted.

STIR ½ cup of the sugar into chocolate mixture. Mix in 1 egg. Stir in flour until well blended. Spread batter in prepared pan.

MICROWAVE remaining chocolate (6 squares if using semi-sweet, 4 squares if using bittersweet) and cream in microwavable bowl on HIGH 1½ minutes. Stir until chocolate is completely melted.

BEAT remaining ¼ cup sugar and 2 eggs in small bowl with electric mixer on high speed 1 minute until thick and lemon yellow colored; beat in chocolate/cream mixture. Pour over batter in pan.

BAKE 35 to 40 minutes or until truffle topping is set and edges begin to pull away from sides of pan. Cool in pan. Run knife around edge of pan to loosen brownies from sides. Lift from pan using foil as handles. Cut into squares. *Makes 16 brownies*

Cindy's Fudgy Brownies

1 (21-ounce) package DUNCAN HINES®
    Family-Style Chewy Fudge
    Brownie Mix
1 egg
⅓ cup water
⅓ cup vegetable oil
¾ cup semi-sweet chocolate chips
½ cup chopped pecans

1. Preheat oven to 350°F. Grease bottom of 13×9×2-inch pan.

2. Combine brownie mix, egg, water and oil in large bowl. Stir with spoon until well blended, about 50 strokes. Stir in chocolate chips. Spread in pan. Sprinkle with pecans. Bake at 350°F 25 to 28 minutes or until set. Cool completely. Cut into bars.   *Makes 24 brownies*

Tip: Overbaking brownies will cause them to become dry. Follow the recommended baking times given in recipes closely.

Peanut Butter Paisley Brownies

½ cup (1 stick) butter or margarine,
    softened
¼ cup REESE'S® Creamy Peanut Butter
1 cup granulated sugar
1 cup packed light brown sugar
3 eggs
1 teaspoon vanilla extract
2 cups all-purpose flour
2 teaspoons baking powder
¼ teaspoon salt
½ cup HERSHEY'S Syrup

1. Heat oven to 350°F. Grease 13×9×2-inch baking pan.

2. Beat butter and peanut butter in large bowl. Add granulated sugar and brown sugar; beat well. Add eggs, 1 at a time, beating well after each addition. Stir in vanilla. Combine flour, baking powder and salt; add to peanut butter mixture.

3. Spread half of batter into prepared pan. Spoon syrup over batter. Carefully spread with remaining batter. Swirl with spatula or knife to marbleize.

4. Bake for 35 to 40 minutes or until lightly browned. Cool; cut into squares.
    Makes about 36 brownies

Cindy's Fudgy Brownies

Blast-Off Brownies

4 (1-ounce) squares unsweetened chocolate
¾ cup (1½ sticks) butter *or* margarine
2 cups sugar
1 cup flour
3 eggs
1 tablespoon TABASCO® brand Pepper
 Sauce
½ cup semisweet chocolate chips
½ cup walnuts, chopped

Preheat oven to 350°F. Grease 9×9-inch baking pan. Melt chocolate and butter in small saucepan over medium-low heat, stirring frequently. Combine sugar, flour, eggs, TABASCO® Sauce and melted chocolate mixture in large bowl until well blended. Stir in chocolate chips and walnuts. Spoon mixture into prepared pan. Bake 35 to 40 minutes or until toothpick inserted in center comes out clean. Cool in pan on wire rack.   *Makes 16 brownies*

Deep Dish Brownies

¾ cup (1½ sticks) butter or margarine,
 melted
1½ cups sugar
1½ teaspoons vanilla extract
 3 eggs
¾ cup all-purpose flour
½ cup HERSHEY'S Cocoa
½ teaspoon baking powder
½ teaspoon salt

1. Heat oven to 350°F. Grease 8-inch square baking pan.

2. Blend butter, sugar and vanilla in medium bowl. Add eggs; using spoon, beat well. Combine flour, cocoa, baking powder and salt; gradually add to egg mixture, beating until well blended. Spread batter into prepared pan.

3. Bake 40 to 45 minutes or until brownies begin to pull away from sides of pan. Cool completely in pan on wire rack. Cut into squares.

Makes about 16 brownies

Variation: Stir 1 cup REESE'S® Peanut Butter Chips or HERSHEY'S Semi-Sweet Chocolate Chips into batter before spreading into pan. Proceed as above.

Blast-Off Brownies

Toffee-Topped Fudgey Brownies

1¼ cups (2½ sticks) butter or margarine
2 cups sugar
2 teaspoons vanilla extract
4 eggs
1½ cups all-purpose flour
¾ cup HERSHEY'S Cocoa
1¾ cups (10-ounce package) HEATH® Almond Toffee Bits
¾ cup HERSHEY'S MINICHIPS™ Chocolate

1. Heat oven to 350°F. Grease 13×9×2-inch baking pan.

2. Melt butter in medium saucepan over low heat. Remove from heat; stir in sugar and vanilla. Add eggs, one at a time, beating just until blended.

3. Combine flour and cocoa; gradually add to butter mixture, stirring just until blended. (Do not overmix.) Spread batter in prepared pan. Sprinkle with toffee bits and chocolate chips.

4. Bake 35 minutes or until wooden pick inserted in center comes out clean. Cool completely in pan on wire rack. Cut into squares.

Makes about 36 brownies

"Blondie" Brownies

½ Butter Flavor CRISCO® Stick or ½ cup Butter Flavor CRISCO® all-vegetable shortening plus additional for greasing
1 tablespoon milk
1 cup firmly packed brown sugar
1 egg
1 cup all-purpose flour
½ teaspoon baking powder
⅛ teaspoon salt
1 teaspoon vanilla
½ cup chopped walnuts

1. Heat oven to 350°F. Grease 8×8×2-inch pan with shortening. Place cooling rack on countertop.

2. Combine ½ cup shortening and milk in large microwave-safe bowl. Microwave at 50% (MEDIUM). Stir after 1 minute. Repeat until melted (or melt on rangetop in large saucepan on low heat). Stir in sugar. Stir in egg quickly. Combine flour, baking powder and salt. Stir into sugar mixture. Stir in vanilla and nuts. Spread in prepared pan.

3. Bake at 350°F for 27 to 30 minutes, or until toothpick inserted in center comes out clean. *Do not overbake.* Cool in pan on cooling rack. Cut into 2×2-inch squares.

Makes 16 squares

Coconutty "M&M's"® Brownies

6 squares (1 ounce each) semi-sweet
    chocolate
¾ cup granulated sugar
½ cup (1 stick) butter
2 large eggs
1 tablespoon vegetable oil
1 teaspoon vanilla extract
1¼ cups all-purpose flour
3 tablespoons unsweetened cocoa powder
1 teaspoon baking powder
½ teaspoon salt
1½ cups "M&M's"® Chocolate Mini Baking
    Bits, divided
    Coconut Topping (recipe follows)

Preheat oven to 350°F. Lightly grease 8×8×2-inch baking pan; set aside. In small saucepan combine chocolate, sugar and butter over low heat; stir constantly until chocolate is melted. Remove from heat; let cool slightly. In large bowl beat eggs, oil and vanilla; stir in chocolate mixture until well blended. In medium bowl combine flour, cocoa powder, baking powder and salt; add to chocolate mixture. Stir in 1 cup "M&M's"® Chocolate Mini Baking Bits. Spread batter evenly in prepared pan. Bake 35 to 40 minutes or until toothpick inserted in center comes out clean. Cool completely on wire rack. Prepare Coconut Topping. Spread over brownies; sprinkle with remaining ½ cup "M&M's"® Chocolate Mini Baking Bits. Cut into bars. Store in tightly covered container. *Makes 16 brownies*

Coconut Topping

½ cup (1 stick) butter
⅓ cup firmly packed light brown sugar
⅓ cup light corn syrup
1 cup sweetened shredded coconut, toasted*
¾ cup chopped pecans
1 teaspoon vanilla extract

To toast coconut, spread evenly on cookie sheet. Toast in preheated 350°F oven 7 to 8 minutes or until golden brown, stirring occasionally.

In large saucepan melt butter over medium heat; add brown sugar and corn syrup, stirring constantly until thick and bubbly. Remove from heat and stir in remaining ingredients.

Coconutty "M&M's"® Brownies

Blue-Ribbon Brownies **151**

Hershey's Chocolate Chip Blondies

6 tablespoons butter or margarine, softened
¾ cup packed light brown sugar
1 egg
1 tablespoon milk
1 teaspoon vanilla extract
1 cup all-purpose flour
½ teaspoon baking soda
⅛ teaspoon salt
2 cups (12-ounce package) HERSHEY'S Semi-Sweet Chocolate Chips
½ cup coarsely chopped nuts (optional)

1. Heat oven to 350°F. Grease 9-inch square baking pan.

2. Beat butter and brown sugar in large bowl until fluffy. Add egg, milk and vanilla; beat well. Stir together flour, baking soda and salt; add to butter mixture. Stir in chocolate chips and nuts, if desired; spread in prepared pan.

3. Bake 20 to 25 minutes or until lightly browned. Cool completely; cut into bars.

Makes about 1½ dozen bars

Bittersweet Brownies

MAZOLA NO STICK® Cooking Spray
4 squares (1 ounce each) unsweetened chocolate, melted
1 cup sugar
½ cup HELLMANN'S® or BEST FOODS® Real or Light Mayonnaise
2 eggs
1 teaspoon vanilla
¾ cup flour
½ teaspoon baking powder
¼ teaspoon salt
½ cup chopped walnuts

1. Preheat oven to 350°F. Spray 8×8×2-inch baking pan with cooking spray.

2. In large bowl, stir chocolate, sugar, mayonnaise, eggs and vanilla until smooth. Stir in flour, baking powder and salt until well blended. Stir in walnuts. Spread evenly in prepared pan.

3. Bake 25 to 30 minutes or until wooden pick inserted into center comes out clean. Cool in pan on wire rack. Cut into 2-inch squares.

Makes 16 brownies

Nuggets o' Gold Brownies

3 ounces unsweetened baking chocolate
¼ cup WESSON® Vegetable Oil
2 eggs
1 cup sugar
1 teaspoon vanilla extract
¼ teaspoon salt
½ cup all-purpose flour
1 (3.8-ounce) BUTTERFINGER®
Candy Bar, coarsely chopped

In microwave-safe measuring cup, heat chocolate 2 minutes on HIGH in microwave oven. Stir and continue heating in 30-second intervals until chocolate is completely melted. Stir in oil and set aside to cool. In mixing bowl, beat eggs until foamy. Whisk in sugar, then add vanilla and salt. Stir in chocolate mixture then mix in flour until all ingredients are moistened. Gently fold in candy. Pour batter into greased 9-inch baking pan and bake at 350°F for 25 to 30 minutes or until edges begin to pull away from sides of pan. Cool before cutting.

Makes 20 brownies

Fudgey Brownie Cut-Outs

1 cup granulated sugar
⅔ cup all-purpose flour
½ cup HERSHEY'S Cocoa
½ cup applesauce
2 egg whites
1 teaspoon vanilla extract
¼ cup finely chopped nuts
½ teaspoon powdered sugar

1. Heat oven to 350°F. Line 8-inch square baking pan with foil, extending foil over sides of pan; spray with vegetable cooking spray.

2. Stir together granulated sugar, flour and cocoa in small bowl. Add applesauce, egg whites and vanilla; beat on medium speed of mixer until well blended. Stir in nuts. Spread batter into prepared pan.

3. Bake 25 minutes or until edges are firm. Cool completely in pan on wire rack. Place in freezer about 15 minutes for easier cutting. Lift brownies from pan using sides of foil; carefully peel off foil. Cut into squares or other desired shapes with small cookie cutters. Sift powdered sugar over tops of brownies. Store, covered, at room temperature.

Makes 16 brownies

Almond Brownies

½ cup (1 stick) butter
2 squares (1 ounce each) unsweetened
   baking chocolate
2 large eggs
1 cup firmly packed light brown sugar
¼ teaspoon almond extract
½ cup all-purpose flour
1½ cups "M&M's"® Chocolate Mini Baking
   Bits, divided
½ cup slivered almonds, toasted and divided
   Chocolate Glaze (recipe follows)

Preheat oven to 350°F. Grease and flour 8×8×2-inch baking pan; set aside. In small saucepan melt butter and chocolate over low heat; stir to blend. Remove from heat; let cool. In medium bowl beat eggs and brown sugar until well blended; stir in chocolate mixture and almond extract. Add flour. Stir in 1 cup "M&M's"® Chocolate Mini Baking Bits and ¼ cup almonds. Spread batter evenly in prepared pan. Bake 25 to 28 minutes or until firm in center. Cool completely on wire rack. Prepare Chocolate Glaze. Spread over brownies; decorate with remaining ½ cup "M&M's"® Chocolate Mini Baking Bits and remaining ¼ cup almonds. Cut into bars. Store in tightly covered container.

Makes 16 brownies

Chocolate Glaze: In small saucepan over low heat combine 4 teaspoons water and 1 tablespoon butter until it comes to a boil. Stir in 4 teaspoons unsweetened cocoa powder. Gradually stir in ½ cup powdered sugar until smooth. Remove from heat; stir in ¼ teaspoon vanilla extract. Let glaze cool slightly.

Fabulous Blonde Brownies

1¾ cups all-purpose flour
1 teaspoon baking powder
¼ teaspoon salt
1 cup (6 ounces) white chocolate chips
1 cup (4 ounces) blanched whole almonds,
   coarsely chopped
1 cup toffee baking pieces
1½ cups packed light brown sugar
⅔ cup butter, softened
2 eggs
2 teaspoons vanilla

Preheat oven to 350°F. Lightly grease 13×9-inch baking pan.

Combine flour, baking powder and salt in small bowl; mix well. Combine white chocolate chips, almonds and toffee pieces in medium bowl; mix well.

Beat brown sugar and butter in large bowl with electric mixer at medium speed until light and fluffy. Beat in eggs and vanilla. Add flour mixture; beat at low speed until well blended. Stir in ¾ cup white chocolate chip mixture. Spread evenly in prepared pan.

Bake 20 minutes. Immediately sprinkle remaining white chocolate chip mixture evenly over brownies. Press lightly. Bake 15 to 20 minutes or until toothpick inserted into center comes out clean. Cool brownies completely in pan on wire rack. Cut into 2×1½-inch bars. *Makes 3 dozen brownies*

Almond Brownies

Cupcakes for the Crowd

Chocolate Peanut Butter Cups

1 package DUNCAN HINES® Moist Deluxe® Swiss Chocolate Cake Mix
1 container DUNCAN HINES® Creamy Home-Style Classic Vanilla Frosting
½ cup creamy peanut butter
15 miniature peanut butter cup candies, wrappers removed, cut in half vertically

1. Preheat oven to 350°F. Place 30 (2½-inch) paper liners in muffin cups.

2. Prepare, bake and cool cupcakes following package directions for basic recipe.

3. Combine vanilla frosting and peanut butter in medium bowl. Stir until smooth. Frost one cupcake. Decorate with peanut butter cup candy, cut-side down. Repeat with remaining cupcakes and candies. *Makes 30 servings*

Tip: You may substitute DUNCAN HINES® Moist Deluxe® Devil's Food, Dark Chocolate Fudge or Butter Recipe Fudge Cake Mix flavors for Swiss Chocolate Cake Mix.

Chocolate Peanut Butter Cups

Cappuccino Cupcakes

1 package (18.25 ounces) dark chocolate
    cake mix
1⅓ cups strong brewed or instant coffee,
    at room temperature
⅓ cup vegetable oil or melted butter
3 large eggs
1 container (16 ounces) prepared vanilla
    frosting
2 tablespoons coffee liqueur, divided
    Grated chocolate*
    Chocolate-covered coffee beans (optional)
    Additional coffee liqueur (optional)

*Grate half of a 3- or 4-ounce milk, dark chocolate or espresso
chocolate candy bar on the large holes of a standing grater.*

1. Preheat oven to 350°F. Line 24 regular-size
(2½-inch) muffin cups with paper muffin cup liners.

2. Beat cake mix, coffee, oil and eggs with electric
mixer at low speed 30 seconds. Beat at medium
speed 2 minutes.

3. Spoon batter into prepared muffin cups filling
⅔ full. Bake 18 to 20 minutes or until toothpick
inserted in centers comes out clean. Cool in pans on
wire racks 10 minutes. Remove cupcakes to racks;
cool completely. (At this point, cupcakes may be
frozen up to 3 months. Thaw at room temperature
before frosting.)

4. Combine frosting and 2 tablespoons liqueur in
small bowl; mix well. Before frosting, poke about
10 holes in cupcake with toothpick. Pour 1 to
2 teaspoons liqueur over top of each cupcake, if
desired. Frost and sprinkle with chocolate. Garnish
with chocolate-covered coffee beans, if desired.

Makes 24 cupcakes

Chocolate-Raspberry Cupcakes

2 cups all-purpose flour
⅔ cup unsweetened cocoa powder
1¾ teaspoons baking soda
½ teaspoon baking powder
½ teaspoon salt
1¾ cups granulated sugar
⅔ cup vegetable shortening
1 cup cold water
2 teaspoons vanilla extract
3 large eggs
⅓ cup seedless raspberry jam
1½ cups "M&M's"® Semi-Sweet Chocolate
    Mini Baking Bits, divided
1 container (16 ounces) white frosting
    Red food coloring

Preheat oven to 350°F. Lightly grease 24 (2¾-inch)
muffin cups or line with paper or foil liners; set
aside. In large bowl combine flour, cocoa powder,
baking soda, baking powder and salt; stir in sugar.
Beat in shortening until well combined. Gradually
beat in water; stir in vanilla. Beat in eggs. Stir in
raspberry jam. Divide batter evenly among
prepared muffin cups. Sprinkle batter with 1 cup
"M&M's"® Semi-Sweet Chocolate Mini Baking Bits.
Bake 20 to 25 minutes or until toothpick inserted
in centers comes out clean. Cool completely on wire
racks. Combine frosting and red food coloring to
make frosting pink. Spread frosting over tops of
cupcakes; decorate with remaining ½ cup "M&M's"®
Semi-Sweet Chocolate Mini Baking Bits. Store in
tightly covered container. *Makes 24 cupcakes*

Cappuccino Cupcakes

Scarecrow Cupcakes

1¼ cups all-purpose flour
¾ teaspoon baking powder
½ teaspoon baking soda
¼ teaspoon salt
¾ teaspoon ground cinnamon
⅛ teaspoon ground cloves
⅛ teaspoon ground nutmeg
⅛ teaspoon ground allspice
¾ cup heavy cream
2 tablespoons molasses
¼ cup butter, softened
¼ cup granulated sugar
¼ cup packed brown sugar
2 eggs
½ teaspoon vanilla
¾ cup sweetened shredded coconut
    Maple Frosting (recipe follows)
    Toasted coconut, chow mein noodles,
    shredded wheat cereal, assorted
    candies and decorator gel

• Preheat oven to 350°F. Line 18 (2¾-inch) muffin cups with paper baking liners. Combine flour, baking powder, baking soda, salt and spices in medium bowl; set aside. Combine cream and molasses in small bowl; set aside.

• Beat butter in large bowl until creamy. Add granulated sugar and brown sugar; beat until light and fluffy. Add eggs, one at a time, beating well after each addition. Blend in vanilla.

• Add flour mixture alternately with cream mixture, beating well after each addition. Stir in coconut; spoon batter into prepared muffin cups, filling about half full.

• Bake 20 to 25 minutes or until toothpick inserted in centers comes out clean. Cool in pan on wire rack 10 minutes. Remove cupcakes to racks; cool completely.

• Prepare Maple Frosting. Frost cupcakes and decorate to make scarecrow faces as shown in photo.
Makes 18 cupcakes

Maple Frosting: Beat 2 tablespoons softened butter and 2 tablespoons maple or pancake syrup in medium bowl until blended. Gradually beat in 1½ cups powdered sugar until smooth.

Tip

To make a gumdrop hat, use a rolling pin to roll out a large gumdrop on a generously sugared surface. Cut 1 rounded piece to look like the top of the hat and 1 straight piece to look like the brim of the hat as shown in the photo. Overlap the pieces to make the hat; pipe decorator gel over the seam for the hat band.

Scarecrow Cupcakes

"Go Fly a Kite" Cupcakes

1⅔ cups all-purpose flour
½ cup unsweetened cocoa powder
1 teaspoon baking powder
½ teaspoon baking soda
¼ teaspoon salt
1¾ cups granulated sugar
¼ cup firmly packed light brown sugar
½ cup vegetable shortening
1 cup buttermilk
3 large eggs
2 tablespoons vegetable oil
¾ teaspoon vanilla extract
1½ cups "M&M's"® Chocolate Mini Baking
      Bits, divided
24 graham cracker squares
1 container (16 ounces) white frosting
      Assorted food colorings

Preheat oven to 350°F. Lightly grease 24 (2¾-inch) muffin cups or line with foil or paper liners; set aside. In large bowl combine flour, cocoa powder, baking powder, baking soda and salt; stir in sugars. Beat in shortening until well combined. Beat in buttermilk, eggs, oil and vanilla. Divide batter among prepared muffin cups. Sprinkle 1 teaspoon "M&M's"® Chocolate Mini Baking Bits over batter in each muffin cup. Bake 20 to 25 minutes or until toothpick inserted in centers comes out clean. Cool completely on wire racks.

Using serrated knife and back and forth sawing motion, gently cut graham crackers into kite shapes. (Do not press down on cracker while cutting.) Reserve 1 cup frosting. Tint remaining frosting desired color. Frost graham crackers and decorate with "M&M's"® Chocolate Mini Baking Bits. Tint reserved frosting sky blue; frost cupcakes. Place

small mound of frosting at one edge of cupcake; stand kites in frosting on cupcakes. Make kite tails with "M&M's"® Chocolate Mini Baking Bits. Store in tightly covered container.

Makes 24 cupcakes

Golden Apple Cupcakes

1 package (18 to 20 ounces) yellow cake mix
1 cup MOTT'S® Chunky Apple Sauce
⅓ cup vegetable oil
3 eggs
¼ cup firmly packed light brown sugar
¼ cup chopped walnuts
½ teaspoon ground cinnamon
      Vanilla Frosting (recipe follows)

Heat oven to 350°F. In bowl, combine cake mix, apple sauce, oil and eggs; blend according to package directions. Spoon batter into 24 paper-lined muffin pan cups. Mix brown sugar, walnuts and cinnamon; sprinkle over prepared batter in muffin cups. Bake 20 to 25 minutes or until toothpick inserted in center comes out clean. Cool in pan 10 minutes. Remove from pan; cool completely on wire rack. Frost cupcakes with Vanilla Frosting.

Makes 24 cupcakes

Vanilla Frosting: In large bowl, beat 1 package (8 ounces) softened cream cheese until light and creamy; blend in ¼ teaspoon vanilla extract. Beat ½ cup heavy cream until stiff; fold into cream cheese mixture.

"Go Fly a Kite" Cupcakes

Mini Turtle Cupcakes

1 package (21.5 ounces) brownie mix plus
  ingredients to prepare mix
½ cup chopped pecans
1 cup prepared or homemade dark
  chocolate frosting
½ cup chopped pecans, toasted
12 caramels, unwrapped
1 to 2 tablespoons whipping cream

1. Heat oven to 350°F. Line 54 mini (1½-inch) muffin cups with paper muffin cup liners.

2. Prepare brownie batter as directed on package. Stir in chopped pecans.

3. Spoon batter into prepared muffin cups filling ⅔ full. Bake 18 minutes or until toothpick inserted into centers comes out clean. Cool in pans on wire racks 5 minutes. Remove cupcakes to racks; cool completely. (At this point, cupcakes may be frozen up to 3 months. Thaw at room temperature before frosting.)

4. Spread frosting over cooled cupcakes; top with pecans.

5. Combine caramels and 1 tablespoon cream in small saucepan. Cook over low heat until caramels are melted and mixture is smooth, stirring constantly. Add additional 1 tablespoon cream if needed. Drizzle caramel decoratively over cupcakes. Store at room temperature up to 24 hours or cover and refrigerate for up to 3 days before serving.

Makes 54 mini cupcakes

Double Chocolate Cocoa Cupcakes

¾ cup shortening
1¼ cups granulated sugar
2 eggs
1 teaspoon vanilla extract
1¾ cups all-purpose flour
½ cup HERSHEY'S Cocoa
1 teaspoon baking soda
½ teaspoon salt
1 cup milk
1 cup HERSHEY'S MINI CHIPS™
  Semi-Sweet Chocolate Chips
Powdered sugar

1. Heat oven to 375°F. Line muffin cups (2½ inches in diameter) with paper bake cups.

2. Beat shortening and granulated sugar in large bowl until fluffy. Add eggs and vanilla; beat well. Stir together flour, cocoa, baking soda and salt; add alternately with milk to shortening mixture, beating well after each addition. Stir in small chocolate chips. Fill prepared muffin cups about ¾ full with batter.

3. Bake 20 to 25 minutes or until cupcake springs back when touched lightly in center. Remove from pans to wire racks. Cool completely. Sift powdered sugar over tops of cupcakes.

Makes about 2 dozen cupcakes

Mini Turtle Cupcakes

Double Malted Cupcakes

Cupcakes
  2 cups all-purpose flour
  ¼ cup malted milk powder
  2 teaspoons baking powder
  ¼ teaspoon salt
  1¾ cups granulated sugar
  ½ cup (1 stick) butter, softened
  1 cup 2% or whole milk
  1½ teaspoons vanilla
  3 large egg whites

Frosting
  4 ounces milk chocolate candy bar,
      broken into chunks
  ¼ cup (½ stick) butter
  ¼ cup whipping cream
  1 tablespoon malted milk powder
  1 teaspoon vanilla
  1¾ cups powdered sugar
  30 chocolate-covered malt ball candies

1. Preheat oven to 350°F. Line 30 regular-size (2½-inch) muffin cups with paper muffin cup liners.

2. For cupcakes, combine flour, ¼ cup malted milk powder, baking powder and salt; mix well and set aside. Beat sugar and ½ cup butter with electric mixer at medium speed 1 minute. Add milk and 1½ teaspoons vanilla. Beat at low speed 30 seconds. Gradually beat in flour mixture; beat at medium speed 2 minutes. Add egg whites; beat 1 minute.

3. Spoon batter into prepared muffin cups filling ⅔ full. Bake 20 minutes or until golden brown and toothpick inserted into centers comes out clean. Cool in pans on wire racks 10 minutes. (Centers of cupcakes will sink slightly upon cooling.) Remove cupcakes to racks; cool completely. (At this point, cupcakes may be frozen up to 3 months.)

4. For frosting, melt chocolate and ¼ cup butter in heavy medium saucepan over low heat, stirring frequently. Stir in cream, 1 tablespoon malted milk powder and 1 teaspoon vanilla; mix well. Gradually stir in powdered sugar. Cook 4 to 5 minutes, stirring constantly, until small lumps disappear. Remove from heat. Chill 20 minutes, beating every 5 minutes until frosting is spreadable.

5. Spread cooled cupcakes with frosting; decorate with chocolate covered malt ball candies. Store at room temperature up to 24 hours or cover and refrigerate for up to 3 days before serving.

Makes 30 cupcakes

Double Malted Cupcakes

Chocolate Frosted Peanut Butter Cupcakes

⅓ cup creamy or chunky reduced-fat
   peanut butter
⅓ cup butter, softened
½ cup granulated sugar
¼ cup packed brown sugar
 2 eggs
 1 teaspoon vanilla
1¾ cups all-purpose flour
1½ teaspoons baking powder
¼ teaspoon salt
1¼ cups milk
   Peanut Butter Chocolate Frosting
   (recipe follows)

1. Preheat oven to 350°F. Line 18 (2½-inch) muffin cups with foil baking cups.

2. Beat peanut butter and butter with elecric mixer in large bowl at medium speed until smooth; beat in sugars until well mixed. Beat in eggs and vanilla.

3. Combine flour, baking powder and salt in medium bowl. Add flour mixture to peanut butter mixture alternately with milk, beginning and ending with flour mixture.

4. Pour batter into prepared muffin cups. Bake 23 to 25 minutes or until cupcakes spring back when touched and wooden picks inserted in centers come out clean. Cool in pans on wire racks 10 minutes; remove from pans and cool completely.

5. Prepare Peanut Butter Chocolate Frosting. Frost each cupcake with about 1½ tablespoons frosting. Garnish as desired.   *Makes 1½ dozen cupcakes*

Tip: If you don't have muffin pans, don't worry. Foil baking cups are sturdy enough to be used without muffin pans; simply place the baking cups on a baking sheet and fill.

Peanut Butter Chocolate Frosting

 4 cups powdered sugar
⅓ cup unsweetened cocoa powder
 4 to 5 tablespoons milk, divided
 3 tablespoons creamy peanut butter

Combine powdered sugar, cocoa, 4 tablespoons milk and peanut butter in large bowl. Beat with electric mixer at low speed until smooth, scraping bowl frequently. Beat in additional 1 tablespoon milk until desired spreading consistency.
          Makes about 2½ cups frosting

Chocolate Frosted Peanut Butter Cupcakes

Play Ball

2 cups plus 1 tablespoon all-purpose flour,
  divided
¾ cup granulated sugar
¾ cup packed brown sugar
1 tablespoon baking powder
1 teaspoon salt
½ teaspoon baking soda
½ cup shortening
1¼ cups milk
3 eggs
1½ teaspoons vanilla
½ cup mini semisweet chocolate chips
1 container (16 ounces) vanilla frosting
  Assorted candies and food colorings

1. Preheat oven to 350°F. Line 24 regular-size
(2½-inch) muffin pan cups with paper muffin
cup liners.

2. Combine 2 cups flour, sugars, baking powder, salt
and baking soda in medium bowl. Beat shortening,
milk, eggs and vanilla with electric mixer at medium
speed until well combined. Add dry ingredients;
blend well. Beat at high speed 3 minutes, scraping
side of bowl frequently. Toss mini chocolate chips
with remaining 1 tablespoon flour; stir into batter.
Divide evenly between prepared muffin cups.

3. Bake 20 minutes or until toothpick inserted
into centers comes out clean. Cool in pan on wire
racks 5 minutes. Remove cupcakes to racks; cool
completely. Decorate with desired frostings and
candies as shown in photo.   *Makes 24 cupcakes*

Chocolate Zucchini Cupcakes

Cupcakes
1½ cups unsifted all-pupose flour
¾ cup sugar
¼ cup unsweetened cocoa
1½ teaspoons baking soda
½ teaspoon salt
1 cup shredded, peeled zucchini
⅓ cup CRISCO® Oil
⅓ cup buttermilk
1 egg
1 teaspoon vanilla

Frosting
1½ cups confectioners' sugar
2 tablespoons butter or margarine, softened
2 to 3 tablespoons milk, divided
¼ tablespoon vanilla

1. Heat oven to 350°F. Place paper liners in
12 muffin cups. Set aside.

2. Mix flour, sugar, cocoa, baking soda and salt in
medium bowl. Add remaining cupcake ingredients.
Beat with electric mixer at low speed until
ingredients are moistened, scraping bowl often. Beat
at high speed 1 minute, scraping bowl occasionally.
Pour into lined muffin cups, filling about ⅔ full.

3. Bake at 350°F 20 to 25 minutes or until wooden
pick inserted in center comes out clean. Remove
from pan. Cool completely on wire rack.

4. For frosting, combine confectioners' sugar, butter,
1 tablespoon milk and vanilla in small mixing bowl.
Beat with electric mixer at low speed until smooth.,
scraping bowl frequently. Beat in additional milk
until desired spreading consistency. Spread on
cooled cupcakes.   *Makes 1 dozen cupcakes*

Play Ball

Peanut Butter Surprise

2 cups all-purpose flour
2 teaspoons baking powder
¼ teaspoon salt
1¾ cups sugar
½ cup (1 stick) butter, softened
¾ cup reduced-fat (2%) or whole milk
1 teaspoon vanilla
3 large egg whites
2 (3-ounce) bittersweet chocolate candy
    bars, melted and cooled
30 mini peanut butter cups
1 container prepared chocolate frosting
3 ounces white chocolate candy bar, broken
    into chunks

1. Preheat oven to 350°F. Line 30 regular-size (2½-inch) muffin cups with paper muffin cup liners.

2. For cupcakes, combine flour, baking powder and salt in medium bowl; mix well and set aside. Beat sugar and butter with electric mixer at medium speed 1 minute. Add milk and vanilla. Beat with electric mixer at low speed 30 seconds. Gradually beat in flour mixture; beat at medium speed 2 minutes. Add egg whites; beat 1 minute. Stir in melted chocolate.

3. Spoon 1 heaping tablespoon batter into each prepared muffin cup; use back of spoon to slightly spread batter over bottom. Place one mini peanut butter cup in center of each cupcake. Spoon 1 heaping tablespoon batter over peanut butter cup; use back of spoon to smooth out batter. (Do not fill cups more than ¾ full.)

4. Bake 24 to 26 minutes or until puffed and golden brown. Cool in pans on wire racks 10 minutes. (Center of cupcakes will sink slightly upon cooling.) Remove cupcakes to racks; cool completely. (At this point, cupcakes may be frozen up to 3 months). Spread frosting over cooled cupcakes.

5. For white drizzle, place white chocolate in small resealable plastic food storage bag. Microwave at HIGH 30 to 40 seconds. Turn bag over; microwave additional 30 seconds or until chocolate is melted. Cut off tiny corner of bag; pipe chocolate decoratively over frosted cupcakes. Store at room temperature up to 24 hours or cover and refrigerate up to 3 days before serving. *Makes 30 cupcakes*

Peanut Butter Surprise

Touchdown Brownie Cups

1 cup (2 sticks) butter or margarine
½ cup HERSHEY'S Cocoa or HERSHEY'S
    Dutch Processed Cocoa
1 cup packed light brown sugar
½ cup granulated sugar
3 eggs
1 teaspoon vanilla extract
1 cup all-purpose flour
1⅓ cup chopped pecans, divided

1. Heat oven to 350°F. Line 2½-inch muffin cups with paper or foil bake cups.

2. Place butter in large microwave-safe bowl; cover. Microwave at HIGH (100%) 1½ minutes or until melted. Add cocoa; stir until smooth. Add brown sugar and granulated sugar; stir until well blended. Add eggs and vanilla; beat well. Add flour and 1 cup pecans; stir until well blended. Fill prepared muffin cups about ¾ full with batter; sprinkle about 1 teaspoon remaining pecans over top of each.

3. Bake 20 to 25 minutes or until tops are beginning to dry and crack on top. Cool completely in cups on wire rack.   *Makes about 17 cupcakes*

Banana Split Cupcakes

1 (18.25 ounces) yellow cake mix, divided
1 cup water
1 cup mashed ripe bananas
3 eggs
1 cup chopped drained maraschino cherries
1½ cups miniature semi-sweet chocolate
    chips, divided
1½ cups prepared vanilla frosting
1 cup marshmallow creme
1 teaspoon shortening
30 whole maraschino cherries, drained and
    patted dry

1. Preheat oven to 350°F. Line 30 regular-size (2½-inch) muffin cups with paper muffin cup liners.

2. Reserve 2 tablespoons cake mix. Combine remaining cake mix, water, bananas and eggs in large bowl. Beat at low speed of electric mixer until moistened, about 30 seconds. Beat at medium speed 2 minutes. Combine chopped cherries and reserved cake mix in small bowl. Stir chopped cherry mixture and 1 cup chocolate chips into batter.

3. Spoon batter into prepared muffin cups. Bake 15 to 20 minutes or until toothpick inserted in centers comes out clean. Cool in pans on wire racks 10 minutes. Remove to wire racks; cool completely.

4. Blend frosting and marshmallow creme in small bowl. Frost each cupcake with frosting mixture. Combine remaining ½ cup chocolate chips and shortening in small microwavable bowl. Microwave at HIGH 30 to 45 seconds, stirring after 30 seconds, or until smooth. Drizzle chocolate mixture over cupcakes. Place one whole cherry on each cupcake.
Makes 30 cupcakes

Touchdown Brownie Cups

Blueberry Crisp Cupcakes

Cupcakes

2 cups all-purpose flour
2 teaspoons baking powder
¼ teaspoon salt
1¾ cups granulated sugar
½ cup (1 stick) butter, softened
¾ cup milk
1½ teaspoons vanilla
3 large egg whites
3 cups fresh or frozen (unthawed) blueberries

Streusel

⅓ cup all-purpose flour
¼ cup uncooked old-fashioned or quick oats
¼ cup packed light brown sugar
½ teaspoon ground cinnamon
¼ cup butter, softened
½ cup chopped walnuts or pecans

1. Preheat oven to 350°F. Line 30 regular-size (2½-inch) muffin cups with paper muffin cup liners.

2. For cupcakes, combine 2 cups flour, baking powder and salt in medium bowl; mix well and set aside. Beat granulated sugar and ½ cup butter with electric mixer at medium speed 1 minute. Add milk and vanilla. Beat at low speed 30 seconds. Gradually beat in flour mixture; beat at medium speed 2 minutes. Add egg whites; beat 1 minute. Spoon batter into prepared muffin cups filling ½ full. Spoon blueberries over batter. Bake 10 minutes.

3. Meanwhile for streusel, combine ⅓ cup flour, oats, brown sugar and cinnamon in small bowl; mix well. Cut in ¼ cup butter with pastry blender or two knives until mixture is well combined. Stir in chopped nuts.

4. Sprinkle streusel over partially baked cupcakes. Return to oven; bake 18 to 20 minutes or until golden brown and toothpick inserted into centers comes out clean. Cool in pans on wire racks 10 minutes. Remove cupcakes to racks; cool completely. (Cupcakes may be frozen up to 3 months.)
Makes 30 cupcakes

Tip

When using frozen blueberries in baked goods, add them at the last minute and never thaw them before using—thawed blueberries are much more likely to "bleed" into the batter and discolor the final product.

Blueberry Crisp Cupcakes

Chocolate Tiramisu Cupcakes

Cupcakes
- 1 package (18.25 ounces) chocolate cake mix
- 1¼ cups water
- 3 large eggs
- ⅓ cup vegetable oil or melted butter
- 2 tablespoons instant espresso powder
- 2 tablespoons brandy (optional)

Frosting
- 8 ounces mascarpone cheese or cream cheese
- 1½ to 1¾ cups powdered sugar
- 2 tablespoons coffee-flavored liqueur
- 1 tablespoon unsweetened cocoa powder

1. Preheat oven to 350°F. Line 30 regular-size (2½-inch) muffin cups with paper muffin cup liners.

2. Beat all cupcake ingredients with electric mixer at low speed 30 seconds. Beat at medium speed 2 minutes.

3. Spoon batter into prepared cups filling ⅔ full. Bake 20 to 22 minutes or until toothpick inserted in centers comes out clean. Cool in pans on wire racks 10 minutes. Remove cupcakes to racks; cool completely. (At this point, cupcakes may be frozen up to 3 months. Thaw at room temperature before frosting.)

4. For frosting, beat mascarpone cheese and 1½ cups powdered sugar with electric mixer at medium speed until well blended. Add liqueur; beat until well blended. If frosting is too soft, beat in additional powdered sugar or chill until spreadable.

5. Frost cooled cupcakes with frosting. Place cocoa in strainer; shake over cupcakes. Store at room temperature up to 24 hours or cover and refrigerate for up to 3 days before serving.

Makes 30 cupcakes

P.B. Chips Brownie Cups

- 1 cup (2 sticks) butter or margarine
- 2 cups sugar
- 2 teaspoons vanilla extract
- 4 eggs
- ¾ cup HERSHEY'S Cocoa or HERSHEY'S Dutch Processed Cocoa
- 1¾ cups all-purpose flour
- ½ teaspoon baking powder
- ½ teaspoon salt
- 1⅔ cups (10-ounce package) REESE'S® Peanut Butter Chips, divided

1. Heat oven to 350°F. Line 18 muffin cups (2½ inches in diameter) with paper or foil bake cups.

2. Place butter in large microwave-safe bowl. Microwave at HIGH (100%) 1 to 1½ minutes or until melted. Stir in sugar and vanilla. Add eggs; beat well. Add cocoa; beat until well blended. Add flour, baking powder and salt; beat well. Stir in 1⅓ cups peanut butter chips. Divide batter evenly into muffin cups; sprinkle with remaining ⅓ cup peanut butter chips.

3. Bake 25 to 30 minutes or until surface is firm; cool completely in pan on wire rack.

Makes about 1½ dozen brownie cups

Chocolate Tiramisu Cupcakes

Red's Rockin' Rainbow Cupcakes

2¼ cups all-purpose flour
1 tablespoon baking powder
½ teaspoon salt
1⅔ cups granulated sugar
½ cup (1 stick) butter, softened
1 cup milk
2 teaspoons vanilla extract
3 large egg whites
    Blue and assorted food colorings
1 container (16 ounces) white frosting
1½ cups "M&M's"® Chocolate Mini Baking
    Bits, divided

Preheat oven to 350°F. Lightly grease 24 (2¾-inch) muffin cups or line with paper or foil liners; set aside. In large bowl combine flour, baking powder and salt. Blend in sugar, butter, milk and vanilla; beat about 2 minutes. Add egg whites; beat 2 minutes. Divide batter evenly among prepared muffin cups. Place 2 drops desired food coloring into each muffin cup. Swirl gently with knife. Sprinkle evenly with ¾ cup "M&M's"® Chocolate Mini Baking Bits. Bake 20 to 25 minutes or until toothpick inserted in center comes out clean. Cool completely on wire racks. Combine frosting and blue food coloring. Spread frosting over cupcakes; decorate with remaining ¾ cup "M&M's"® Chocolate Mini Baking Bits to make rainbows. Store in tightly covered container.   *Makes 24 cupcakes*

Chocolate Sundae Cupcakes

24 REYNOLDS® Baking Cups
1 package (about 18 ounces) devil's food
    cake mix
1 container (16 ounces) ready-to-spread
    chocolate frosting
½ cup caramel ice cream topping
1½ cups frozen whipped topping, thawed
24 maraschino cherries with stems, drained

PREHEAT oven to 350°F. Place Reynolds Baking Cups in muffin pans; set aside. Prepare cake mix following package directions for 24 cupcakes. Spoon batter into baking cups. Bake as directed. Cool.

FROST cupcakes. Top each cupcake with 1 teaspoon caramel topping and 1 tablespoon whipped topping. Garnish each cupcake with a cherry. Refrigerate until serving time.

Makes 24 cupcakes

Red's Rockin' Rainbow Cupcakes

Pumpkin Bread

1 package (about 18 ounces) yellow cake mix
1 can (16 ounces) solid pack pumpkin
⅓ cup GRANDMA'S® Molasses
4 eggs
1 teaspoon cinnamon
1 teaspoon nutmeg
⅓ cup nuts, chopped (optional)
⅓ cup raisins (optional)

Preheat oven to 350°F. Grease two 9×5-inch loaf pans.

Combine all ingredients in a large bowl and mix well. Beat at medium speed 2 minutes. Pour into prepared pans. Bake 60 minutes or until toothpick inserted into center comes out clean.   *Makes 2 loaves*

Hint: Serve with cream cheese or preserves, or top with cream cheese frosting or ice cream.

Pumpkin Bread

Tempting Breakfast Treats **187**

Fudgey Peanut Butter Chip Muffins

½ cup applesauce
½ cup quick-cooking rolled oats
¼ cup (½ stick) butter or margarine, softened
½ cup granulated sugar
½ cup packed light brown sugar
1 egg
½ teaspoon vanilla extract
¾ cup all-purpose flour
¼ cup HERSHEY'S Dutch Processed Cocoa or HERSHEY'S Cocoa
½ teaspoon baking soda
¼ teaspoon ground cinnamon (optional)
1 cup REESE'S® Peanut Butter Chips
Powdered sugar (optional)

1. Heat oven to 350°F. Line muffin cups (2½ inches in diameter) with paper bake cups.

2. Blend applesauce and oats in small bowl; set aside. In large bowl, beat butter, granulated sugar, brown sugar, egg and vanilla until well blended. Add applesauce mixture; blend well. Stir together flour, cocoa, baking soda and cinnamon, if desired. Add to butter mixture, blending well. Stir in peanut butter chips. Fill muffin cups ¾ full with batter.

3. Bake 22 to 26 minutes or until wooden pick inserted in center comes out almost clean. Cool slightly in pan on wire rack. Sprinkle muffin tops with powdered sugar, if desired. Serve warm.

Makes 12 to 15 muffins

Fudgey Chocolate Chip Muffins: Omit Peanut Butter Chips. Add 1 cup HERSHEY'S Semi-Sweet Chocolate Chips.

Apricot Oatmeal Muffins

1 cup QUAKER® Oats (quick or old fashioned, uncooked)
1 cup low-fat buttermilk
¼ cup egg substitute or 2 egg whites
2 tablespoons margarine, melted
1 cup all-purpose flour
⅓ cup finely chopped dried apricots
¼ cup chopped nuts (optional)
3 tablespoons granulated sugar or 1¾ teaspoons EQUAL® MEASURE™ (7 packets) or 2 tablespoons fructose
1 teaspoon baking powder
½ teaspoon baking soda
¼ teaspoon salt (optional)

Heat oven to 400°F. Lightly spray 12 medium muffin cups with vegetable oil cooking spray. Combine oats and buttermilk; let stand 10 minutes. Add egg substitute and margarine; mix well. In large bowl, combine remaining ingredients; mix well. Add wet ingredients to dry ingredients; mix just until moistened. Fill muffin cups almost full. Bake 20 to 25 minutes or until golden brown. Let muffins stand a few minutes; remove from pan.

Makes 1 dozen

Tip: To toast nuts for extra flavor, spread evenly in small baking pan. Bake in 400°F oven 5 to 7 minutes or until light golden brown. Or, spread nuts on plate. Microwave on HIGH 1 minute; stir. Continue microwaving, checking every 30 seconds, until nuts are crunchy.

Fudgey Peanut Butter Chip Muffins

Cranberry Oat Bran Muffins

Prep Time: 15 minutes
Bake Time: 17 minutes

    2 cups flour
    1 cup oat bran
    ½ cup packed brown sugar
    2 teaspoons CALUMET® Baking Powder
    ½ teaspoon baking soda
    ½ teaspoon salt (optional)
    ½ cup MIRACLE WHIP® Light Dressing
    3 egg whites, slightly beaten
    ½ cup skim milk
    ⅓ cup orange juice
    1 teaspoon grated orange peel
    1 cup coarsely chopped cranberries

• **LINE** 12 medium muffin cups with paper baking cups or spray with nonstick cooking spray.

• **MIX** dry ingredients.

• **MIX** dressing, egg whites, milk, juice and peel.

• **ADD** to dry ingredients; mix just until moistened. Gently stir in cranberries. Spoon evenly into prepared muffin cups filling each cup ⅔ full.

• **BAKE** at 375°F for 15 to 17 minutes or until golden brown.

Makes 12 muffins

Banana Coffee Cake

    6 tablespoons margarine, softened
    ¾ cup sugar
    1 egg
    1 tablespoon grated lemon peel
    1 teaspoon vanilla extract
    ½ cup milk
    2 cups all-purpose flour
    1 tablespoon baking powder
    ¼ teaspoon salt
    3 ripe, large DOLE® Bananas, sliced
      (3 cups)
    Streusel Topping (recipe follows)

• Beat margarine and sugar in large bowl until light and fluffy. Beat in egg, lemon peel and vanilla until smooth. Stir in milk.

• Combine flour, baking powder and salt in medium bowl; add to margarine mixture, stirring until blended. Fold in bananas.

• Spoon batter into well greased 9-inch square baking pan; smooth top. Sprinkle with Streusel Topping. Bake at 375°F 45 to 50 minutes until toothpick inserted in center comes out clean. Cool 20 minutes before cutting.

Makes 9 servings

Streusel Topping: Combine ⅓ cup packed brown sugar, ⅓ cup all-purpose flour and ¾ teaspoon cinnamon. Cut in ¼ cup margarine until mixture is crumbly.

Cranberry Oat Bran Muffins

Blueberry Kuchen

Prep Time: 20 minutes
Cook Time: 35 minutes

  1½ cups all-purpose flour
   2 teaspoons baking powder
  ½ cup EGG BEATERS® Healthy Real
      Egg Product
  ⅓ cup skim milk
   1 teaspoon vanilla extract
  ½ cup granulated sugar
  ¼ cup FLEISCHMANN'S® Original
      Margarine, softened
   1 (21-ounce) can blueberry pie filling and
      topping
      Streusel Topping (recipe follows)
      Powdered Sugar Glaze, optional
      (recipe follows)

In small bowl, combine flour and baking powder; set aside. In another small bowl, combine Egg Beaters®, milk and vanilla; set aside.

In medium bowl, with electric mixer at medium speed, beat granulated sugar and margarine until creamy. Alternately add flour mixture and egg mixture, blending well after each addition. Spread batter into greased 9-inch square baking pan.

Bake at 350°F for 20 minutes. Spoon blueberry pie filling over batter; sprinkle Streusel Topping over filling. Bake for 10 to 15 minutes more or until toothpick inserted in center comes out clean. Cool in pan on wire rack. Drizzle with Powdered Sugar Glaze if desired. Cut into 12 (3×2-inch) pieces.

Makes 12 servings

Streusel Topping: In small bowl, combine 3 tablespoons all-purpose flour, 3 tablespoons powdered sugar and ¼ teaspoon ground cinnamon. Cut in 1 tablespoon Fleischmann's Original Margarine until crumbly.

Powdered Sugar Glaze: In small bowl, combine 1 cup powdered sugar and 5 to 6 teaspoons water until smooth.

Tip

A kuchen is a fruit- or cheese-filled coffee cake that is German in origin. ("Kaffeekuchen" is the German word for coffee cake.) Kuchen is generally served for breakfast but is also eaten as a dessert.

Blueberry Kuchen

Toll House® Crumbcake

Topping
- ⅓ cup packed brown sugar
- 1 tablespoon all-purpose flour
- 2 tablespoons butter or margarine, softened
- ½ cup chopped nuts
- 2 cups (12-ounce package) NESTLÉ® TOLL HOUSE® Semi-Sweet Chocolate Mini Morsels, *divided*

Cake
- 1¾ cups all-purpose flour
- 1 teaspoon baking powder
- 1 teaspoon baking soda
- ¼ teaspoon salt
- ¾ cup granulated sugar
- ½ cup (1 stick) butter or margarine, softened
- 1 teaspoon vanilla extract
- 3 large eggs
- 1 cup sour cream

PREHEAT oven to 350°F. Grease 13×9-inch baking pan.

For Topping
COMBINE brown sugar, flour and butter in small bowl with pastry blender or two knives until crumbly. Stir in nuts and *½ cup* morsels.

For Cake
COMBINE flour, baking powder, baking soda and salt in small bowl. Beat granulated sugar, butter and vanilla extract in large mixer bowl until creamy. Add eggs one at a time, beating well after each addition. Gradually add flour mixture alternately with sour cream. Fold in *remaining* morsels. Spread into prepared baking pan; sprinkle with topping.

BAKE for 25 to 35 minutes or until wooden toothpick inserted in center comes out clean. Cool in pan on wire rack. *Makes 12 servings*

Tip

If you use margarine when baking, make sure it is not the reduced-fat type—this contains less fat and more water and will affect the taste and texture of your baked goods.

Pineapple Citrus Muffins

⅓ cup honey
¼ cup butter or margarine, softened
1 egg
1 can (8 ounces) DOLE® Crushed Pineapple
1 tablespoon grated orange peel
1 cup all-purpose flour
1 cup whole wheat flour
1½ teaspoons baking powder
¼ teaspoon salt
¼ teaspoon ground nutmeg
1 cup DOLE® Chopped Dates
½ cup chopped walnuts, optional

• Preheat oven to 375°F. In large mixer bowl, beat together honey and butter 1 minute. Beat in egg, then undrained crushed pineapple and orange peel. In medium bowl, combine remaining ingredients; stir into pineapple mixture until just blended.

• Spoon batter into 12 greased muffin cups. Bake in preheated oven 25 minutes or until wooden pick inserted in center comes out clean. Cool slightly in pan before turning out onto wire rack. Serve warm.

Makes 12 muffins

Peanut Butter and Jelly Muffins

Prep Time: 15 minutes
Bake Time: 25 minutes

PAM® No-Stick Cooking Spray
2½ cups all-purpose flour
¾ cup sugar
1½ tablespoons baking powder
1 teaspoon salt
⅔ cup PETER PAN® Extra Crunchy Peanut Butter
¾ cup milk
⅓ cup WESSON® Vegetable Oil
2 eggs, room temperature and beaten
1 jar (10 ounces) KNOTT'S BERRY FARM® Jelly or Preserves, any flavor

Preheat oven to 400°F. Spray 12 muffin cups with PAM® Cooking Spray. In a large mixing bowl, stir together flour, sugar, baking powder and salt. Using a pastry cutter or two knives, cut Peter Pan® Peanut Butter into flour until mixture resembles coarse crumbs. Add milk, Wesson® Oil and eggs; stir until just moistened. Spoon muffin cups ½ *full* with batter, creating a well in the center of each cup. Place a heaping *1 tablespoon* of Knott's® Jelly into well. Evenly distribute remaining batter over jelly. Bake 20 to 25 minutes or until wooden pick inserted into center comes out clean. Cool completely on wire rack.

Makes 1 dozen muffins

Chunky Apple Molasses Muffins

2 cups all-purpose flour
¼ cup sugar
1 tablespoon baking powder
1 teaspoon ground cinnamon
¼ teaspoon salt
1 Fuji apple, peeled, cored, and finely
    chopped
½ cup milk
¼ cup molasses
¼ cup vegetable oil
1 large egg

1. Heat oven to 450°F. Lightly grease eight 3-inch muffin pan cups. In large bowl, combine flour, sugar, baking powder, cinnamon and salt. Add apple and stir to distribute evenly.

2. In small bowl, beat together milk, molasses, oil and egg. Stir into dry ingredients and mix just until blended. Fill muffin pan cups with batter. Bake 5 minutes, then reduce heat to 350°F and bake 12 to 15 minutes longer or until centers of muffins spring back when gently pressed. Cool in pan 5 minutes. Remove muffins from pan and cool to warm; serve.   *Makes 8 (3-inch) muffins*

Favorite recipe from **Washington Apple Commission**

Butterscotch Sticky Buns

3 tablespoons butter or margarine, *divided*
2 packages (8 ounces *each*) refrigerated
    crescent dinner rolls
1⅔ cups (11-ounce package) NESTLÉ®
    TOLL HOUSE® Butterscotch Flavored
    Morsels, *divided*
½ cup chopped pecans
¼ cup granulated sugar
1½ teaspoons lemon juice
1½ teaspoons water
1 teaspoon ground cinnamon

PREHEAT oven to 375°F.

PLACE *1 tablespoon* butter in 13×9-inch baking pan; melt in oven for 2 to 4 minutes or until butter sizzles. Unroll dinner rolls; separate into 16 triangles. Sprinkle triangles with *1⅓ cups* morsels. Starting at shortest side, roll up each triangle; arrange in prepared baking pan.

BAKE for 15 to 20 minutes or until lightly browned.

MICROWAVE *remaining* morsels and *remaining* butter in medium, microwave-safe bowl on MEDIUM-HIGH (70%) power for 30 seconds; stir. Microwave at additional 10- to 20-second intervals, stirring until smooth. Stir in nuts, sugar, lemon juice, water and cinnamon. Pour over hot rolls.

BAKE for 5 minutes or until bubbly. Immediately loosen buns from pan. Cool in pan on wire rack for 10 minutes; serve warm.   *Makes 16 buns*

Star-Of-The-East Fruit Bread

½ cup (1 stick) butter or margarine,
    softened
1 cup sugar
2 eggs
1 teaspoon vanilla extract
2 cups all-purpose flour
1 teaspoon baking soda
¼ teaspoon salt
1 cup mashed ripe bananas (about
    3 medium)
½ cup chopped maraschino cherries,
    well-drained
1 can (11 ounces) mandarin orange
    segments, well-drained
½ cup chopped dates or Calimyrna figs
1 cup HERSHEY'S Semi-Sweet Chocolate
    Chips
    Chocolate Drizzle (recipe follows)

1. Heat oven to 350°F. Grease two 8½×4½×2⅝-inch loaf pans.

2. Beat butter and sugar in large bowl until fluffy. Add eggs and vanilla; beat well. Stir together flour, baking soda and salt; add alternately with mashed bananas to butter mixture, blending well. Stir in cherries, orange segments, dates and chocolate chips. Divide batter evenly between prepared pans.

3. Bake 40 to 50 minutes or until golden brown. Cool; remove from pans. Drizzle tops of loaves with Chocolate Drizzle. Store tightly wrapped.

Makes 2 loaves

Chocolate Drizzle: Combine ½ cup HERSHEY'S Semi-Sweet Chocolate Chips and 2 tablespoons whipping cream in small microwave-safe bowl. Microwave at HIGH (100%) 30 seconds; stir. If necessary, microwave at HIGH an additional 15 seconds; stir until chips are melted and mixture is smooth. Makes about ½ cup.

Tip

For the best flavor, use very ripe bananas. A yellow peel flecked with tiny brown spots indicates that a banana is ripe, but for baking the peel can be even darker. If your bananas ripen before you're ready to bake, store them in a tightly sealed plastic bag in the refrigerator. The peels will turn dark brown, but the flesh inside will still be perfectly good.

Star-Of-The-East Fruit Bread

Cranberry Streusel Coffee Cake

        1 egg
        ½ cup plus 3 tablespoons sugar, divided
        ½ cup milk
        1 tablespoon vegetable oil
        1 tablespoon orange juice
        1 teaspoon grated orange peel
        ¼ teaspoon almond extract
    1½ cups all-purpose flour, divided
        2 teaspoons baking powder
        ½ teaspoon salt
        8 ounces (2 cups) fresh cranberries
        2 tablespoons butter

1. Preheat oven to 375°F.

2. Beat egg in large bowl. Add ½ cup sugar, milk, oil, orange juice, orange peel and almond extract; mix thoroughly. Combine 1 cup flour, baking powder and salt; add to egg mixture and stir, being careful not to overmix. Pour into 8×8×2-inch pan sprayed with nonstick cooking spray.

3. Chop cranberries in blender or food processor; spoon over batter. Mix remaining ½ cup flour and remaining 3 tablespoons sugar. Cut in butter. Sprinkle mixture over cranberries.

4. Bake 25 to 30 minutes. Serve warm.

Makes 9 servings

Chocolate Chunk Banana Bread

Prep Time: 15 minutes
Bake Time: 55 minutes

        2 eggs, lightly beaten
        1 cup mashed ripe bananas
        ⅓ cup oil
        ¼ cup milk
        2 cups flour
        1 cup sugar
        2 teaspoons CALUMET® Baking Powder
        ¼ teaspoon salt
        1 package (4 ounces) BAKER'S®
            GERMAN'S® Sweet Baking Chocolate,
            coarsely chopped
        ½ cup chopped nuts

HEAT oven to 350°F.

STIR eggs, bananas, oil and milk until well blended. Add flour, sugar, baking powder and salt; stir until just moistened. Stir in chocolate and nuts. Pour into greased 9×5-inch loaf pan.

BAKE for 55 minutes or until toothpick inserted into center comes out clean. Cool in pan 10 minutes. Remove from pan; cool completely on wire rack.

Makes 18 (½-inch) servings

Note: For easier slicing, wrap bread and store overnight.

Sour Cream Coffee Cake

     Streusel Topping (recipe follows)
- ¾ cup sugar
- 6 tablespoons butter
- 2 eggs
- 1 cup sour cream
- 1½ teaspoons vanilla
- 1 tablespoon grated lemon peel
- 1½ cups all-purpose flour
- 1½ teaspoons ground cardamom
- 1 teaspoon baking powder
- 1 teaspoon baking soda
- ⅛ teaspoon salt

1. Prepare Streusel Topping. Set aside. Grease and flour bottom and sides of 8-inch springform pan.

2. Preheat oven to 350°F. Beat sugar and butter in large bowl with electric mixer at medium speed until light and fluffy. Beat in eggs, 1 at a time, until well blended. Beat in sour cream, vanilla and lemon peel. Add flour, cardamom, baking powder, baking soda and salt; beat at low speed just until blended.

3. Spoon half of batter into prepared pan. Sprinkle half of streusel over batter. Repeat layers ending with streusel. Bake 50 to 60 minutes or until wooden pick inserted in center comes out clean. Cool in pan on wire rack 15 minutes.

4. Run long slender knife around edge of pan to loosen cake. Unhinge side; lift off. Cool until cake is just warm to touch. Slide long slender knife under cake; rotate cake to loosen from bottom. Slide off onto serving plate. Wrap in plastic wrap. Store at room temperature up to 1 week.

Makes 10 servings

Streusel Topping

- ¾ cup chopped walnuts or pecans
- ⅓ cup packed light brown sugar
- 2 tablespoons all-purpose flour
- ½ teaspoon ground cardamom
- ½ teaspoon ground nutmeg
- ½ teaspoon ground cinnamon
- 3 tablespoons butter or margarine, melted

Combine walnuts, sugar, flour, cardamom, nutmeg and cinnamon in small bowl. Stir in butter until well blended.

Makes about ¾ cup

Sour Cream Coffee Cake

Oreo® Muffins

1¾ cups all-purpose flour
½ cup sugar
1 tablespoon baking powder
½ teaspoon salt
¾ cup milk
⅓ cup sour cream
1 egg
¼ cup margarine or butter, melted
20 OREO® Chocolate Sandwich Cookies, coarsely chopped

1. Mix flour, sugar, baking powder and salt in medium bowl; set aside.

2. Blend milk, sour cream and egg in small bowl; stir into flour mixture with margarine or butter until just blended. Gently stir in cookie pieces. Spoon batter into 12 greased 2½-inch muffin-pan cups.

3. Bake at 400°F for 20 to 25 minutes or until toothpick inserted in center comes out clean. Remove from pan; cool on wire rack. Serve warm or cold.   *Makes 1 dozen muffins*

Breakfast Cookies

1 Butter Flavor CRISCO® Stick or 1 cup Butter Flavor CRISCO® all-vegetable shortening
1 cup JIF® Crunchy Peanut Butter
¾ cup granulated sugar
¾ cup firmly packed brown sugar
2 eggs, beaten
1½ cups all-purpose flour
1 teaspoon baking powder
1 teaspoon baking soda
1 teaspoon ground cinnamon
1¾ cups quick oats, uncooked
1¼ cups raisins
1 medium Granny Smith apple, finely grated, including juice
⅓ cup finely grated carrot
¼ cup flake coconut (optional)

1. Heat oven to 350°F. Place sheets of foil on countertop for cooling cookies.

2. Combine 1 cup shortening, peanut butter and sugars in large bowl. Beat at medium speed with electric mixer until blended. Beat in eggs.

3. Combine flour, baking powder, baking soda and cinnamon. Add gradually to creamed mixture at low speed. Beat until blended. Stir in oats, raisins, apple, carrot and coconut. Drop by measuring tablespoonfuls onto ungreased baking sheet.

4. Bake for 9 to 11 minutes or until just brown around edges. *Do not overbake.* Cool 2 minutes on baking sheet. Remove cookies to foil to cool completely.   *Makes 5 to 6 dozen cookies*

Hint: Freeze cookies between sheets of waxed paper in sealed container. Use as needed for breakfast on-the-run or as a nutritious snack.

Oreo® Muffins

Pumpkin Apple Streusel Muffins

Muffins
- 2½ cups all-purpose flour
- 2 cups granulated sugar
- 1 tablespoon pumpkin pie spice
- 1 teaspoon baking soda
- ½ teaspoon salt
- 1¼ cups LIBBY'S® 100% Pure Pumpkin
- 2 large eggs
- ¼ cup vegetable oil
- 2 cups (2 small) peeled, cored and finely chopped apples

Streusel Topping
- ¼ cup granulated sugar
- 2 tablespoons all-purpose flour
- ½ teaspoon ground cinnamon
- 2 tablespoons butter or margarine

For Muffins
PREHEAT oven to 350°F. Grease or paper-line 24 muffin cups.

COMBINE flour, sugar, pumpkin pie spice, baking soda and salt in large bowl. Combine pumpkin, eggs and vegetable oil in medium bowl, mix well. Stir into flour mixture just until moistened. Stir in apples. Spoon batter into prepared muffin cups, filling ¾ full.

For Streusel Topping
COMBINE sugar, flour and cinnamon in medium bowl. Cut in butter with pastry blender or two knives until mixture is crumbly. Sprinkle over muffin batter.

BAKE for 30 to 35 minutes or until wooden pick inserted in center comes out clean. Cool pans for 5 minutes; remove to wire racks to cool slightly.

Makes 18 muffins

Tip

For fuss-free filling of muffin cups, use an ice cream scoop with a release mechanism. The scoop uniformly portions the thick batter neatly into the cups with minimal mess. Ice cream scoops are available in various sizes at kitchenware stores.

Lemon Cranberry Loaves

1¼ cups finely chopped fresh cranberries
½ cup finely chopped walnuts
¼ cup granulated sugar
1 package DUNCAN HINES® Moist Deluxe®
    Lemon Supreme Cake Mix
¾ cup milk
1 (3-ounce) package cream cheese, softened
4 eggs
    Confectioners' sugar

1. Preheat oven to 350°F. Grease and flour two 8½×4½-inch loaf pans.

2. Stir together cranberries, walnuts and granulated sugar in large bowl; set aside.

3. Combine cake mix, milk and cream cheese in large bowl. Beat at medium speed with electric mixer for 2 minutes. Add eggs, 1 at a time, beating for 2 minutes. Fold in cranberry mixture. Pour into prepared pans. Bake 45 to 50 minutes or until toothpick inserted in centers comes out clean. Cool in pans 15 minutes. Loosen loaves from pans. Invert onto cooling rack. Turn right side up. Cool completely. Dust with confectioners' sugar.

Makes 24 slices

Tip: To quickly chop cranberries or walnuts, use food processor fitted with steel blade and pulse until evenly chopped.

Yellow's Sticky Cinnamon Buns

½ cup (1 stick) butter, softened
⅔ cup firmly packed light brown sugar
2½ teaspoons ground cinnamon
1 package (1 pound) frozen white bread
    dough, thawed
½ cup chopped pecans
    White Icing (recipe follows)
½ cup "M&M's"® Semi-Sweet Chocolate
    Mini Baking Bits

Lightly grease 9-inch round cake pan; set aside. In large bowl cream butter and brown sugar until light and fluffy; add cinnamon. On lightly floured surface, roll dough to 18×8-inch rectangle. Spread with butter mixture; sprinkle with pecans. Roll dough up from long side; slice into 12 (1½-inch-wide) pieces. Arrange rolls in prepared pan; cover with damp towel. Let rolls rise at room temperature until doubled in size, about 30 minutes. Preheat oven to 350°F. Bake 30 to 35 minutes. Cool slightly on wire rack. Prepare White Icing and spread over warm rolls. Sprinkle with "M&M's"® Semi-Sweet Chocolate Mini Baking Bits. Store in tightly covered container.

Makes 12 servings

White Icing: In small bowl combine 1 cup powdered sugar and 2 tablespoons milk until smooth

Walnut-Chocolate Quick Bread

1½ cups milk
1 cup sugar
⅓ cup vegetable oil
1 egg, beaten
1 tablespoon molasses
1 teaspoon vanilla
3 cups all-purpose flour
3 tablespoons unsweetened cocoa powder
2 teaspoons baking soda
2 teaspoons baking powder
1 teaspoon salt
1 cup chocolate chips
½ cup walnuts, coarsely chopped

1. Preheat oven to 350°F. Grease four 5×3-inch loaf pans; set aside.

2. Combine milk, sugar, oil, egg, molasses and vanilla in medium bowl. Stir until sugar is dissolved.

3. Whisk flour, cocoa, baking soda, baking powder and salt in large bowl. Add chocolate chips, nuts and sugar mixture; stir just until combined. Pour into prepared pans.

4. Bake 30 minutes or until toothpick inserted near center of loaf comes out clean. Cool in pan 15 minutes. Remove from pan and cool on wire rack.

Makes 4 loaves

Muffin Variation: Preheat oven to 375°F. Spoon batter into 12 greased muffin cups. Bake 20 minutes or until toothpick inserted near center of muffin comes out clean. Makes 12 muffins.

Peanut Butter Coffeecake

1⅔ cups (10-ounce package) REESE'S® Peanut Butter Chips
2 tablespoons shortening (do *not* use butter, margarine, spread or oil)
2¼ cups all-purpose flour
1½ cups packed light brown sugar
½ cup (1 stick) butter or margarine, softened
1 teaspoon baking powder
½ teaspoon baking soda
1 cup milk
3 eggs
1 teaspoon vanilla extract
1 cup REESE'S® Peanut Butter Chips or HERSHEY'S MINI CHIPS Semi-Sweet Chocolate Chips

1. Heat oven to 350°F. Grease bottom of 13×9×2-inch baking pan. Place 1⅔ cups peanut butter chips and shortening in microwave-safe bowl. Microwave at HIGH (100%) 1 minute; stir. If necessary, microwave at HIGH an additional 15 seconds at a time, stirring after each heating, just until chips are melted when stirred.

2. Combine flour, brown sugar, butter and peanut butter chip mixture in large bowl. Beat on low speed of mixer until mixture resembles small crumbs; reserve 1 cup crumbs. To remaining crumb mixture, add baking powder, baking soda, milk, eggs and vanilla; beat until well combined. Pour batter into prepared pan; sprinkle with reserved crumbs.

3. Bake 35 to 40 minutes or until wooden pick inserted in center comes out clean. Remove from oven to wire rack; immediately sprinkle 1 cup peanut butter or small chocolate chips over top. Cool completely.

Makes 12 to 15 servings

Walnut-Chocolate Quick Bread

Cranberry Oat Bread

¾ cup honey
⅓ cup vegetable oil
2 eggs
½ cup milk
2½ cups all-purpose flour
1 cup quick-cooking rolled oats
1 teaspoon baking soda
1 teaspoon baking powder
½ teaspoon salt
½ teaspoon ground cinnamon
2 cups fresh or frozen cranberries
1 cup chopped nuts

Combine honey, oil, eggs and milk in large bowl; mix well. Combine flour, oats, baking soda, baking powder, salt and cinnamon in medium bowl; mix well. Stir into honey mixture. Fold in cranberries and nuts. Spoon into two 8½×4½×2½-inch greased and floured loaf pans.

Bake in preheated 350°F oven 40 to 45 minutes or until wooden toothpick inserted near center comes out clean. Cool in pans on wire racks 15 minutes. Remove from pans; cool completely on wire racks.

Makes 2 loaves

Favorite recipe from **National Honey Board**

Chocolate Fleck Coffee Cake

1 package (4 ounces) BAKER'S®
    GERMAN'S® Sweet Baking Chocolate,
    chopped
½ cup chopped nuts
1¼ cups sugar, divided
1 teaspoon ground cinnamon
1¾ cups flour
½ teaspoon CALUMET® Baking Powder
¼ teaspoon salt
1 container (8 ounces) BREAKSTONE'S®
    or KNUDSEN® Sour Cream
1 teaspoon baking soda
½ cup (1 stick) butter or margarine
2 eggs
½ teaspoon vanilla

HEAT oven to 350°F.

MIX chocolate, nuts, ¼ cup of the sugar and cinnamon; set aside. Stir together flour, baking powder and salt; set aside. Mix sour cream and baking soda; set aside.

BEAT butter and remaining 1 cup sugar until light and fluffy. Add eggs, 1 at a time, beating well after each addition. Add vanilla. Add flour mixture alternately with sour cream mixture, beginning and ending with flour mixture. Spoon ½ the batter into greased 9-inch square baking pan. Top with ½ the chocolate-nut mixture, spreading carefully with spatula. Repeat layers.

BAKE 30 to 35 minutes or until cake just begins to pull away from sides of pan. Cool in pan on wire rack. Cut into squares. *Makes 9 servings*

Note: For 12 servings, cake may be baked in 13×9-inch pan.

Cranberry Oat Bread

Gingerbread Streusel Raisin Muffins

1 cup raisins
½ cup boiling water
⅓ cup margarine or butter, softened
¾ cup GRANDMA'S® Molasses
    (Unsulphured)
1 egg
2 cups all-purpose flour
1½ teaspoons baking soda
½ teaspoon salt
1 teaspoon cinnamon
1 teaspoon ginger

Topping
⅓ cup all-purpose flour
¼ cup firmly packed brown sugar
¼ cup chopped nuts
3 tablespoons margarine or butter
1 teaspoon cinnamon

Preheat oven to 375°F. Grease bottoms only of 12 muffin cups or line with paper baking cups. In small bowl, cover raisins with boiling water; let stand 5 minutes. In large bowl, beat ⅓ cup margarine and molasses until fluffy. Add egg; beat well. Stir in 2 cups flour, baking soda, salt, 1 teaspoon cinnamon and ginger. Blend just until dry ingredients are moistened. Gently stir in raisins and water. Fill prepared muffin cups ¾ full. For topping, combine all ingredients in small bowl. Sprinkle over muffins.

Bake 20 to 25 minutes or until toothpick inserted in centers comes out clean. Cool 5 minutes; remove from pan. Serve warm.   *Makes 12 muffins*

Chippy Banana Bread

⅓ cup butter or margarine, softened
⅔ cup sugar
2 eggs
2 tablespoons milk
1¾ cups all-purpose flour
1¼ teaspoons baking powder
¾ teaspoon salt
½ teaspoon baking soda
1 cup mashed ripe bananas
1 cup HERSHEY'S Semi-Sweet Chocolate
    Chips

1. Heat oven to 350°F. Lightly grease 8×4×2-inch loaf pan.

2. Beat butter and sugar in large bowl on medium speed of mixer until creamy. Add eggs, one at a time, beating well after each addition. Add milk; beat until blended.

3. Stir together flour, baking powder, salt and baking soda; add alternately with bananas to butter mixture, beating until smooth after each addition. Gently fold in chocolate chips. Pour batter into prepared pan.

4. Bake 60 to 65 minutes or until wooden pick inserted near center come sout clean. Cool 10 minutes. Remove from pan to wire rack; cool completely. For easier slicing, wrap in foil and store overnight.   *Makes 12 servings*

Gingerbread Streusel Raisin Muffins

Cherry and Almond Coffeecake

1 sheet (½ of 17¼-ounce package) frozen
    puff pastry
1 package (3 ounces) cream cheese,
    softened
⅓ cup plus 2 tablespoons powdered sugar,
    divided
1 egg, separated
¼ teaspoon almond extract
1 tablespoon water
½ cup dried cherries or cranberries,
    coarsely chopped
½ cup sliced almonds

1. Thaw pastry sheet according to package directions.

2. Preheat oven to 375°F. Spray baking sheet with nonstick cooking spray.

3. Combine cream cheese, ⅓ cup powdered sugar, egg yolk and almond extract in large bowl. Beat with electric mixer at medium speed until smooth; set aside. In separate small bowl, mix egg white and water; set aside.

4. On lightly floured board, roll out pastry into 14×10-inch rectangle. Spread cream cheese mixture over dough leaving 1-inch border. Sprinkle evenly with cherries. Reserve 2 tablespoons almonds; sprinkle remaining almonds over cherries.

5. Starting with long side, loosely roll up dough jelly-roll style. Place roll on baking sheet, seam side down. Form into circle, pinching ends together. Using scissors, cut at 1-inch intervals from outside of ring toward (but not through) center. Twist each section half a turn, allowing filling to show.

6. Brush top of ring with egg white mixture. Sprinkle with reserved almonds. Bake 25 to 30 minutes or until light brown. Using large spatula, carefully remove ring to wire rack. Cool 15 minutes; sprinkle with remaining 2 tablespoons powdered sugar. *Makes 1 (12-inch) coffeecake*

Tip

Baking often requires dough to be rolled out or shaped into specific sizes, such as rolling pastry into a 10-inch square or shaping cookie dough into 1-inch balls. For easy, accurate measuring, keep a washable plastic ruler in the kitchen that is used just for baking.

Cherry Oatmeal Muffins

1 cup old-fashioned or quick-cooking oats
1 cup all-purpose flour
½ cup firmly packed brown sugar
1½ teaspoons baking powder
¼ teaspoon ground nutmeg
¾ cup buttermilk
1 egg, slightly beaten
¼ cup vegetable oil
1 teaspoon almond extract
1 cup frozen tart cherries, coarsely chopped
Granulated sugar

Combine oats, flour, brown sugar, baking powder and nutmeg in large mixing bowl; mix well. Combine buttermilk, egg, oil and almond extract in small bowl. Pour buttermilk mixture into oats mixture; stir just to moisten ingredients. Quickly stir in cherries. (It is not necessary to thaw cherries before chopping and adding to batter.)

Spray muffin pan with nonstick cooking spray. Fill muffin cups two-thirds full. Sprinkle with granulated sugar.

Bake in preheated 400°F oven 15 to 20 minutes or until golden brown. *Makes 12 muffins*

Note: 1 cup canned tart cherries, drained and coarsely chopped, may be substituted for 1 cup frozen tart cherries.

Favorite recipe from **Cherry Marketing Institute**

Cocoa Orange Muffins

2 cups all-purpose flour
¾ cup sugar
¼ cup HERSHEY'S Cocoa
1 tablespoon baking powder
⅔ cup milk
¼ cup orange juice
¼ cup vegetable oil
1 egg
1 tablespoon freshly grated orange peel
Orange Sugar Topping (recipe follows)

1. Heat oven to 400°F. Grease or line twelve muffin cups (2½ inches in diameter) with paper bake cups.

2. Stir together flour, sugar, cocoa and baking powder in large bowl. In small bowl, stir together milk, orange juice, oil, egg and orange peel; add to dry ingredients, stirring just until moistened. Fill muffin cups ¾ full with batter. Sprinkle Orange Sugar Topping over muffins.

3. Bake 20 minutes or until wooden pick inserted in center comes out clean. Serve warm.
Makes 1 dozen muffins

Orange Sugar Topping: Mix together 2 tablespoons sugar and 1½ teaspoons finely grated orange peel.

Apple Streusel Coffeecake

1½ cups all-purpose flour
2 teaspoons baking powder
½ cup EGG BEATERS® Healthy Real
 Egg Product
⅓ cup skim milk
1 teaspoon vanilla extract
½ cup granulated sugar
¼ cup FLEISCHMANN'S® Original
 Margarine, softened
1½ cups chopped apples
 Streusel Topping (recipe follows)
 Powdered Sugar Glaze, optional
 (recipe follows)

In small bowl, combine flour and baking powder; set aside. In another small bowl, combine Egg Beaters®, milk and vanilla; set aside.

In medium bowl, with electric mixer at medium speed, beat granulated sugar and margarine until creamy. Alternately add flour mixture and egg mixture, blending well after each addition. Spread batter into greased 9-inch round cake pan. Arrange apple pieces over top, gently pressing into batter.

Bake at 350°F for 20 minutes. Sprinkle top with Streusel Topping. Bake for 10 to 15 minutes more or until toothpick inserted in center comes out clean. Cool in pan on wire rack. Drizzle with Powdered Sugar Glaze, if desired. *Makes 12 servings*

Streusel Topping: In small bowl, combine 3 tablespoons flour, 3 tablespoons powdered sugar and ¾ teaspoon ground cinnamon. Cut in 2 tablespoons Fleischmann's Spread until crumbly.

Powdered Sugar Glaze: In small bowl, combine 1 cup powdered sugar and 5 to 6 teaspoons water until smooth.

Banana Chocolate Chip Muffins

Prep Time: 20 minutes
Bake Time: 30 minutes

2 ripe, medium DOLE® Bananas
2 eggs
1 cup packed brown sugar
½ cup margarine, melted
1 teaspoon vanilla extract
2¼ cups all-purpose flour
2 teaspoons baking powder
½ teaspoon ground cinnamon
½ teaspoon salt
1 cup chocolate chips
½ cup chopped walnuts

• Purée bananas in blender (1 cup). Beat bananas, eggs, sugar, margarine and vanilla in medium bowl until well blended.

• Combine flour, baking powder, cinnamon and salt in large bowl. Stir in chocolate chips and nuts. Make well in center of dry ingredients. Add banana mixture. Stir just until blended. Spoon into well greased 2½-inch muffin pan cups.

• Bake at 350°F 25 to 30 minutes or until toothpick inserted in center comes out clean. Cool slightly; remove from pan and place on wire rack.
Makes 12 muffins

Sun Dried Cherry-Orange Coffee Cake

2 cups all-purpose flour
½ cup granulated sugar
3 teaspoons baking powder
½ teaspoon salt
½ cup CRISCO® Canola Oil
½ cup milk
1 egg, beaten
½ cup chopped sun dried cherries
2 teaspoons grated fresh orange peel
½ cup fresh orange juice
½ cup packed light brown sugar
2 tablespoons butter, softened
1 teaspoon ground cinnamon
½ teaspoon ground nutmeg
½ cup chopped pecans

1. Heat oven to 375°F. Sift together flour, sugar, baking powder and salt in large bowl. Combine oil, milk and egg in small bowl; mix well. Add to flour mixture; stir until blended. Combine cherries, orange peel and orange juice in large bowl; mix well. Add to batter until just well blended.

2. Spray 9-inch square baking pan with CRISCO® No-Stick Cooking Spray. Dust pan with flour. Pour batter into pan; spread evenly. Combine brown sugar, butter, cinnamon, nutmeg and chopped pecans in large bowl; mix well. Sprinkle over batter.

3. Bake at 375°F for 25 to 30 minutes or until wooden pick inserted in center comes out clean. Remove from oven and let rest 5 minutes before serving.   *Makes 6 to 8 servings*

Oatmeal-Almond Bread

½ cup BLUE DIAMOND® sliced natural almonds
1½ cups sifted flour
2 teaspoons baking powder
1 teaspoon salt
1 cup oats, uncooked
¾ cup sugar
½ cup dark seedless raisins
1 tablespoon grated orange peel
½ cup milk
½ cup orange juice
⅓ cup salad oil
1 egg

Spread almonds in shallow pan and toast at 350°F for 5 minutes. Sift flour with baking powder and salt into large mixing bowl. Stir in oats, sugar, toasted almonds, raisins and orange peel. All at once add milk, orange juice, oil and egg; mix just until dry ingredients are moistened. Pour batter into greased and floured 8½×4½- or 9×5-inch loaf pan; bake at 350°F for 50 to 60 minutes or until wooden toothpick inserted in center of loaf comes out clean. Cool 10 minutes in pan; remove from pan and cool completely.
Makes 1 loaf

Sun Dried Cherry-Orange Coffee Cake

Tex-Mex Quick Bread

1½ cups all-purpose flour
1 cup shredded Monterey Jack cheese
½ cup cornmeal
½ cup sun-dried tomatoes, coarsely chopped
1 can (4¼ ounces) black olives, drained and chopped
¼ cup sugar
1½ teaspoons baking powder
1 teaspoon baking soda
1 cup milk
1 can (4½ ounces) green chilies, drained and chopped
¼ cup olive oil
1 large egg, beaten

1. Preheat oven to 325°F. Grease 9×5-inch loaf pan or four 5×3-inch loaf pans; set aside.

2. Combine flour, cheese, cornmeal, tomatoes, olives, sugar, baking powder and baking soda in large bowl.

3. Combine remaining ingredients in small bowl. Add to flour mixture; stir just until combined. Pour into prepared pan. Bake 9×5-inch loaf 45 minutes and 5×3-inch loaves 30 minutes or until toothpick inserted near center of loaf comes out clean. Cool in pan 15 minutes. Remove from pan and cool on wire rack.   *Makes 1 large loaf or 4 small loaves*

Muffin Variation: Preheat oven to 375°F. Spoon batter into 12 well-greased muffin cups. Bake 20 minutes or until toothpick inserted near center of muffin comes out clean. Makes 12 muffins.

Orange Brunch Muffins

3 cups all-purpose baking mix
¾ cup all-purpose flour
⅔ cup granulated sugar
2 large eggs, lightly beaten
½ cup plain yogurt
½ cup orange juice
1 tablespoon grated orange peel
2 cups (12-ounce package) NESTLÉ® TOLL HOUSE® Premier White Morsels, *divided*
½ cup chopped macadamia nuts or walnuts

PREHEAT oven to 375°F. Grease or paper-line 18 muffin cups.

COMBINE baking mix, flour and sugar in large bowl. Add eggs, yogurt, juice and orange peel; stir just until blended. Stir in *1⅓ cups* morsels. Spoon into prepared muffin cups, filling ¾ full. Sprinkle with nuts.

BAKE for 18 to 22 minutes or until wooden pick inserted into centers comes out clean. Cool in pans for 10 minutes; remove to wire racks to cool slightly.

MICROWAVE *remaining* morsels in small, *heavy-duty* plastic bag on MEDIUM-HIGH (70%) power for 1 minute; knead. Microwave at additional 10- to 20-second intervals, kneading until smooth. Cut tiny corner from bag; squeeze to drizzle over muffins. Serve warm.   *Makes 18 muffins*

Tex-Mex Quick Bread

Streusel Coffeecake

Prep Time: 25 minutes
Cook Time: 40 minutes
Cooling Time: 2 hours
Total Time: 3 hours and 5 minutes

  **32 CHIPS AHOY!® Chocolate Chip Cookies,
     divided**
  **1 (18- to 18.5-ounce) package yellow or
     white cake mix**
  **½ cup BREAKSTONE'S® or KNUDSEN®
     Sour Cream**
  ½ cup PLANTERS® Pecans, chopped
  ½ cup BAKER'S® ANGEL FLAKE® Coconut
  ¼ cup packed brown sugar
  1 teaspoon ground cinnamon
  ⅓ cup margarine or butter, melted
     Powdered sugar glaze (optional)

1. Coarsely chop 20 cookies; finely crush remaining 12 cookies. Set aside.

2. Prepare cake mix batter according to package directions; blend in sour cream. Stir in chopped cookies. Pour batter into greased and floured 13×9×2-inch baking pan.

3. Mix cookie crumbs, pecans, coconut, brown sugar and cinnamon; stir in margarine or butter. Sprinkle over cake batter.

4. Bake at 350°F for 40 minutes or until toothpick inserted in center of cake comes out clean. Cool completely. Drizzle with powdered sugar glaze if desired. Cut into squares to serve.

Makes 24 servings

Lemon Raisin Quick Bread

  1¼ cups all-purpose flour
  ¾ cup whole wheat flour
  4 tablespoons sugar, divided
  2 teaspoons baking powder
  ½ teaspoon baking soda
  ¼ teaspoon salt
  1½ cups lemon-flavored low-fat yogurt
  **¼ cup unsalted butter, melted and cooled
     slightly**
  1 egg
  ½ teaspoon lemon peel
  1 cup raisins
  ¾ cup chopped walnuts (optional)

Preheat oven to 350°F. Grease 8½×4½-inch loaf pan. Combine flours, 3 tablespoons sugar, baking powder, baking soda and salt in large bowl. Combine yogurt, butter, egg and lemon peel in medium bowl; stir until well blended. Pour yogurt mixture into flour mixture. Add raisins and walnuts; stir just until dry ingredients are moistened. Pour into prepared pan and smooth top. Sprinkle top with remaining 1 tablespoon sugar.

Bake 40 to 45 minutes or until lightly brown and toothpick inserted in center comes out clean. Cool in pan on wire rack 30 minutes. Remove from pan; cool completely.

Makes 1 loaf

Chocolate Quickie Stickies

8 tablespoons (1 stick) butter or margarine, divided
¾ cup packed light brown sugar
4 tablespoons HERSHEY'S Cocoa, divided
5 teaspoons water
1 teaspoon vanilla extract
½ cup coarsely chopped nuts (optional)
2 cans (8 ounces each) refrigerated quick crescent dinner rolls
2 tablespoons granulated sugar

1. Heat oven to 350°F.

2. Melt 6 tablespoons butter in small saucepan over low heat; add brown sugar, 3 tablespoons cocoa and water. Cook over medium heat, stirring constantly, just until mixture comes to boil. Remove from heat; stir in vanilla. Spoon about 1 teaspoon chocolate mixture into each of 48 small muffin cups (1¾ inches in diameter). Sprinkle ½ teaspoon nuts, if desired, into each cup; set aside.

3. Unroll dough; separate into 8 rectangles; firmly press perforations to seal. Melt remaining 2 tablespoons butter; brush over rectangles. Stir together granulated sugar and remaining 1 tablespoon cocoa; sprinkle over rectangles. Starting at longer side, roll up each rectangle; pinch seams to seal. Cut each roll into 6 equal pieces. Press gently into prepared pans, cut-side down.

4. Bake 11 to 13 minutes or until light brown. Remove from oven; let cool 30 seconds. Invert onto cookie sheet. Let stand 1 minute; remove pans. Serve warm or cool completely.

Makes 4 dozen small rolls

Note: Rolls can be baked in two 8-inch round baking pans. Heat oven to 350°F. Cook chocolate mixture as directed; spread half of mixture in each pan. Prepare rolls as directed; place 24 pieces, cut-side down, in each pan. Bake 20 to 22 minutes. Cool and remove pans as directed above

The flavor of vanilla extract is greatly reduced by heat, which is why it should be added to hot mixtures after—not during—cooking.

Peach Streusel Coffee Cake

Streusel
- ½ cup QUAKER® Oats (quick or old fashioned, uncooked)
- ⅓ cup sugar
- 3 tablespoons margarine, melted
- ½ teaspoon ground cinnamon
- ⅛ teaspoon ground nutmeg (optional)

Coffee Cake
- 1 cup sugar
- ½ cup (1 stick) margarine, softened
- 1½ teaspoons vanilla
- 4 egg whites
- 1½ cups all-purpose flour
- ¾ cup QUAKER® Oats (quick or old fashioned, uncooked)
- 1 tablespoon baking powder
- ½ teaspoon baking soda
- ¾ cup light sour cream
- 1 (16-ounce) can sliced peaches, drained, or 1 cup sliced fresh peaches

Heat oven to 350°F. Spray 9-inch square baking pan with no-stick cooking spray or grease lightly. For streusel, combine all ingredients; mix well. Set aside. For coffee cake, beat sugar, margarine and vanilla until fluffy. Add egg whites; mix until smooth. Combine flour, oats, baking powder and baking soda; mix well. Add to sugar mixture alternately with sour cream, beginning and ending with dry ingredients; mix well after each addition. Spread into prepared pan. Pat canned peach slices dry with paper towels; arrange over batter. Sprinkle with streusel. Bake 50 to 55 minutes or until wooden pick inserted in center comes out clean. Serve warm.

Makes 16 servings

Oatmeal Pumpkin Bread

- 1 cup quick-cooking oats
- 1 cup hot low-fat milk
- ¾ cup cooked or canned pumpkin
- 2 eggs, beaten
- ¼ cup margarine, melted
- 2 cups all-purpose flour
- 1 cup sugar
- 1 tablespoon baking powder
- 1 teaspoon ground cinnamon
- ¼ teaspoon ground nutmeg
- ¼ teaspoon salt
- 1 cup raisins
- ½ cup chopped pecans

Preheat oven to 350°F. In large bowl, combine oats and milk; allow to stand about 5 minutes. Stir in pumpkin, eggs and margarine. In separate bowl, mix together flour, sugar, baking powder, cinnamon, nutmeg and salt. Gradually add dry ingredients to oatmeal mixture; stir in raisins and nuts and mix well. Place in greased 9×5-inch loaf pan. Bake 55 to 60 minutes or until done. Cool on wire rack.

Makes one loaf (16 slices)

Favorite recipe from **The Sugar Association, Inc.**

Nutty Cinnamon Sticky Buns

Prep Time: 10 minutes
Cook Time: 25 minutes
Total Time: 35 minutes

⅓ cup margarine or butter
½ cup packed brown sugar
½ cup PLANTERS® Pecans, chopped
1 teaspoon ground cinnamon
1 (17.3-ounce) package refrigerated
   biscuits (8 large biscuits)

1. Melt margarine or butter in 9-inch round baking pan in 350°F oven.

2. Mix brown sugar, pecans and cinnamon in small bowl; sprinkle over melted margarine or butter in pan. Arrange biscuits in pan with sides touching (biscuits will fit tightly in pan).

3. Bake at 350°F for 25 to 30 minutes or until biscuits are golden brown and center biscuit is fully cooked. Invert pan immediately onto serving plate. Spread any remaining topping from pan on buns. Serve warm.

Makes 8 buns

Cran-Lemon Coffee Cake

1 package (about 18 ounces) yellow cake
   mix with pudding in the mix
1 cup water
3 eggs
⅓ cup butter, melted and cooled
¼ cup fresh lemon juice
1 tablespoon grated lemon peel
1½ cups coarsely chopped cranberries

Preheat oven to 350°F. Grease and flour 12-inch tube pan. Beat cake mix, water, eggs, butter, lemon juice and lemon peel in large bowl with electric mixer on low speed 2 minutes. Fold in cranberries. Spread batter evenly in prepared pan.

Bake about 55 minutes or until wooden pick inserted 1 inch from edge comes out clean. Cool on wire rack 10 minutes. Remove from pan; cool on wire rack. Coffee cake may be served warm or at room temperature.

Makes 12 servings

Nutty Cinnamon Sticky Buns

Blueberry Orange Muffins

1¾ cups all-purpose flour
⅓ cup sugar
2½ teaspoons baking powder
½ teaspoon baking soda
½ teaspoon salt
½ teaspoon ground cinnamon
¾ cup fat-free (skim) milk
1 egg, slightly beaten
¼ cup butter, melted and slightly cooled
3 tablespoons orange juice concentrate, thawed
1 teaspoon vanilla
¾ cup fresh or frozen blueberries, thawed

Preheat oven to 400°F. Grease muffin pan or line with paper baking cups.

Combine flour, sugar, baking powder, baking soda, salt and cinnamon in large bowl. Set aside. Beat milk, egg, butter, orange juice concentrate and vanilla in medium bowl on medium speed of electric mixer until well combined. Add milk mixture to dry ingredients. Mix lightly until dry ingredients are barely moistened (mixture will be lumpy). Add blueberries. Stir gently just until berries are evenly distributed.

Fill muffin cups ¾ full. Bake 20 to 25 minutes (25 to 30 minutes if using frozen berries) or until toothpick inserted in center comes out clean. Remove pan and allow to cool 5 minutes. Remove to wire rack. Serve warm.

Makes 12 muffins

Banana Nut Bread

2 ripe, large DOLE® Bananas
⅔ cup sugar
⅓ cup butter
2 eggs
2 cups all-purpose flour
2 teaspoons baking powder
½ teaspoon baking soda
½ cup buttermilk
¾ cup chopped nuts

• Purée bananas in blender (1¼ cups). Cream sugar and butter until light and fluffy. Beat in bananas and eggs. Combine flour, baking powder and baking soda. Add dry ingredients to banana mixture alternately in thirds with buttermilk, blending well after each addition. Stir in nuts.

• Pour into greased 9×5-inch loaf pan. Bake at 350°F 50 to 60 minutes or until wooden toothpick inserted in center comes out clean. Cool in pan on wire rack 10 minutes. Remove from pan and cool completely.

Makes 1 loaf

Blueberry Orange Muffins

Cranberry Orange Coffee Cake

1½ cups biscuit baking mix
⅓ cup granulated sugar
⅓ cup sour cream
1 teaspoon vanilla
1 egg
2 tablespoons orange juice
1 tablespoon plus 1 teaspoon grated orange peel, divided
1 cup fresh or frozen whole cranberries
⅓ cup coarsely chopped walnuts
½ cup chopped dried fruit (such as apricots, golden raisins and figs)
½ cup brown sugar
2 tablespoons butter, softened
Whipped cream

Preheat oven to 350°F. Grease 12½-inch removable-bottom tart pan.

Stir together baking mix and granulated sugar in large bowl. Beat together sour cream, vanilla, egg, orange juice and 1 tablespoon orange peel in medium bowl. Add sour cream mixture to baking mix and sugar; stir just until moistened. Spread into tart pan.

Sprinkle cranberries, walnuts and dried fruit over top of coffee cake. Stir together brown sugar, butter and remaining 1 teaspoon orange peel in small bowl; sprinkle over fruit.

Bake 25 to 30 minutes or until lightly browned. Serve warm with whipped cream.

Makes 12 servings

Fruit Muffins

Muffins
⅔ cup milk
1 tablespoon oil
1 egg
2 cups packaged baking mix
2 tablespoons sugar
¼ cup SMUCKER'S® Preserves (any flavor)

Glaze
⅔ cup powdered sugar
3 to 4 teaspoons milk

Grease bottom only of 12 medium muffin cups or line with paper baking cups. Combine milk, oil and egg; blend until well mixed. Add baking mix and sugar; stir just until moistened. Fill greased muffin cups ⅔ full. Drop 1 level teaspoon of preserves onto center of batter in each cup.

Bake at 400°F for 13 to 18 minutes or until golden brown. Cool slightly and remove from pan.

Stir together glaze ingredients until smooth, adding enough milk for desired glaze consistency. Drizzle over cooled muffins.

Makes 12 muffins

Cranberry Orange Coffee Cake

Streusel-Topped Blueberry Muffins

1½ cups plus ⅓ cup all-purpose flour, divided
½ cup plus ⅓ cup sugar, divided
1 teaspoon ground cinnamon
3 tablespoons butter, cut into small pieces
2 teaspoons baking powder
½ teaspoon salt
1 cup milk
¼ cup butter, melted and slightly cooled
1 egg, beaten
1 teaspoon vanilla
1 cup fresh blueberries

Preheat oven to 375°F. Grease or paper-line 12 (2½-inch) muffin cups; set aside.

Combine ⅓ cup flour, ⅓ cup sugar and cinnamon in small bowl. Cut in 3 tablespoons butter with pastry blender until mixture resembles coarse crumbs; set aside. Combine remaining 1½ cups flour, ½ cup sugar, baking powder and salt in large bowl. Combine milk, ¼ cup melted butter, egg and vanilla in small bowl. Stir into flour mixture just until moistened. Fold in blueberries. Spoon evenly into prepared muffin cups. Sprinkle reserved topping over top of each muffin.

Bake 20 to 25 minutes or until toothpick inserted in center comes out clean. Remove from pan; cool completely. *Makes 12 muffins*

Pumpkin Corn Muffins

1¼ cups all-purpose flour
1 cup ALBERS® Yellow Corn Meal
⅓ cup granulated sugar
4 teaspoons baking powder
½ teaspoon salt
2 large eggs
1¼ cups LIBBY'S® 100% Pure Pumpkin
⅓ cup milk
¼ cup vegetable oil

PREHEAT oven to 375°F. Grease or paper-line 12 muffin cups.

COMBINE flour, cornmeal, sugar, baking powder and salt in large bowl. Beat eggs, pumpkin, milk and oil in medium bowl until combined. Add to flour mixture; mix thoroughly. Spoon batter into prepared muffin cups.

BAKE for 25 to 30 minutes or until wooden pick inserted in center comes out clean. Serve warm.

Makes 12 muffins

Peach Orchard Muffins

PAM® No-Stick Cooking Spray
1 (16-ounce) can sliced peaches in heavy
    syrup, diced, syrup reserved
⅓ cup WESSON® Vegetable Oil
2 eggs, slightly beaten
1 teaspoon vanilla
2 cups all-purpose flour
⅓ cup sugar
3 teaspoons baking powder
½ teaspoon salt
½ cup KNOTT'S BERRY FARM® Peach
    Preserves
Sugar for topping

Preheat oven to 400°F. Spray 12 muffin cups with PAM® Cooking Spray. In a small bowl, combine syrup, Wesson® Oil, eggs and vanilla; mix well. In a large bowl, mix together flour, sugar, baking powder and salt. Pour egg mixture into flour mixture; stir just until dry ingredients are moistened. Fold in diced peaches. Fill muffin cups to rim. Bake for 15 to 22 minutes or until wooden pick inserted into center comes out clean. Cool 5 minutes. Remove muffins to wire racks. Brush with Knott's® preserves and sprinkle with desired amount of sugar.

Makes 1 dozen muffins

Lemon Bread

1¼ cup sugar, divided
⅓ cup margarine
2 teaspoons grated lemon peel
2 eggs
1½ cups all-purpose flour
1 teaspoon baking powder
¼ teaspoon salt
½ cup milk
2 to 3 tablespoons lemon juice

Cream together ¾ cup sugar, margarine and lemon peel. Add eggs; beat together. Sift together flour, baking powder and salt. Mix flour mixture into batter alternately with milk, beginning and ending with flour mixture.

Pour into 8×4-inch loaf pan coated with nonstick cooking spray. Bake at 325°F for 50 to 60 minutes. Mix lemon juice and remaining ½ cup sugar thoroughly. Pour over bread while still hot. Let set in pan 5 to 10 minutes. Remove from pan and cool on cooling rack. *Makes 1 loaf (18 slices)*

Favorite recipe from **North Dakota Wheat Commission**

Date Nut Bread

2 cups all-purpose flour
½ cup packed light brown sugar
1 tablespoon baking powder
½ teaspoon salt
¼ cup butter
1 cup toasted chopped walnuts
1 cup chopped dates
1¼ cups milk
1 egg
½ teaspoon grated lemon peel

Preheat oven to 375°F. Spray 9×5-inch loaf pan with nonstick cooking spray; set aside.

Combine flour, sugar, baking powder and salt in large bowl. Cut in butter with pastry blender or 2 knives until mixture resembles fine crumbs. Add walnuts and dates; stir until coated. Beat milk, egg and lemon peel in small bowl with fork. Add to flour mixture; stir just until moistened. Pour into prepared pan.

Bake 45 to 50 minutes or until toothpick inserted into center comes out clean. Cool in pan on wire rack 10 minutes. Remove from pan and cool completely on wire rack.   *Makes 12 servings*

Chocolate Quicky Sticky Bread

2 loaves (16 ounces each) frozen bread
    dough
¾ cup granulated sugar
1 tablespoon HERSHEY'S Cocoa
1 teaspoon ground cinnamon
½ cup (1 stick) butter or margarine,
    melted and divided
½ cup packed light brown sugar
¼ cup water
    HERSHEY'S MINI KISSES™
    Semi-Sweet or Milk Chocolates

1. Thaw loaves as directed on package; let rise until doubled.

2. Stir together granulated sugar, cocoa and cinnamon. In small microwave-safe bowl, stir together ¼ cup butter, brown sugar and water. Microwave at HIGH (100%) 30 to 60 seconds or until smooth when stirred. Pour mixture into 12-cup fluted tube pan.

3. Heat oven to 350°F. Pinch off pieces of bread dough; form into balls, 1½ inches in diameter, placing 3 Mini Kisses™ inside each ball. Dip each ball in remaining ¼ cup butter; roll in cocoa-sugar mixture. Place balls in prepared pan.

4. Bake 45 to 50 minutes or until golden brown. Cool 20 minutes in pan; invert onto serving plate. Cool until lukewarm.   *Makes 12 servings*

Date Nut Bread

Cranberry Orange Ring

2 cups all-purpose flour
1 cup sugar
1½ teaspoons baking powder
1 teaspoon salt
½ teaspoon baking soda
¼ teaspoon ground cloves
1 tablespoon minced orange peel
¾ cup orange juice
1 egg, slightly beaten
2 tablespoons vegetable oil
1 teaspoon vanilla
¼ teaspoon orange extract
1 cup whole cranberries

Preheat oven to 350°F. Grease 12-cup tube pan and set aside.

Combine flour, sugar, baking powder, salt, baking soda and cloves in large bowl. Add orange peel; mix well. Set aside. Combine orange juice, egg, oil, vanilla and orange extract in medium bowl. Beat until well blended. Add orange juice mixture to flour mixture. Stir until just moistened. Gently fold in cranberries. Do not overmix.

Spread batter evenly in prepared pan. Bake 30 to 35 minutes (35 to 40 minutes if using frozen cranberries) or until toothpick inserted in center comes out clean. Cool in pan on wire rack 15 to 20 minutes. Invert onto serving plate. Serve warm or at room temperature.   *Makes 12 servings*

Cherry Corn Muffins

1¼ cups all-purpose flour
¾ cup yellow cornmeal
⅔ cup dried tart cherries
½ cup sugar
2 teaspoons baking powder
¼ teaspoon salt
1 cup milk
¼ cup vegetable oil
1 egg, slightly beaten
1 teaspoon vanilla extract

Combine flour, cornmeal, cherries, sugar, baking powder and salt in medium mixing bowl; mix well. Stir in milk, oil, egg and vanilla just until dry ingredients are moistened. Fill paper-lined muffin cups three-fourths full with batter.

Bake in preheated 400°F oven 20 to 25 minutes or until wooden pick inserted in center comes out clean. Let cool in pan 5 minutes. Remove from pan and serve warm or at room temperature.

Makes 12 muffins

Favorite recipe from **Cherry Marketing Institute**

Cranberry Orange Ring

That Takes the Cake

Chocolate Pudding Poke Cake

Prep Time: 30 minutes plus refrigerating

- 1 package (2-layer size) white cake mix
- 2 egg whites
- 1⅓ cups water
- 4 cups cold fat free milk
- 2 packages (4-serving size each) JELL-O® Chocolate Flavor Fat Free Sugar Free Instant Reduced Calorie Pudding & Pie Filling

PREPARE cake as directed on package for 13×9-inch baking pan using 2 egg whites and 1⅓ cup water. Remove from oven. Immediately poke holes down through cake to pan with round handle of a wooden spoon. (Or poke holes with a plastic drinking straw, using turning motion to make large holes.) Holes should be at 1-inch intervals.

POUR milk into large bowl. Add pudding mixes. Beat with wire whisk 2 minutes. Quickly pour about ½ of the thin pudding mixture evenly over warm cake and into holes to make stripes. Let remaining pudding mixture stand to thicken slightly. Spoon over top of cake, swirling to "frost" cake.

REFRIGERATE at least 1 hour or until ready to serve. Store cake in refrigerator.

Makes 15 servings

Chocolate Pudding Poke Cake

Philadelphia® 3-Step® Chocolate Swirl Cheesecake

Prep Time: 10 minutes
Bake Time: 40 minutes

    2 packages (8 ounces each)
        PHILADELPHIA® Cream Cheese,
        softened
    ½ cup sugar
    ½ teaspoon vanilla
    2 eggs
    1 square BAKER'S® Semi-Sweet Chocolate,
        melted, slightly cooled
    1 OREO® Pie Crust (6 ounces)

BEAT cream cheese, sugar and vanilla with electric mixer on medium speed until well blended. Add eggs, 1 at a time, mixing on low speed after each addition just until blended. Stir melted chocolate into ¾ cup of the cream cheese batter.

POUR remaining cream cheese batter into crust. Spoon chocolate batter over cream cheese batter; cut through batter with knife several times for marble effect.

BAKE at 350°F for 35 to 40 minutes or until center is almost set. Cool. Refrigerate 3 hours or overnight.

Makes 8 servings

Carrot Cake

    1 package DUNCAN HINES® Moist Deluxe®
        Yellow Cake Mix
    2 cups grated fresh carrots
    1 (8-ounce) can crushed pineapple with
        juice, undrained
    ½ cup water
    3 eggs
    ½ cup vegetable oil
    ½ cup finely chopped pecans
    2 teaspoons ground cinnamon
    1 container DUNCAN HINES® Cream
        Cheese Frosting

Preheat oven to 350°F. Grease and flour 13×9-inch baking pan.

Combine cake mix, carrots, pineapple with juice, water, eggs, oil, pecans and cinnamon in large mixing bowl. Beat at low speed with electric mixer until moistened. Beat at medium speed for 2 minutes. Pour into prepared pan. Bake 35 to 40 minutes or until toothpick inserted in center comes out clean. Cool in pan.

Spread frosting on cooled cake. Refrigerate until ready to serve.

Makes 12 to 16 servings

Philadelphia® 3-Step® Chocolate Swirl Cheesecake

Rich & Gooey Apple-Caramel Cake

Cake

PAM® No-Stick Cooking Spray
2 cups all-purpose flour
1 teaspoon salt
1 teaspoon baking soda
1 teaspoon pumpkin pie spice
1½ cups sugar
¾ cup WESSON® Vegetable Oil
3 eggs
2 teaspoons vanilla
3 cups peeled, cored and sliced tart apples, such as Granny Smith (½-inch slices)
1 cup chopped walnuts

Glaze

1 cup firmly packed light brown sugar
½ cup (1 stick) butter
¼ cup milk
Whipped cream

For cake, preheat oven to 350°F. Spray 13×9×2-inch baking pan with PAM® Cooking Spray; set aside. In medium bowl, combine flour, salt, baking soda and pumpkin pie spice; mix well. Set aside. In large bowl, with electric mixer, beat sugar, Wesson® Oil, eggs and vanilla for 3 minutes at medium speed. Add flour mixture and stir until dry ingredients are moistened; fold in apples and walnuts. Pour batter into baking pan and spread evenly; bake 50 to 55 minutes or until wooden pick inserted into center comes out clean. Cool cake in pan on wire rack.

Meanwhile, for glaze, in small saucepan over medium heat, bring brown sugar, butter and milk to a boil, stirring until sugar has dissolved. Boil 1 minute. Spoon half of glaze over warm cake; set *remaining* aside. Allow cake to stand 5 minutes. Top *each* serving with *remaining* glaze and whipped cream. *Makes 12 to 15 servings*

Tip

It's important to beat the fat and sugar in cake recipes for as long as the recipe directs. Batters that are underbeaten can result in an overly dense or coarse-textured cake. Electric mixers are the best tool for beating heavy batters, as they incorporate more air and help lighten the texture of the cake.

Rich & Gooey Apple-Caramel Cake

Easy Cappuccino Cake

Prep Time: 25 minutes

> 1 package (2-layer size) white cake mix
> 4 tablespoons MAXWELL HOUSE® Instant Coffee, divided
> ¼ cup milk plus 1 tablespoon milk
> 4 squares BAKER'S® Semi-Sweet Baking Chocolate, melted
> 2 tubs (8 ounces each) COOL WHIP® Whipped Topping, thawed, divided

HEAT oven to 350°F.

PREPARE and bake cake mix as directed on package for 8- or 9-inch round pans, adding 2 tablespoons instant coffee to cake mix.

POUR ¼ cup milk and 1 tablespoon instant coffee into small bowl, stirring until coffee is dissolved. Slowly stir into melted chocolate until smooth. Cool completely. Gently stir in 1 tub of whipped topping. Refrigerate 20 minutes, or until well chilled.

MEANWHILE, mix 1 tablespoon milk and 1 tablespoon coffee until dissolved. Gently stir into remaining tub of whipped topping.

COVER one cake layer with chocolate mixture. Place second cake layer on top. Frost top and side of cake with coffee-flavored whipped topping. Refrigerate until ready to serve.

Makes 14 servings

Variation: If desired, omit the coffee for a delicious plain chocolate filled layer cake.

Country Oat Cake

Cake

> 1 package (18.5 ounces) spice cake mix
> 1 cup QUAKER® Oats (quick or old fashioned, uncooked)
> 1 carton (8 ounces) plain lowfat yogurt
> 3 eggs or ¾ cup egg substitute
> ¼ cup vegetable oil
> ¼ cup water
> 1½ cups peeled, finely chopped apples (about 2 medium)

Topping

> 1 cup QUAKER® Oats (quick or old fashioned, uncooked)
> ½ cup firmly packed brown sugar
> ¼ cup (½ stick) margarine or butter, softened
> ½ teaspoon ground cinnamon
> Whipped cream (optional)

Heat oven to 350°F. Grease and flour 13×9-inch baking pan. For cake, combine cake mix, oats, yogurt, eggs, oil and water. Blend on low speed of electric mixer until moistened; mix at medium speed for 2 minutes. Stir in apples. Pour into prepared pan. For topping, combine oats, brown sugar, margarine and cinnamon; mix well. Sprinkle evenly over batter. Bake 40 to 45 minutes or until wooden pick inserted in center comes out clean. Serve warm or at room temperature with whipped cream, if desired.

Makes 16 servings

Classic New York Cheesecake

Prep Time: 15 minutes plus refrigerating
Bake Time: 1 hour 10 minutes

Crust
  1 cup HONEY MAID® Graham Cracker
    Crumbs
  3 tablespoons sugar
  3 tablespoons butter *or* margarine, melted

Filling
  4 packages (8 ounces each)
    PHILADELPHIA® Cream Cheese,
    softened
  1 cup sugar
  3 tablespoons flour
  1 tablespoon vanilla
  1 cup BREAKSTONE'S® *or* KNUDSEN®
    Sour Cream
  4 eggs

Crust
MIX crumbs, 3 tablespoons sugar and butter; press onto bottom of 9-inch springform pan. Bake at 325°F for 10 minutes if using a silver springform pan. (Bake at 300°F for 10 minutes if using a dark nonstick springform pan.)

Filling
BEAT cream cheese, 1 cup sugar, flour and vanilla with electric mixer on medium speed until well blended. Blend in sour cream. Add eggs, 1 at a time, mixing on low speed after each addition just until blended. Pour over crust.

BAKE at 325°F for 1 hour to 1 hour 5 minutes or until center is almost set if using a silver springform pan. (Bake at 300°F for 1 hour to 1 hour 5 minutes or until center is almost set if using a dark nonstick springform pan.) Run knife or metal spatula around rim of pan to loosen cake; cool before removing rim of pan. Refrigerate 4 hours or overnight.

Makes 12 servings

Tip

The secret to a smooth, perfectly mixed cheesecake batter is to make sure the cream cheese is at room temperature. This allows it to blend thoroughly with the other ingredients.

Classic New York Cheesecake

Glazed Chocolate Pound Cake

Prep Time: about 30 minutes
Bake Time: 75 to 85 minutes

Cake
1¾ cups Butter Flavor CRISCO®
    all-vegetable shortening or
    1¾ Butter Flavor CRISCO® Stick
3 cups granulated sugar
5 eggs
1 teaspoon vanilla
3¼ cups all-purpose flour
½ cup unsweetened cocoa powder
1 teaspoon baking powder
½ teaspoon salt
1⅓ cups milk
1 cup miniature semi-sweet chocolate chips

Glaze
1 cup miniature semi-sweet chocolate chips
¼ cup Butter Flavor CRISCO® all-vegetable
    shortening or ¼ Butter Flavor CRISCO®
    Stick
1 tablespoon light corn syrup

1. For cake, heat oven to 325°F. Grease and flour 10-inch tube pan.

2. Combine 1¾ cups shortening, sugar, eggs and vanilla in large bowl. Beat at low speed of electric mixer until blended, scraping bowl constantly. Beat on high speed 6 minutes, scraping bowl occasionally. Combine flour, cocoa, baking powder and salt in medium bowl. Mix in dry ingredients alternately with milk, beating after each addition until batter is smooth. Stir in 1 cup chocolate chips. Spoon into prepared pan.

3. Bake at 325°F for 75 to 85 minutes or until wooden pick inserted in center comes out clean. Cool on cooling rack 20 minutes. Invert onto serving dish. Cool completely.

4. For glaze, combine 1 cup chocolate chips, ¼ cup shortening and corn syrup in top part of double boiler over hot, not boiling, water. Stir until just melted and smooth. Cool slightly. (Or place mixture in microwave-safe bowl. Microwave at 50% power (Medium) for 1 minute and 15 seconds. Stir. Repeat at 15 second intervals, if necessary, until just melted and smooth. Cool slightly.) Spoon glaze over cake. Let stand until glaze is firm.

Makes 1 (10-inch) tube cake

Coconut Candy Bar Cake

Prep Time: 45 minutes
Bake Time: 30 minutes

14 squares BAKER'S® Semi-Sweet Baking
Chocolate, divided
½ cup (1 stick) plus 2 tablespoons butter *or*
margarine, divided
1 cup sugar
2 eggs
1½ teaspoons vanilla
1⅔ cups flour, divided
¾ teaspoon baking soda
⅛ teaspoon salt
1 cup water
1 package (14 ounces) BAKER'S® ANGEL
FLAKE® Coconut (5⅓ cups)
1 can (14 ounces) sweetened condensed
milk
¾ cup whipping (heavy) cream

HEAT oven to 350°F.

MICROWAVE 4 squares of the chocolate and
½ cup of the butter in large microwavable bowl
on HIGH 2 minutes or until butter is melted. Stir
until chocolate is completely melted.

STIR sugar into chocolate mixture until well
blended. Mix in eggs and vanilla. Stir in ⅓ cup of
the flour, baking soda and salt until well blended.
Beat in remaining 1⅓ cups flour alternately with
water until well blended. Pour into greased and
floured 13×9-inch baking pan.

BAKE 30 minutes or until toothpick inserted in
center comes out clean. Cool completely in pan on
wire rack.

MIX coconut and milk until well blended. Spread
over top of cake.

MICROWAVE cream and remaining 2 tablespoons
butter in large microwavable bowl on HIGH
2 minutes; stir. Microwave 30 seconds or until
mixture boils. Add remaining 10 squares chocolate;
stir until completely melted. Stir frequently until
mixture is cool and of spreading consistency.

SPREAD over coconut layer. Let stand until
chocolate is firm. Cut into bars.

Makes 3 dozen bars

Karen Ann's Lemon Cake

2 cups all-purpose flour
1½ teaspoons baking powder
½ teaspoon baking soda
¼ teaspoon salt
⅔ cup butter or margarine, softened
1¼ cups granulated sugar
3 eggs, separated
¾ cup sour cream
Grated peel of 1 SUNKIST® lemon
Lemony Frosting (recipe follows)

Line two 8-inch round cake pans with waxed paper. Preheat oven to 350°F. In medium bowl, combine flour, baking powder, baking soda and salt. In large bowl, with electric mixer, cream butter and sugar. Beat in egg yolks one at a time; beat until light in color. Add flour mixture alternately with sour cream, beating just until smooth. With clean beaters, beat egg whites until soft peaks form. Fold beaten egg whites and lemon peel into batter. Pour batter into prepared pans. Bake at 350°F for 30 to 35 minutes or until wooden pick inserted in center comes out clean. Cool 10 minutes. Remove from pans and peel off waxed paper. Cool on wire racks. Fill and frost with Lemony Frosting.

Makes 12 servings

Lemony Frosting

½ cup butter or margarine, softened
3 cups confectioners' sugar, divided
Grated peel of ½ SUNKIST® lemon
2 tablespoons fresh squeezed SUNKIST® lemon juice

In medium bowl, cream together butter and 1 cup confectioners' sugar. Add lemon peel, lemon juice and remaining 2 cups sugar; beat until smooth.

Makes about 1¾ cups frosting

Take-Along Cake

1 package DUNCAN HINES® Moist Deluxe®
  Swiss Chocolate Cake Mix
1 (12-ounce) package semisweet chocolate
  chips
1 cup miniature marshmallows
¼ cup butter or margarine, melted
½ cup packed brown sugar
½ cup chopped pecans or walnuts

Preheat oven to 350°F. Grease and flour 13×9-inch baking pan.

Prepare cake mix as directed on package. Add chips and marshmallows to batter. Pour into prepared pan. Drizzle melted butter over batter. Sprinkle with sugar and top with pecans. Bake 45 to 55 minutes or until toothpick inserted in center comes out clean. Serve warm or cool completely in pan.   *Makes 12 to 16 servings*

Tip: To keep leftover pecans fresh, store them in the freezer in an airtight container.

Butterscotch Banana Cake

1⅔ cups (11-ounce package) NESTLÉ® TOLL
  HOUSE® Butterscotch Flavored
  Morsels, *divided*
1 package (18.5 ounces) yellow cake mix
4 large eggs
¾ cup (2 medium) mashed ripe bananas
½ cups vegetable oil
¼ cup water
¼ cup granulated sugar

PREHEAT oven to 375°F. Grease 10-cup bundt or round tube pan.

MICROWAVE *1⅓ cups* morsels in medium, microwave-safe bowl on MEDIUM-HIGH (70%) power for 1 minute; stir. Microwave at additional 10- to 20-second intervals, stirring until smooth. Combine cake mix, eggs, bananas, vegetable oil, water and granulated sugar in large mixer bowl. Beat on low speed until moistened. Beat on high speed for 2 minutes. Stir *2 cups* batter into melted morsels. Alternately spoon batters into prepared pan.

BAKE for 35 to 45 minutes or until wooden pick inserted in cake comes out clean. Cool in pan for 20 minutes; invert onto wire rack to cool completely.

PLACE *remaining* morsels in small, *heavy-duty* plastic bag. Microwave on MEDIUM-HIGH (70%) power for 30 seconds; knead. Microwave at additional 10- to 20-second intervals. kneading until smooth. Cut tiny corner from bag; squeeze to drizzle over cake.   *Makes 24 servings*

Oreo® Cheesecake

Prep Time: 25 minutes
Cook Time: 55 minutes

    1 (1-pound 4-ounce) package OREO®
        Chocolate Sandwich Cookies, divided
    ⅓ cup margarine or butter, melted
    3 (8-ounce) packages PHILADELPHIA®
        Cream Cheese, softened
    ¾ cup sugar
    4 eggs
    1 cup BREAKSTONE'S® or KNUDSEN®
        Sour Cream
    1 teaspoon vanilla extract
        Whipped cream and mint sprigs,
        for garnish
        Additional OREO® Chocolate Sandwich
        Cookies, halved, for garnish

1. Finely crush 30 cookies and coarsely chop 20 cookies. Mix finely crushed cookie crumbs and margarine or butter in bowl. Press on bottom and 2 inches up side of 9-inch springform pan; set aside.

2. Beat cream cheese and sugar in medium bowl with electric mixer at medium speed until creamy. Blend in eggs, sour cream and vanilla; fold in chopped cookies. Spread mixture into prepared crust. Bake at 350°F for 55 to 60 minutes or until set. (If necessary to prevent top from overbrowning, tent with foil for final 15 to 20 minutes of baking.)

3. Cool on wire rack at room temperature. Refrigerate at least 4 hours.

4. Remove side of pan; garnish with whipped cream, mint sprigs and cookie halves to serve.

Makes 16 servings

Fudgy Peanut Butter Cake

    1 (18.25-ounce) box chocolate fudge
        cake mix
    2 eggs
    1½ cups plus ⅔ cup water, divided
    1 (16-ounce) package chocolate fudge
        frosting mix
    1¼ cups SMUCKER'S® Chunky Natural
        Peanut Butter or LAURA SCUDDER'S®
        Nutty Old-Fashioned Peanut Butter

Grease and flour 10-inch tube pan. In large bowl, blend cake mix, eggs and 1½ cups water until moistened; mix as directed on cake package. Pour batter into pan.

In medium bowl, combine frosting mix, peanut butter and ⅔ cup water; blend until smooth. Spoon over batter in pan.

Bake in preheated 350°F oven 35 to 45 minutes or until top springs back when touched lightly in center. Cool upright in pan 1 hour; remove from pan. Cool completely.   *Makes 12 to 15 servings*

Oreo® Cheesecake

Hershey's Red Velvet Cake

½ cup (1 stick) butter or margarine,
    softened
1½ cups sugar
2 eggs
1 teaspoon vanilla extract
1 cup buttermilk or sour milk*
2 tablespoons (1-ounce bottle) red food
    color
2 cups all-purpose flour
⅓ cup HERSHEY'S Cocoa
1 teaspoon salt
1½ teaspoons baking soda
1 tablespoon white vinegar
1 can (16 ounces) ready-to-spread vanilla
    frosting
    HERSHEY'S MINI CHIPS™ Semi-Sweet
    Chocolate Chips or HERSHEY'S Milk
    Chocolate Chips (optional)

To sour milk: Use 1 tablespoon white vinegar plus milk to equal 1 cup.

1. Heat oven to 350°F. Grease and flour 13×9×2-inch baking pan.**

2. Beat butter and sugar in large bowl; add eggs and vanilla, beating well. Stir together buttermilk and food color. Stir together flour, cocoa and salt; add alternately to butter mixture with buttermilk mixture, mixing well. Stir in baking soda and vinegar. Pour into prepared pan.

3. Bake 30 to 35 minutes or until wooden pick inserted in center comes out clean. Cool completely in pan on wire rack. Frost; garnish with chocolate chips, if desired. *Makes about 15 servings*

**This recipe can be made in 2 (9-inch) cake pans. Bake at 350°F for 30 to 35 minutes.*

Fresh Apple Cake

3 cups flour, divided
3 cups finely chopped apples
1 cup finely chopped pecans or walnuts
3 eggs *or* ¾ cup egg substitute
2 cups sugar
1 cup vegetable oil
2 teaspoons ground cinnamon
2 teaspoons vanilla
1 teaspoon ARM & HAMMER® Baking
    Soda
1 teaspoon nutmeg
½ teaspoon salt

Toss ¼ cup flour with apples and nuts. Beat eggs thoroughly in large bowl; blend in sugar. Alternately add remaining 2¾ cups flour and oil. Stir in cinnamon, vanilla, Baking Soda, nutmeg and salt; mix well. Fold in apple mixture. Pour batter into greased and floured 10-inch tube pan. Bake at 350°F 1 hour. *Makes 16 servings*

Hershey's Red Velvet Cake

Brownie Bottom Cheesecake

Prep Time: 20 minutes plus refrigerating
Bake Time: 1 hour 5 minutes

Crust

1 package (10 to 16 ounces) brownie mix, any variety (8×8 pan size)

Filling

3 packages (8 ounces each) PHILADELPHIA® Cream Cheese, softened
¾ cup sugar
1 teaspoon vanilla
½ cup BREAKSTONE'S® or KNUDSEN® Sour Cream
3 eggs

Crust
PREPARE and bake brownie mix as directed on package for 8-inch square pan in bottom of well-greased 9-inch springform pan.

Filling
MIX cream cheese, sugar and vanilla with electric mixer on medium speed until well blended. Blend in sour cream. Add eggs, mixing on low speed just until blended. Pour over brownie crust.

BAKE at 325°F for 1 hour to 1 hour and 5 minutes or until center is almost set if using a silver springform pan. (Bake at 300°F for 1 hour to 1 hour and 5 minutes or until center is almost set if using a dark nonstick springform pan.) Run knife or metal spatula around rim of pan to loosen cake; cool before removing rim of pan. Refrigerate 4 hours or overnight. *Makes 12 servings*

Mississippi Nilla Mud Cake

1½ cups margarine or butter, divided
4 eggs
1 cup unsweetened cocoa, divided
2 cups granulated sugar
1½ cups all-purpose flour
1¼ cups PLANTERS® Pecans, chopped
¼ teaspoon salt
3 cups miniature marshmallows
35 NILLA® Wafers
1 (1-pound) package powdered sugar
½ cup milk
½ teaspoon vanilla extract

1. Beat 1 cup margarine or butter, eggs and ½ cup cocoa in large bowl with electric mixer at medium speed until well combined. Blend in granulated sugar, flour, pecans and salt. Spread batter into greased 13×9×2-inch baking pan. Bake at 350°F for 30 to 35 minutes or until cake pulls away from sides of pan.

2. Sprinkle marshmallows over hot cake; return to oven for 2 minutes or until marshmallows are slightly puffed. Arrange wafers over marshmallow layer.

3. Beat remaining ½ cup margarine or butter, powdered sugar, remaining ½ cup cocoa, milk and vanilla in medium bowl with electric mixer at medium speed until smooth; spread immediately over wafer layer. Cool cake completely on wire rack. Cut into squares to serve. *Makes 24 servings*

Brownie Bottom Cheesecake

Philadelphia® 3-Step® Midwest Cheesecake

Prep Time: 10 minutes plus refrigerating
Bake Time: 40 minutes

> 2 packages (8 ounces each)
>   PHILADELPHIA® Cream Cheese,
>   softened
> ½ cup sugar
> ½ teaspoon vanilla
> 2 eggs
> 1 HONEY MAID® Graham Pie Crust
>   (6 ounces)
> ½ cup BREAKSTONE'S® or KNUDSEN®
>   Sour Cream
> 3 cups whole strawberries, stems removed
> 2 tablespoons strawberry jelly, heated

1. **BEAT** cream cheese, sugar and vanilla with electric mixer on medium speed until well blended. Add eggs; mix just until blended.

2. **POUR** into crust.

3. **BAKE** at 350°F for 40 minutes or until center is almost set. Cool. Refrigerate 3 hours or overnight. Spread sour cream over cheesecake. Top with strawberries, stem-sides down. Drizzle with jelly.

Makes 8 servings

Pineapple Orange Pound Cake

> 1 package DUNCAN HINES® Moist Deluxe®
>   Pineapple Supreme Cake Mix
> 1 (4-serving size) package vanilla-flavor
>   instant pudding and pie filling mix
> 4 eggs
> 1 cup plus 4 tablespoons orange juice,
>   divided
> ⅓ cup vegetable oil
> 1 tablespoon grated orange peel
> ⅓ cup granulated sugar

Preheat oven to 350°F. Grease and flour 10-inch Bundt pan.

Combine cake mix, pudding mix, eggs, 1 cup orange juice, oil and orange peel in large mixing bowl. Beat at medium speed with electric mixer for 2 minutes. Pour into prepared pan. Bake 50 to 60 minutes or until toothpick inserted in center comes out clean. Cool 25 minutes in pan. Invert onto serving plate.

Combine sugar and 4 tablespoons orange juice in small saucepan. Simmer 3 minutes. Brush warm glaze on cake. *Makes 12 to 16 servings*

Tip: Serve cake with peach ice cream.

Philadelphia® 3-Step® Midwest Cheesecake

Choca-Cola Cake

Cake
  1¾ cups granulated sugar
   ¾ cup CRISCO® Stick or ¾ cup CRISCO®
      all-vegetable shortening
   2 eggs
   2 tablespoons cocoa
   1 tablespoon vanilla
   ¼ teaspoon salt
   ½ cup buttermilk or sour milk*
   1 teaspoon baking soda
  2½ cups all-purpose flour
   1 cup cola soft drink (not sugar-free)

Frosting
   1 box (1 pound) confectioners' sugar
      (3½ to 4 cups)
   6 tablespoons or more cola soft drink
      (not sugar-free)
   ¼ cup cocoa
   ¼ cup CRISCO® Stick or ¼ cup CRISCO®
      all-vegetable shortening
   1 cup chopped pecans, divided

To sour milk: Combine 1½ teaspoons white vinegar plus enough milk to equal ½ cup. Stir. Wait 5 minutes before using.

1. Heat oven to 350°F. Line bottom of 13×9×2-inch baking pan with waxed paper.

2. For cake, combine granulated sugar and ¾ cup shortening in large bowl. Beat at medium speed of electric mixer 1 minute. Add eggs. Beat until blended. Add 2 tablespoons cocoa, vanilla and salt. Beat until blended.

3. Combine buttermilk and baking soda in small bowl. Add to creamed mixture. Beat until blended. Reduce speed to low. Add flour alternately with 1 cup cola, beginning and ending with flour, beating at low speed after each addition until well blended. Pour into pan.

4. Bake at 350°F for 30 to 35 minutes or until cake begins to pull away from sides of pan. *Do not overbake.* Cool 10 minutes before removing from pan. Invert cake on wire rack. Remove waxed paper. Cool completely. Place cake on serving tray.

5. For frosting, combine confectioners' sugar, 6 tablespoons cola, ¼ cup cocoa and ¼ cup shortening in medium bowl. Beat at low, then medium speed until blended, adding more cola, if necessary, until of desired spreading consistency. Stir in ½ cup nuts. Frost top and sides of cake. Sprinkle remaining nuts over top of cake. Let stand at least 1 hour before serving.
   Makes 1 (13×9×2-inch) cake (12 to 16 servings)

Note: Flavor of cake improves if made several hours or a day before serving.

Choca-Cola Cake

White Chocolate Pound Cake

3 cups flour
1 teaspoon CALUMET® baking powder
½ teaspoon salt
1 container (8 ounces) BREAKSTONE'S®
    or KNUDSEN® Sour Cream
1 can (8 ounces) crushed pineapple in juice,
    undrained
1 cup (2 sticks) butter, softened
2 cups sugar
5 eggs
1 package (6 squares) BAKER'S® Premium
    White Baking Chocolate, melted, cooled
    slightly
2 teaspoons vanilla
½ cup BAKER'S® ANGEL FLAKE® Coconut

HEAT oven to 350°F. Lightly grease and flour
12-cup fluted tube pan or 10-inch tube pan.

MIX flour, baking powder and salt; set aside. Mix
sour cream and pineapple; set aside.

BEAT butter and sugar in large bowl with electric
mixer on medium speed until light and fluffy. Add
eggs, 1 at a time, beating well after each addition.
Beat in melted chocolate and vanilla. Add flour
mixture alternately with sour cream mixture.
Beat in coconut. Pour into prepared pan.

BAKE 70 to 75 minutes or until toothpick inserted
near center comes out clean. Cool in pan 10 minutes
on wire rack. Loosen cake from side of pan with
small knife or spatula. Invert cake onto rack; gently
remove pan. Cool completely on wire rack. Sprinkle
with powdered sugar, if desired.

Makes 12 to 16 servings

Southern Jam Cake

Cake
    ¾ cup butter or margarine, softened
    1 cup granulated sugar
    3 eggs
    1 cup (12-ounce jar) SMUCKER'S®
        Seedless Blackberry Jam
    2½ cups all-purpose flour
    1 teaspoon baking soda
    1 teaspoon ground cinnamon
    1 teaspoon ground cloves
    1 teaspoon ground allspice
    1 teaspoon ground nutmeg
    ¾ cup buttermilk

Caramel Icing (optional)
    2 tablespoons butter
    ½ cup firmly packed brown sugar
    3 tablespoons milk
    1¾ cups powdered sugar

Grease and flour tube pan. Combine ¾ cup butter
and granulated sugar; beat until light and fluffy.
Add eggs one at a time, beating well after each
addition. Fold in jam.

Blend flour, baking soda and spices. Add to batter
alternately with buttermilk, stirring just enough to
blend after each addition. Spoon into prepared pan.

Bake at 350°F for 50 minutes or until toothpick
inserted in center comes out clean. Cool in pan for
10 minutes. Remove from pan; cool completely.

In saucepan, melt 2 tablespoons butter; stir in
brown sugar. Cook, stirring constantly, until
mixture boils; remove from heat. Cool 5 minutes.
Stir in milk; blend in powdered sugar. Frost cake.

Makes 12 to 16 servings

White Chocolate Pound Cake

Fudge Ribbon Cake

Prep Time: 20 minutes
Bake Time: 40 minutes

    1 (18.25-ounce) package chocolate cake mix
    1 (8-ounce) package cream cheese, softened
    2 tablespoons butter or margarine, softened
    1 tablespoon cornstarch
    1 (14-ounce) can EAGLE® BRAND
        Sweetened Condensed Milk
        (NOT evaporated milk)
    1 egg
    1 teaspoon vanilla extract
    Chocolate Glaze (recipe follows)

1. Preheat oven to 350°F. Grease and flour 13×9-inch baking pan. Prepare cake mix as package directs. Pour batter into prepared pan.

2. In small mixing bowl, beat cream cheese, butter and cornstarch until fluffy. Gradually beat in Eagle Brand. Add egg and vanilla; beat until smooth. Spoon evenly over cake batter.

3. Bake 40 minutes or until wooden pick inserted near center comes out clean. Cool. Prepare Chocolate Glaze and drizzle over cake. Store covered in refrigerator. *Makes 10 to 12 servings*

Chocolate Glaze: In small saucepan over low heat, melt 1 (1-ounce) square unsweetened or semi-sweet chocolate and 1 tablespoon butter or margarine with 2 tablespoons water. Remove from heat. Stir in ¾ cup powdered sugar and ½ teaspoon vanilla extract. Stir until smooth and well blended. Makes about ⅓ cup.

Fudge Ribbon Bundt Cake: Preheat oven to 350°F. Grease and flour 10-inch Bundt pan. Prepare cake mix as package directs. Pour batter into prepared pan. Prepare cream cheese layer as directed above; spoon evenly over batter. Bake 50 to 55 minutes or until wooden pick inserted near center comes out clean. Cool 10 minutes. Remove from pan. Cool. Prepare Chocolate Glaze and drizzle over cake. Store covered in refrigerator.

Tip

Many ovens have hot spots. To prevent cakes from baking unevenly, change the position of the cake pans from side to side and front to back after 20 minutes of baking time. (For best results, don't open the oven door before that time.)

Fudge Ribbon Cake

Apple-Pecan Cheesecake

2 packages (8 ounces each) cream cheese,
    softened
⅔ cup sugar, divided
2 eggs
½ teaspoon vanilla
1 (9-inch) prepared graham cracker
    pie crust
½ teaspoon ground cinnamon
4 cups Golden Delicious apples,
    peeled, cored and thinly sliced
    (about 2½ pounds apples)
½ cup chopped pecans

1. Preheat oven to 350°F.

2. Beat cream cheese and ⅓ cup sugar in large bowl
with electric mixer at medium speed until well
blended. Add eggs, 1 at a time, beating well after
each addition. Blend in vanilla; pour into crust.

3. Combine remaining ⅓ cup sugar and cinnamon
in large bowl. Add apples; toss gently to coat. Spoon
or arrange apple mixture over cream cheese mixture.
Sprinkle with pecans.

4. Bake 1 hour and 10 minutes or until set. Cool
completely. Store in refrigerator.

Makes one 9-inch cheesecake

Quick & Easy Chocolate Cake

4 bars (4 ounces) HERSHEY'S
    Unsweetened Baking Chocolate,
    broken into pieces
¼ cup (½ stick) butter or margarine
1⅔ cups boiling water
2⅓ cups all-purpose flour
2 cups sugar
½ cup dairy sour cream
2 eggs
2 teaspoons baking soda
1 teaspoon salt
1 teaspoon vanilla extract

1. Heat oven to 350°F. Grease and flour 13×9×2-
inch baking pan.

2. Combine chocolate, butter and water in large
bowl; with spoon, stir until chocolate is melted
and mixture is smooth. Add flour, sugar, sour cream,
eggs, baking soda, salt and vanilla; beat on low
speed of mixer until smooth. Pour batter into
prepared pan.

3. Bake 35 to 40 minutes or until wooden pick
inserted in center comes out clean. Cool completely
in pan on wire rack. Frost as desired.

Makes 12 to 15 servings

Apple-Pecan Cheesecake

Pumpkin Cake with Orange Glaze

Cake
2 cups firmly packed light brown sugar
¾ Butter Flavor CRISCO® Stick or ¾ cup Butter Flavor CRISCO® all-vegetable shortening plus additional for greasing
4 eggs
1 can (16 ounces) solid-pack pumpkin (not pumpkin pie filling)
¼ cup water
2½ cups cake flour
1 tablespoon plus 1 teaspoon baking powder
1 tablespoon pumpkin pie spice
1½ teaspoons baking soda
1 teaspoon salt
½ cup chopped walnuts
½ cup raisins

Glaze
1 cup confectioners' sugar
¾ teaspoon grated orange peel
1 tablespoon plus 1 teaspoon orange juice
Additional chopped walnuts

1. Heat oven to 350°F. Grease 10-inch (12-cup) Bundt pan. Flour lightly.

2. For cake, combine brown sugar and ¾ cup shortening in large bowl. Beat at low speed of electric mixer until creamy. Add eggs, 1 at a time, beating well after each addition. Stir in pumpkin and water.

3. Combine flour, baking powder, pumpkin pie spice, baking soda and salt in medium bowl. Add to pumpkin mixture. Beat at low speed of electric mixer until blended. Beat 2 minutes at medium speed. Fold in ½ cup nuts and raisins. Spoon into prepared pan.

4. Bake at 350°F for 55 to 60 minutes or until toothpick inserted near center comes out clean. Cool 10 minutes before removing from pan. Place cake, fluted side up, on serving plate. Cool completely.

5. For glaze, combine confectioners' sugar, orange peel and orange juice in small bowl. Stir with spoon to blend. Spoon over top of cake, letting excess glaze run down side. Sprinkle with additional nuts before glaze hardens.

Makes one 10-inch bundt cake (12 to 16 servings)

Pumpkin Cake with Orange Glaze

Lemon Crumb Cake

1 package DUNCAN HINES® Moist Deluxe®
    Lemon Supreme Cake Mix
3 eggs
1⅓ cups water
⅓ cup vegetable oil
1 cup all-purpose flour
½ cup packed light brown sugar
½ teaspoon baking powder
½ cup butter or margarine

Preheat oven to 350°F. Grease and flour 13×9-inch baking pan.

Combine cake mix, eggs, water and oil in large mixing bowl. Beat at medium speed with electric mixer for 2 minutes. Pour into prepared pan. Combine flour, sugar and baking powder in small bowl. Cut in butter until crumbly. Sprinkle evenly over batter. Bake 35 to 40 minutes or until toothpick inserted in center comes out clean. Cool completely in pan. *Makes 12 to 16 servings*

Tip: Butter or margarine will cut more easily into the flour mixture if it is chilled. Use two knives or a pastry cutter to cut the mixture into crumbs.

Chocolate Spice Cake

1¾ cups all-purpose flour
1¼ cups sugar
⅓ cup HERSHEY'S Cocoa
2 teaspoons baking soda
1 teaspoon ground cinnamon
½ teaspoon ground nutmeg
¼ teaspoon ground allspice
⅛ teaspoon salt
1½ cups applesauce
½ cup milk
½ cup (1 stick) butter or margarine, melted
1 teaspoon vanilla extract
1 cup chopped nuts (optional)
½ cup raisins
    Vanilla Glaze (recipe follows)

1. Heat oven to 350°F. Grease and flour 13×9×2-inch baking pan.

2. Stir together flour, sugar, cocoa, baking soda, cinnamon, nutmeg, allspice and salt in large bowl. Stir in applesauce, milk, butter and vanilla; beat until well blended. Add nuts, if desired, and raisins. Pour batter into prepared pan.

3. Bake 40 to 45 minutes or until wooden pick inserted in center comes out clean. Cool completely in pan on wire rack. Drizzle with Vanilla Glaze.
Makes 12 to 15 servings

Vanilla Glaze: Combine 1¼ cups powdered sugar, 2 tablespoons softened butter or margarine, 1 to 2 tablespoons hot water or milk and ½ teaspoon vanilla extract in medium bowl; beat with whisk until smooth and of desired consistency. Makes about ¾ cup glaze.

Lemon Crumb Cake

Black & White Cheesecake

Prep Time: 15 minutes
Bake Time: 35 minutes

> 2 (3-ounce) packages cream cheese, softened
> 1 (14-ounce) can EAGLE® BRAND Sweetened Condensed Milk (NOT evaporated milk)
> 1 egg
> 1 teaspoon vanilla extract
> 1 cup mini chocolate chips, divided
> 1 teaspoon all-purpose flour
> 1 (6-ounce) chocolate crumb pie crust
> Chocolate Glaze (recipe follows)

1. Preheat oven to 350°F. In medium mixing bowl, beat cream cheese until fluffy. Gradually beat in Eagle Brand until smooth. Add egg and vanilla; mix well.

2. In small mixing bowl, toss ½ cup chips with flour to coat; stir into cheese mixture. Pour into crust.

3. Bake 35 minutes or until center springs back when lightly touched. Cool. Prepare Chocolate Glaze and spread over cheesecake. Serve chilled. Store covered in refrigerator. *Makes 6 to 8 servings*

Chocolate Glaze: In small saucepan over low heat, melt remaining ½ cup chips with ¼ cup whipping cream. Cook and stir until thickened and smooth. Use immediately.

Pebbles and Stones Chocolate Cake

> 2 cups semisweet chocolate morsels, divided
> ½ cup WESSON® Vegetable Oil
> ½ cup sour cream, at room temperature
> 2 eggs, lightly beaten
> 2 cups granulated sugar
> 1½ cups all-purpose flour
> ¾ teaspoon baking soda
> ½ teaspoon salt
> PAM® No-Stick Cooking Spray
> 4 tablespoons instant coffee
> 1 cup warm milk
> ½ cup chopped nuts

In a small microwave-safe bowl, microwave 1 cup morsels on HIGH for 1 minute; stir. Cook at additional 10-second intervals, stirring between intervals until smooth. Cool to room temperature. In a large mixing bowl, beat melted chocolate, Wesson® Oil, sour cream and eggs until well blended. Add sugar, flour, baking soda and salt; mix batter well. Preheat oven to 350°F. Spray a 13×9×2-inch baking pan with PAM® Cooking Spray; lightly dust pan with flour. Set aside. In a small bowl, dissolve coffee in warm milk; slowly mix into batter. Pour into baking pan and bake 40 to 50 minutes or until wooden pick inserted into center comes out clean. Remove and sprinkle with *remaining* morsels and nuts. Cool cake completely. *Makes 12 servings*

Black & White Cheesecake

Sock-It-To-Me Cake

Streusel Filling
- 1 package DUNCAN HINES® Moist Deluxe® Butter Recipe Golden Cake Mix, divided
- 2 tablespoons brown sugar
- 2 teaspoons ground cinnamon
- 1 cup finely chopped pecans

Cake
- 4 eggs
- 1 cup dairy sour cream
- 1/3 cup vegetable oil
- 1/4 cup water
- 1/4 cup granulated sugar

Glaze
- 1 cup confectioners' sugar
- 1 or 2 tablespoons milk

1. Preheat oven to 375°F. Grease and flour 10-inch tube pan.

2. For streusel filling, combine 2 tablespoons cake mix, brown sugar and cinnamon in medium bowl. Stir in pecans. Set aside.

3. For cake, combine remaining cake mix, eggs, sour cream, oil, water and granulated sugar in large bowl. Beat at medium speed with electric mixer 2 minutes. Pour two-thirds of batter into pan. Sprinkle with streusel filling. Spoon remaining batter evenly over filling. Bake at 375°F 45 to 55 minutes or until toothpick inserted in center comes out clean. Cool in pan 25 minutes. Invert onto serving plate. Cool completely.

4. For glaze, combine confectioners' sugar and milk in small bowl. Stir until smooth. Drizzle over cake.

Makes 12 to 16 servings

Tip: For a quick glaze, place 1/2 cup Duncan Hines® Creamy Homestyle Vanilla Frosting in small microwave-safe bowl. Microwave at HIGH (100% power) 10 seconds; add 5 to 10 seconds, if needed. Stir until smooth and thin.

Egg- and oil- or butter-rich cakes freeze well. Wrap the plain cake (do not frost or decorate before freezing) in a double layer of foil to protect it from freezer burn. Thaw the cake 24 hours in advance in the refrigerator. Bring to room temperature and decorate.

Sock-It-To-Me Cake

German Chocolate Cake

Prep Time: 15 minutes
Bake Time: 40 to 45 minutes

> 1 (18.25-ounce) package chocolate cake mix
> 1 cup water
> 3 eggs
> ½ cup vegetable oil
> 1 (14-ounce) can EAGLE® BRAND
>   Sweetened Condensed Milk
>   (NOT evaporated milk), divided
> 3 tablespoons butter or margarine
> 1 egg yolk
> ⅓ cup chopped pecans
> ⅓ cup flaked coconut
> 1 teaspoon vanilla extract

1. Preheat oven to 350°F. Grease and flour 13×9-inch baking pan. In large mixing bowl, combine cake mix, water, 3 eggs, oil and ⅓ cup Eagle Brand. Beat at low speed of electric mixer until moistened; beat at high speed 2 minutes.

2. Pour into prepared pan. Bake 40 to 45 minutes or until wooden pick inserted near center comes out clean.

3. In small saucepan over medium heat, combine remaining Eagle Brand, butter and egg yolk. Cook and stir until thickened, about 6 minutes. Add pecans, coconut and vanilla; spread over warm cake. Store covered in refrigerator.

Makes 10 to 12 servings

Spicy Applesauce Cake

> 2¼ cups all-purpose flour
> 2 teaspoons baking soda
> 1 teaspoon ground cinnamon
> 1 teaspoon ground nutmeg
> ½ teaspoon ground cloves
> 1 cup firmly packed brown sugar
> ½ cup FILIPPO BERIO® Olive Oil
> 1½ cups applesauce
> 1 cup raisins
> 1 cup coarsely chopped walnuts
>   Powdered sugar or sweetened whipped
>   cream (optional)

Preheat oven to 375°F. Grease 9-inch square pan with olive oil. In medium bowl, combine flour, baking soda, cinnamon, nutmeg and cloves.

In large bowl, mix brown sugar and olive oil with electric mixer at medium speed until blended. Add applesauce; mix well. Add flour mixture all at once; beat on low speed until well blended. Stir in raisins and nuts. Spoon batter into prepared pan.

Bake 20 to 25 minutes or until lightly browned. Cool completely on wire rack. Cut into squares. Serve plain, dusted with powdered sugar or frosted with whipped cream, if desired.

Makes 9 servings

German Chocolate Cake

Refreshing Choco-Orange Cheesecake

1 cup graham cracker crumbs
¼ cup (½ stick) butter or margarine, melted
2 cups sugar, divided
1 cup HERSHEY'S Semi-Sweet Chocolate Chips
3 packages (8 ounces each) cream cheese, softened
4 eggs
1½ cups dairy sour cream
2 teaspoons orange extract
1 teaspoon freshly grated orange peel
Whipped topping

1. Stir together graham cracker crumbs, melted butter and ¼ cup sugar in small bowl; pat firmly onto bottom of 9-inch springform pan.

2. Place chocolate chips in medium microwave-safe bowl. Microwave at HIGH (100%) 1 minute or just until chips are melted when stirred.

3. Beat cream cheese and remaining 1¾ cups sugar in large bowl; add eggs, one at a time, beating after each addition. Stir in sour cream and orange extract. Stir 3 cups cream cheese mixture into melted chocolate chips; pour into crust. Freeze 10 to 15 minutes or until chocolate sets.

4. Heat oven to 325°F. Stir orange peel into remaining cream cheese mixture; gently spread over chocolate mixture.

5. Bake 1 hour 15 minutes or until set except for 3-inch circle in center; turn off oven. Let stand in oven, with door ajar, 1 hour; remove from oven. With knife, loosen cheesecake from side of pan. Cool completely; remove side of pan. Cover; refrigerate. Garnish with whipped topping and orange wedges, if desired. Cover; refrigerate leftover cheesecake.

Makes 12 servings

Tip

To help avoid cracks in the top of your cheesecake, beat the batter at low speed using an electric mixer, and let the cake cool to room temperature before refrigerating. The texture and flavor of cheesecakes improve with chilling, so these are good items to make one or two days before a bake sale. Simply cover them and store in the refrigerator.

Refreshing Choco-Orange Cheesecake

Carrot Layer Cake

Cake
    1 package DUNCAN HINES® Moist Deluxe®
        Classic Yellow Cake Mix
    4 eggs
    ½ cup vegetable oil
    3 cups grated carrots
    1 cup finely chopped nuts
    2 teaspoons ground cinnamon

Cream Cheese Frosting
    1 (8-ounce) package cream cheese, softened
    ¼ cup butter or margarine, softened
    2 teaspoons vanilla extract
    4 cups confectioners' sugar

1. Preheat oven to 350°F. Grease and flour
2 (8- or 9-inch) round baking pans.

2. For cake, combine cake mix, eggs, oil, carrots,
nuts and cinnamon in large bowl. Beat at low speed
with electric mixer until moistened. Beat at medium
speed for 2 minutes. Pour into pans. Bake at 350°F
for 35 to 40 minutes or until toothpick inserted in
centers comes out clean. Cool.

3. For frosting, place cream cheese, butter and
vanilla extract in large bowl. Beat at low speed
until smooth and creamy. Add confectioners' sugar
gradually, beating until smooth. Add more sugar to
thicken, or milk or water to thin frosting, as needed.
Fill and frost cooled cake. Garnish with whole
pecans. *Makes 12 to 16 servings*

Chocolate Raspberry Cheesecake

Prep Time: 15 minutes
Chill Time: 3 hours

    2 (3-ounce) packages cream cheese,
        softened
    1 (14-ounce) can sweetened condensed milk
    1 egg
    3 tablespoons lemon juice
    1 teaspoon vanilla
    1 cup fresh or frozen raspberries
    1 (6-ounce) READY CRUST® Chocolate
        Pie Crust
    Chocolate Glaze (recipe follows)

1. Preheat oven to 350°F. Beat cream cheese in
medium bowl with electric mixer at medium speed
until fluffy. Gradually beat in sweetened condensed
milk until smooth. Add egg, lemon juice and vanilla;
mix well. Arrange raspberries on bottom of crust.
Slowly pour cream cheese mixture over raspberries.

2. Bake 30 to 35 minutes or until center is almost
set. Cool on wire rack.

3 . Prepare Chocolate Glaze; spread over cheesecake.
Refrigerate 3 hours. Garnish as desired. Refrigerate
leftovers. *Makes 8 servings*

Chocolate Glaze: Melt 2 (1-ounce) squares
semisweet baking chocolate with ¼ cup whipping
cream in small saucepan over low heat. Cook and
stir until thickened and smooth. Remove from heat.

Carrot Layer Cake

Reese's® Chocolate Peanut Butter Cheesecake

1¼ cups graham cracker crumbs
⅓ cup plus ¼ cup sugar
⅓ cup HERSHEY'S Cocoa
⅓ cup butter or margarine, melted
3 packages (8 ounces each) cream cheese, softened
1 can (14 ounces) sweetened condensed milk (not evaporated milk)
1⅔ cup (10-ounce package) REESE'S® Peanut Butter Chips, melted
4 eggs
2 teaspoons vanilla extract
Chocolate Drizzle (recipe follows)
Whipped topping
HERSHEY'S MINI KISSES™ Semi-Sweet or Milk Chocolates

1. Heat oven to 300°F. Combine graham cracker crumbs, ⅓ cup sugar, cocoa and butter; press onto bottom of 9-inch springform pan.

2. Beat cream cheese and remaining ¼ cup sugar until fluffy. Gradually beat in sweetened condensed milk, then melted chips, until smooth. Add eggs and vanilla; beat well. Pour over crust.

3. Bake 60 to 70 minutes or until center is almost set. Remove from oven. With knife, loosen cake from side of pan. Cool. Remove side of pan. Refrigerate until cold. Garnish with Chocolate Drizzle, whipped topping and Mini Kisses™. Store, covered, in refrigerator. *Makes 12 servings*

Chocolate Drizzle: Melt 2 tablespoons butter in small saucepan over low heat; add 2 tablespoons HERSHEY'S Cocoa and 2 tablespoons water. Cook and stir until slightly thickened. Do not boil. Cool slightly. Gradually add 1 cup powdered sugar and ½ teaspoon vanilla extract, beating with whisk until smooth. Makes about ¾ cup.

Tip: If desired, spoon drizzle into small heavy seal-top plastic bag. With scissors, make small diagonal cut in bottom corner of bag. Squeeze drizzle over top of cake.

Tip

Not all cream cheeses are created equally. Soft and whipped cream cheeses contain more air and should not be used for baking. Reduced-fat cream cheese, also called Neufchâtel cheese, can be used for baking, but fat-free cream cheese should not be used.

Reese's® Chocolate Peanut Butter Cheesecake

Sour Cream Pound Cake

1 orange
1 cup butter, softened
2¾ cups sugar
1 tablespoon vanilla
6 eggs
3 cups all-purpose flour
½ teaspoon salt
¼ teaspoon baking soda
1 cup sour cream
Citrus Topping (recipe follows)

Preheat oven to 325°F. Grease 10-inch tube pan. Finely grate colored portion of orange peel. Measure 2 teaspoons orange peel; set aside. Beat butter in large bowl with electric mixer at medium speed until creamy, scraping down side of bowl once. Gradually add sugar, beating until light and fluffy. Beat in vanilla and orange peel. Add eggs, 1 at a time, beating 1 minute after each addition. Combine flour, salt and baking soda in small bowl. Add to butter mixture alternately with sour cream, beginning and ending with flour mixture. Beat well after each addition. Pour into prepared pan. Bake 1 hour 15 minutes or until wooden pick inserted in center comes out clean.

Meanwhile, prepare Citrus Topping. Spoon over hot cake; cool in pan 15 minutes. Remove from pan to wire rack; cool completely.

Makes 10 to 12 servings

Citrus Topping

2 oranges
3 teaspoons salt
Water
½ cup sugar, divided
⅓ cup lemon juice
1 teaspoon vanilla

With citrus zester or vegetable peeler, remove colored peel, not white pith, from oranges. Measure ⅓ cup orange peel. Cut oranges in half. Squeeze juice from oranges into measuring cup or small bowl. Measure ⅓ cup orange juice. Combine orange peel and salt in medium saucepan. Add enough water to cover. Bring to a boil over high heat. Boil 2 minutes.

Drain in fine-meshed sieve. Return orange peel to saucepan. Add orange juice and ¼ cup sugar to saucepan. Bring to a boil over high heat. Reduce heat; simmer 10 minutes. Remove from heat. Add remaining ¼ cup sugar, lemon juice and vanilla; stir until smooth.

Sour Cream Pound Cake

Peachy Pecan Cake

1 (8-ounce) package cream cheese, softened
1 cup packed brown sugar
4 eggs, beaten
½ cup half-and-half
1½ teaspoons vanilla
1 cup ginger snap crumbs
1 (6-ounce) package almond brickle chips
¾ cup chopped pecans, toasted*
½ cup coconut flakes
1 (16-ounce) can sliced peaches, well
  drained and chopped
Whipped cream (optional)

To toast pecans, spread in single layer on baking sheet. Bake in preheated 350°F oven 10 to 12 minutes or until lightly toasted, stirring occasionally.

1. Preheat oven to 350°F. Grease 9-inch square baking pan.

2. Beat cream cheese and sugar in large bowl until well blended.

3. Add eggs, one at a time, beating well after each addition. Blend in half-and-half and vanilla. Stir in crumbs, chips, pecans and coconut. Stir in peaches; pour into prepared pan.

4. Bake 35 to 40 minutes or until center is firm and edges are golden brown. Serve warm or chilled. Garnish with whipped cream, if desired.

Makes one 9-inch cake

Chocolate Syrup Swirl Cake

1 cup (2 sticks) butter or margarine,
  softened
2 cups sugar
2 teaspoons vanilla extract
3 eggs
2¾ cups all-purpose flour
1¼ teaspoons baking soda, divided
½ teaspoon salt
1 cup buttermilk or sour milk*
1 cup HERSHEY'S Syrup
1 cup MOUNDS® Sweetened Coconut
  Flakes (optional)

To sour milk: Use 1 tablespoon white vinegar plus milk to equal 1 cup.

1. Heat oven to 350°F. Grease and flour 12-cup fluted tube pan or 10-inch tube pan.

2. Beat butter, sugar and vanilla in large bowl until fluffy. Add eggs; beat well. Stir together flour, 1 teaspoon baking soda and salt; add alternately with buttermilk to butter mixture, beating until well blended.

3. Measure 2 cups batter in small bowl; stir in syrup and remaining ¼ teaspoon baking soda. Add coconut, if desired, to remaining batter; pour into prepared pan. Pour chocolate batter over vanilla batter in pan; do not mix.

4. Bake 60 to 70 minutes or until wooden pick inserted in center comes out clean. Cool 15 minutes; remove from pan to wire rack. Cool completely on wire rack; glaze or frost as desired.

Makes 20 servings

Peachy Pecan Cake

Perfect Pies

Heavenly Chocolate Mousse Pie

Prep Time: 20 minutes
Chill Time: 15 minutes

 4 (1-ounce) squares unsweetened chocolate, melted
 1 (14-ounce) can EAGLE® BRAND Sweetened Condensed Milk
  (NOT evaporated milk)
 1½ teaspoons vanilla extract
 1 cup (½ pint) whipping cream, whipped
 1 (6-ounce) chocolate crumb pie crust

1. In medium mixing bowl, beat melted chocolate with Eagle Brand and vanilla until well blended.

2. Chill 15 minutes or until cooled; stir until smooth. Fold in whipped cream.

3. Pour into crust. Chill thoroughly. Garnish as desired. Refrigerate leftovers.

Makes 1 pie

Heavenly Chocolate Mousse Pie

Best-Ever Apple Pie

2⅓ cups all-purpose flour, divided
¾ cup plus 1 tablespoon sugar, divided
½ teaspoon baking powder
½ teaspoon salt
¾ cup plus 3 tablespoons cold unsalted
    butter, cut into small pieces, divided
4 to 5 tablespoons ice water
1 egg, separated
7 medium apples such as Jonathan or
    Granny Smith, peeled, cored and sliced
1 tablespoon lemon juice
1¼ teaspoons ground cinnamon
1 tablespoon sour cream

1. Combine 2 cups flour, 1 tablespoon sugar, baking powder and salt in large bowl until well blended. Cut in ¾ cup butter using pastry blender or 2 knives until mixture resembles coarse crumbs. Add water, 1 tablespoon at a time, to flour mixture. Toss with fork until mixture holds together. Form dough into 2 discs. Wrap discs in plastic wrap; refrigerate 30 minutes or until firm.

2. Roll out 1 disc dough on lightly floured surface with lightly floured rolling pin into 12-inch circle, ⅛ inch thick. Ease dough into 9-inch glass pie plate. *Do not stretch dough.* Trim dough leaving ½-inch overhang; brush with beaten egg white. Set aside.

3. Preheat oven to 450°F.

4. Place apple slices in large bowl; sprinkle with lemon juice. Combine remaining ⅓ cup flour, ¾ cup sugar and cinnamon in small bowl until well blended. Add to apple mixture; toss to coat apples evenly. Spoon filling into prepared pie crust; place remaining 3 tablespoons butter on top of filling.

5. Moisten edge of dough with water. Roll out remaining disc of dough. Place onto filling. Trim dough leaving ½-inch overhang.

6. Flute edge. Cut slits in dough at ½-inch intervals around edge to form flaps. Press 1 flap in toward center of pie and the next out toward rim of pie plate. Continue around edge as shown in photo. Cut 4 small slits in top of dough to allow steam to escape.

7. Combine egg yolk and sour cream in small bowl until well blended. Cover; refrigerate until ready to use.

8. Bake 10 minutes; *reduce oven temperature to 375°F.* Bake 35 minutes. Brush egg yolk mixture evenly on pie crust with pastry brush. Bake 20 to 25 minutes or until crust is deep golden brown. Cool completely on wire rack. Store loosely covered at room temperature 1 day or refrigerate up to 4 days.

Makes one (9-inch) pie

Easy Chocolate Lover's Cheesepie

Prep Time: 15 minutes
Bake Time: 40 minutes
Cool Time: 1 hour

> 3 packages (8 ounces each) cream cheese, softened
> ¾ cup sugar
> 3 eggs
> 1 teaspoon vanilla extract
> 2 cups (12-ounce package) HERSHEY'S MINI CHIPS™ Semi-Sweet Chocolate Chips, divided
> 1 extra serving-size packaged graham cracker crumb crust (9 ounces)
> 2 tablespoons whipping cream

1. Heat oven to 450°F.

2. Beat cream cheese and sugar in large bowl in large bowl with mixer until well blended. Add eggs and vanilla; beat well. Stir in 1⅔ cups small chocolate chips; pour into crust.

3. Bake 10 minutes. Without opening oven door, reduce temperature to 250°F; continue baking 30 minutes or just until set. Remove from oven to wire rack. Cool completely. Cover; refrigerate until thoroughly chilled.

4. Place remaining ⅓ cup chips and whipping cream in small microwave-safe bowl. Microwave at HIGH (100%) 20 to 30 seconds or just until chips are melted and mixture is smooth when stirred. Cool slightly; spread over top of cheesepie. Refrigerate 15 minutes or until topping is set. Cover; refrigate leftover cheesepie. *Makes 10 servings*

Coconut Peach Crunch Pie

Prep Time: 15 minutes
Bake Time: 35 to 40 minutes

> 1 (6-ounce) READY CRUST® Shortbread Pie Crust
> 1 egg yolk, beaten
> 1 (21-ounce) can peach pie filling
> 1 cup flaked coconut
> ½ cup all-purpose flour
> ½ cup sugar
> ¼ cup wheat germ
> ¼ cup margarine, melted

1. Preheat oven to 375°F. Brush bottom and sides of crust with egg yolk; bake on baking sheet 5 minutes or until golden brown.

2. Spoon peach filling into crust. Combine coconut, flour, sugar, wheat germ and margarine in small bowl. Mix until well blended. Spread over peach filling.

3. Bake on baking sheet 30 to 35 minutes or until filling is bubbly and topping is light brown. Cool on wire rack. *Makes 8 servings*

Easy Chocolate Lover's Cheesepie

Michigan Blueberry Pie

Crust
> Classic CRISCO® Double Crust
> (page 320)

Filling
> 3 packages (12 ounces each) frozen
> blueberries, thawed and drained,
> reserving liquid
> ¼ cup quick-cooking tapioca
> 1½ cups sugar
> ¼ cup cornstarch
> 2 tablespoons grated orange peel
> 1 tablespoon butter or margarine
> 1 tablespoon cinnamon

Glaze
> Milk
> Sugar (optional)

1. For crust, prepare as directed. Press bottom crust into 9-inch pie plate. Do not bake. Heat oven to 425°F.

2. For filling, pour reserved liquid into medium saucepan. Stir in tapioca. Let stand 5 minutes. Stir in 1½ cups sugar and cornstarch. Cook and stir on medium heat until mixture comes to a boil and thickens. Stir in orange peel, butter and cinnamon. Fold in blueberries. Bring to a boil. Pour into unbaked pie crust. Moisten pastry edge with water.

3. Roll top crust same as bottom. Lift onto filled pie. Trim ½ inch beyond edge of pie plate. Fold top edge under bottom crust. Flute.

4. For glaze, brush with milk. Sprinkle with sugar, if desired. Cut slits in top crust to allow steam to escape.

5. Bake at 425°F for 45 minutes, or until filling in center is bubbly and crust is golden brown. *Do not overbake.* Cover edge with foil, if necessary, to prevent overbrowning. Serve barely warm or at room temperature.   *Makes 1 (9-inch) pie*

Caramel-Pecan Pie

> 3 eggs
> ⅔ cup sugar
> 1 cup (12-ounce jar) SMUCKER'S®
> Caramel Topping
> ¼ cup butter or margarine, melted
> 1½ cups pecan halves
> 1 (9-inch) unbaked pie shell

In mixing bowl, beat eggs slightly with fork. Add sugar, stirring until dissolved. Stir in topping and butter; mix well. Stir in pecan halves. Pour filling into pie shell.

Bake at 350°F for 45 minutes or until knife inserted near center comes out clean. Cool thoroughly on rack before serving. Cover and store in refrigerator.

Makes 6 to 8 servings

Caramel-Pecan Pie

White Chocolate Cranberry Tart

1 refrigerated pie crust (half of
   15-ounce package)
1 cup sugar
2 eggs
¼ cup butter, melted
2 teaspoons vanilla
½ cup all-purpose flour
1 package (6 ounces) white chocolate
   baking bar, chopped
½ cup chopped macadamia nuts, lightly
   toasted*
½ cup dried cranberries, coarsely chopped

*Toast chopped macadamia nuts in hot skillet about
3 minutes or until fragrant.*

1. Preheat oven to 350°F. Line 9-inch tart pan
with removable bottom or pie pan with pie crust
(refrigerate or freeze other crust for another use).

2. Combine sugar, eggs, butter and vanilla in large
bowl; mix well. Stir in flour until well blended.
Add white chocolate, nuts and cranberries.

3. Pour filling into unbaked crust. Bake 50 to
55 minutes or until top of tart is crusty and deep
golden brown and knife inserted in center comes
out clean.

4. Cool completely on wire rack. Cover and store
at room temperature until serving time.

Makes 8 servings

Serving Suggestion: Top each serving with a
dollop of whipped cream flavored with ground
cinnamon, a favorite liqueur and grated orange peel.

Chocolate Coconut Marshmallow Pie

Prep Time: 45 minutes plus refrigerating
Bake Time: 20 minutes

2 cups BAKER'S® ANGEL FLAKE® Coconut
½ cup chopped pecans
¼ cup (½ stick) butter *or* margarine, melted
4 squares BAKER'S® Semi-Sweet Baking
   Chocolate *or* 1 package (4 ounces)
   BAKER'S® GERMAN'S® Sweet Baking
   Chocolate
2 cups miniature marshmallows
½ cup milk
4 ounces (½ of 8-ounce package)
   PHILADELPHIA® Cream Cheese,
   softened
1 tub (8 ounces) COOL WHIP® Whipped
   Topping, thawed

HEAT oven to 350°F.

MIX coconut, pecans and butter in 9-inch pie plate;
press evenly onto bottom and up side of pie plate.

BAKE 20 minutes or until lightly browned. Cool.

MICROWAVE chocolate, marshmallows and milk
in large microwavable bowl on HIGH 3 minutes or
until marshmallows are melted. Stir until chocolate
is completely melted. Beat in cream cheese until
smooth. Refrigerate until slightly thickened. Gently
stir in whipped topping. Spoon into crust.

REFRIGERATE 3 hours. Just before serving, dip
pie plate briefly in hot water to loosen crust from
plate. Garnish with additional whipped topping and
chocolate curls, if desired. *Makes 8 servings*

Country Peach Tart

Pastry for single crust 9-inch pie
1 tablespoon all-purpose flour
2½ teaspoons EQUAL® FOR RECIPES *or*
   8 packets EQUAL® sweetener *or*
   ⅓ cup EQUAL® SPOONFUL™
4 cups sliced pitted peeled fresh peaches
   (about 4 medium) or frozen peaches,
   thawed
   Ground nutmeg

• Roll pastry on floured surface into 12-inch circle; transfer to ungreased cookie sheet. Combine flour and Equal®; sprinkle over peaches and toss. Arrange peaches on pastry, leaving 2-inch border around edge of pastry. Sprinkle peaches lightly with nutmeg. Bring pastry edge toward center, overlapping as necessary.

• Bake tart in preheated 425°F oven until crust is browned and fruit is tender, 25 to 30 minutes.

Makes 8 servings

Nestlé® Toll House® Chocolate Chip Pie

1 *unbaked* 9-inch (4-cup volume) deep-dish
  pie shell*
2 large eggs
½ cup all-purpose flour
½ cup granulated sugar
½ cup packed brown sugar
¾ cup (1½ sticks) butter, softened
1 cup (6 ounces) NESTLÉ® TOLL HOUSE®
  Semi-Sweet Chocolate Morsels
1 cup chopped nuts
  Sweetened whipped cream or ice cream
  (optional)

If using frozen pie shell, use deep-dish style, thawed completely. Bake on baking sheet; increase baking time slightly.

PREHEAT oven to 325°F.

BEAT eggs in large mixer bowl on high speed until foamy. Beat in flour, granulated sugar and brown sugar. Beat in butter. Stir in morsels and nuts. Spoon into pie shell.

BAKE for 55 to 60 minutes or until knife inserted halfway between outside edge and center comes out clean. Cool on wire rack. Serve warm with whipped cream.

Makes 8 servings

Chocolate Pecan Caramel Pie

20 NABISCO® Famous Chocolate Wafers,
    finely crushed (about 1 cup crumbs)
½ cup PLANTERS® Pecans, finely chopped
7 tablespoons margarine or butter, melted,
    divided
1 envelope KNOX® Unflavored Gelatine
¼ cup cold water
2 cups heavy cream, divided
1 (6-ounce) package semisweet chocolate
    chips
1 teaspoon vanilla extract
24 KRAFT® Caramels
    PLANTERS® Pecans, for garnish

1. Mix wafer crumbs, chopped pecans and
5 tablespoons margarine or butter. Press on
bottom and up side of 9-inch pie plate. Bake at
350°F for 10 minutes. Cool completely; set aside.

2. Sprinkle gelatine over cold water in small
saucepan; let stand 1 minute. Stir over low heat
until gelatine completely dissolves, about 2 minutes.
Stir in 1 cup cream. Heat mixture over medium heat
just to a boil.

3. Immediately blend hot gelatine mixture and
chocolate chips in electric blender until chocolate
melts, about 1 minute. Add ½ cup cream and vanilla
through feed tube while processing; process until
blended. Pour into bowl and chill until slightly
thickened, about 1 hour.

4. Heat caramels, ¼ cup cream and remaining
2 tablespoons margarine or butter in small saucepan
over low heat until caramels melt and mixture is
smooth. Pour into prepared crust; let cool for
10 minutes.

5. Beat gelatine mixture until smooth. Pour into
prepared crust; refrigerate until firm, about 3 hours.
Whip remaining ¼ cupheavy cream until stiff.
Garnish pie with whipped cream and pecans.

Makes 8 servings

Decadent Brownie Pie

Prep Time: 25 minutes
Bake Time: 45 to 50 minutes

1 (9-inch) unbaked pastry shell
1 cup (6 ounces) semi-sweet chocolate
    chips
¼ cup (½ stick) butter or margarine
1 (14-ounce) can EAGLE® BRAND
    Sweetened Condensed Milk
    (NOT evaporated milk)
½ cup biscuit baking mix
2 eggs
1 teaspoon vanilla extract
1 cup chopped nuts
    Vanilla ice cream

1. Preheat oven to 375°F. Bake pastry shell
10 minutes; remove from oven. Reduce oven
temperature to 325°F.

2. In small saucepan over low heat, melt chips
with butter until smooth.

3. In large mixing bowl, beat chocolate mixture
with Eagle Brand, biscuit mix, eggs and vanilla
until smooth. Add nuts. Pour into baked pastry
shell.

4. Bake 35 to 40 minutes or until center is set.
Serve warm or at room temperature with ice cream.
Refrigerate leftovers.
Makes 1 (9-inch) pie

Decadent Brownie Pie

Triple Layer Butterscotch Pie

2 squares BAKER'S® Semi-Sweet Baking
　　Chocolate, melted
¼ cup sweetened condensed milk
1 prepared chocolate flavor crumb crust
　　(6 ounces or 9 inches)
¾ cup chopped pecans, toasted
1¾ cups cold milk
2 packages (4-serving size each) JELL-O®
　　Butterscotch Flavor Instant Pudding
　　& Pie Filling
1 tub (8 ounces) COOL WHIP® Whipped
　　Topping, thawed, divided

POUR chocolate and sweetened condensed milk
into bowl; stir until smooth. Pour into crust. Press
nuts evenly onto chocolate in crust. Refrigerate
10 minutes.

POUR milk into large bowl. Add pudding mixes.
Beat with wire whisk 1 minute or until well blended.
(Mixture will be thick.) Spread 1½ cups of the
pudding over chocolate in crust. Immediately stir
½ of the whipped topping into remaining pudding.
Spread over pudding in crust. Top with remaining
whipped topping.

REFRIGERATE 3 hours or until set. Garnish as
desired. 　　　　　　　　　　*Makes 8 servings*

Great Substitute: If you are a chocolate lover,
simply substitute Chocolate Flavor Pudding for
the Butterscotch Flavor.

Luscious Brownie Chip Pie

25 CHIPS AHOY!® Chocolate Chip Cookies,
　　divided
½ cup margarine or butter, melted, divided
½ cup light corn syrup
3 eggs
½ cup sugar
⅓ cup unsweetened cocoa
2 teaspoons vanilla extract
　　Whipped cream, for garnish
　　Chocolate curls, for garnish

1. Cut 5 cookies in half; set aside. Roll remaining
cookies between two pieces of waxed paper until
fine crumbs form. Combine cookie crumbs and
¼ cup melted margarine or butter; press on bottom
and up side of 9-inch pie plate.

2. Heat remaining ¼ cup margarine or butter and
corn syrup in saucepan until warm; remove from
heat. Beat in eggs, sugar, cocoa and vanilla; pour
into crust. Bake at 350°F 15 minutes; insert cookie
halves around edge of pie crust.

3. Bake 15 to 20 minutes more or until set, tenting
with foil during last 5 to 10 minutes if excessive
browning occurs. Cool. Garnish with whipped cream
and chocolate curls. 　　　　　*Makes 8 servings*

Triple Layer Butterscotch Pie

Blueberry Crumble Pie

Prep Time: 15 minutes
Baking Time: 40 minutes

> 1 (6-ounce) READY CRUST® Graham
>   Cracker Pie Crust
> 1 egg yolk, beaten
> 1 (21-ounce) can blueberry pie filling
> ⅓ cup all-purpose flour
> ⅓ cup quick-cooking oats
> ¼ cup sugar
> 3 tablespoons margarine, melted

1. Preheat oven to 375°F. Brush bottom and sides of crust with egg yolk; bake on baking sheet 5 minutes or until light brown.

2. Pour blueberry pie filling into crust. Combine flour, oats and sugar in small bowl; mix in margarine. Spoon over pie filling.

3. Bake on baking sheet about 35 minutes or until filling is bubbly and topping is browned. Cool on wire rack.

Makes 8 servings

Chocolate Satin Pie

> 1 *prepared* 8-inch (6 ounces) graham
>   cracker crust
> 1 can (12 fluid ounces) NESTLÉ®
>   CARNATION® Evaporated Milk
> 2 large egg yolks
> 2 cups (12-ounce package) NESTLÉ®
>   TOLL HOUSE® Semi-Sweet
>   Chocolate Morsels
> Whipped cream (optional)
> Chopped nuts (optional)

WHISK together evaporated milk and egg yolks in medium saucepan. Heat over medium-low heat, stirring constantly, until mixture is very hot and thickens slightly; do not boil. Remove from heat; stir in morsels until chocolate is completely melted and mixture is very smooth.

POUR into crust; refrigerate for 3 hours or until firm. Top with whipped cream before serving; sprinkle with nuts.

Makes 10 servings

Blueberry Crumble Pie

Candy Bar Pie

Prep Time: 15 minutes
Chill Time: 4 hours

  4 ounces cream cheese, softened
1¾ cups plus 1 tablespoon cold milk, divided
  1 (12-ounce) tub COOL WHIP® Whipped
    Topping, thawed, divided
  2 chocolate-covered caramel peanut nougat
    bars (2.07 ounces each), chopped
  1 (4-serving size) package JELL-O®
    Chocolate Flavor Instant Pudding
    & Pie Filling
  1 (6-ounce) READY CRUST® Chocolate
    Pie Crust

1. Mix cream cheese and 1 tablespoon milk in medium bowl with wire whisk until smooth. Gently stir in 2 cups whipped topping and chopped candy bars; set aside.

2. Pour remaining 1¾ cups milk into another medium bowl. Add pudding mix. Beat with wire whisk 1 minute. Gently stir in ½ cup whipped topping. Spread half of pudding mixture on bottom of crust. Spread cream cheese mixture over pudding mixture. Top with remaining pudding mixture.

3. Refrigerate 4 hours or until set. Garnish with remaining whipped topping. Refrigerate leftovers.

Makes 8 servings

Apple Crumb Pie

  1 (6-ounce) HONEY MAID® Graham
    Pie Crust
  1 egg white, slightly beaten
  1 (21-ounce) can apple pie filling
  ½ cup all-purpose flour
  ¼ cup sugar
1½ teaspoons ground cinnamon
  ¼ cup margarine or butter
  ¾ cup PLANTERS® Pecans, chopped
    Powdered sugar, optional
    Apple slices and mint sprig, for garnish

1. Brush pie crust lightly with egg white. Bake at 375°F for 5 minutes; cool.

2. Spoon pie filling into pie crust. Combine flour, sugar and cinnamon in small bowl. Cut in margarine or butter until mixture is crumbly; stir in pecans. Sprinkle over pie filling.

3. Bake at 375°F for 25 to 30 minutes or until topping is golden brown. Cool slightly on wire rack. Serve warm, sprinkled with powdered sugar, if desired. Garnish with apple slices and mint sprig.

Makes 6 servings

Candy Bar Pie

Black & White Brownie Bottom Pudding Pie

4 squares BAKER'S® Semi-Sweet Baking
    Chocolate
¼ cup (½ stick) butter *or* margarine
¾ cup sugar
2 eggs
1 teaspoon vanilla
½ cup flour
2½ cups cold milk
2 packages (4-serving size each) JELL-O®
    White Chocolate *or* Vanilla Flavor
    Instant Pudding & Pie Filling

HEAT oven to 350°F (325°F for glass pie plate).

MICROWAVE chocolate and butter in small microwavable bowl on HIGH 2 minutes or until butter is melted. Stir until chocolate is completely melted.

STIR in sugar, eggs and vanilla. Blend in flour. Spread batter in greased 9-inch pie plate. Bake 25 minutes or until toothpick inserted in center comes out with fudgy crumbs. (DO NOT OVERBAKE.) Lightly press center with bottom of measuring cup or back of spoon to form slight depression. Cool on wire rack.

POUR milk into large bowl. Add pudding mixes. Beat with wire whisk 2 minutes or until blended. Let stand 2 minutes. Spread over brownie pie. Top with thawed COOL WHIP® Whipped Topping and grated chocolate, if desired. Refrigerate until ready to serve. *Makes 8 servings*

Great Substitute: For an added crunch, stir in ½ cup chopped nuts after the flour and proceed as directed above.

Brown Sugar Apple Pie

Crust
    Classic CRISCO® Double Crust (page 320)

Filling
7 cups sliced, peeled Granny Smith apples
    (about 2⅓ pounds or 7 medium apples)
½ cup granulated sugar
¼ cup firmly packed light brown sugar
¼ cup all-purpose flour
1 teaspoon ground cinnamon
½ cup butter or margarine, cut into pieces

Glaze
    Milk

1. For crust, prepare, roll and press bottom crust into 9-inch pie plate. Do not bake. Heat oven to 350°F.

2. For filling, place apple slices in unbaked pie crust. Combine granulated sugar, brown sugar and flour in small bowl. Sprinkle over apples. Sprinkle with cinnamon. Dot with butter. Moisten pastry edge with water.

3. Roll top crust same as bottom. Lift onto filled pie. Trim ½ inch beyond edge of pie plate. Fold top edge under bottom crust. Flute. Cut slits in top crust to allow steam to escape.

4. For glaze, brush top crust with milk.

5. Bake at 350°F for 1 hour or until filling in center is bubbly and crust is golden brown. DO NOT OVERBAKE. Cool to room temperature before serving. *Makes one 9-inch pie (8 servings)*

Black & White Brownie Bottom Pudding Pie

Very Cherry Pie

4 cups frozen unsweetened tart cherries
1 cup dried tart cherries
1 cup sugar
2 tablespoons quick-cooking tapioca
½ teaspoon almond extract
   Pastry for double-crust 9-inch pie
¼ teaspoon ground nutmeg
1 tablespoon butter

Combine frozen cherries, dried cherries, sugar, tapioca and almond extract in large mixing bowl; mix well. (It is not necessary to thaw cherries before using.) Let cherry mixture stand 15 minutes.

Line 9-inch pie plate with pastry; fill with cherry mixture. Sprinkle with nutmeg. Dot with butter. Cover with top crust, cutting slits for steam to escape. Or, cut top crust into strips for lattice top and cherry leaf cutouts.

Bake in preheated 375°F oven about 1 hour or until crust is golden brown and filling is bubbly. If necessary, cover edge of crust with foil to prevent overbrowning.   *Makes 8 servings*

Note: Two (16-ounce) cans unsweetened tart cherries, well drained, can be substituted for frozen tart cherries. Dried cherries are available at gourmet and specialty food stores and at selected supermarkets.

Favorite recipe from **Cherry Marketing Institute**

Fudge Brownie Pie

2 eggs
1 cup sugar
½ cup (1 stick) butter or margarine, melted
½ cup all-purpose flour
⅓ cup HERSHEY'S Cocoa
¼ teaspoon salt
1 teaspoon vanilla extract
½ cup chopped nuts (optional)
   Ice cream
   Hot Fudge Sauce (recipe follows)

1. Heat oven to 350°F. Lightly grease 8-inch pie plate.

2. Beat eggs in small bowl; blend in sugar and melted butter. Stir together flour, cocoa and salt; add to butter mixture. Stir in vanilla and nuts, if desired. Pour into prepared pie plate.

3. Bake 25 to 30 minutes or until almost set. (Pie will not test done in center.) Cool; cut into wedges. Serve topped with scoop of ice cream and drizzled with Hot Fudge Sauce.   *Makes 6 to 8 servings*

Hot Fudge Sauce: Stir together ¾ cup sugar and ½ cup HERSHEY'S Cocoa in small saucepan; blend in one 5-ounce can evaporated milk and ⅓ cup light corn syrup. Cook over medium heat, stirring constantly, until mixture boils; boil and stir 1 minute. Remove from heat; stir in ⅓ cup butter and 1 teaspoon vanilla extract. Serve warm. Makes about 1¾ cups sauce.

Very Cherry Pie

Orange Pecan Pie

3 eggs
½ cup GRANDMA'S® Molasses
½ cup light corn syrup
¼ cup orange juice
1 teaspoon grated orange peel
1 teaspoon vanilla
1½ cups whole pecan halves
1 (9-inch) unbaked pie shell
   Whipping cream (optional)

Heat oven to 350°F. In large bowl, beat eggs. Add molasses, corn syrup, orange juice, orange peel and vanilla; beat until well blended. Stir in pecans. Pour into unbaked pie shell. Bake 30 to 45 minutes or until filling sets. Cool on wire rack. Serve with whipping cream, if desired.   *Makes 8 servings*

Quick & Easy Chocolate Chip Cherry Pie

1 can (21 ounces) cherry pie filling
1 tablespoon cornstarch
1 extra serving-size packaged graham
   cracker crumb crust (9 ounces)
1 package (8 ounces) cream cheese,
   softened
¼ cup sugar
2 eggs
½ teaspoon vanilla extract
½ teaspoon almond extract
½ cup HERSHEY'S Semi-Sweet Chocolate
   Chips *or* HERSHEY'S MINI CHIPS™
   Semi-Sweet Chocolate Chips

1. Heat oven to 350°F.

2. Stir together pie filling and cornstarch in medium bowl until blended; pour into crust. Beat cream cheese, sugar, eggs, vanilla and almond extract in small bowl until blended; pour over pie filling. Sprinkle chocolate chips evenly over top.

3. Bake 35 to 40 minutes or until almost set in center. Cool completely on wire rack. Refrigerate until firm. Cover; refrigerate leftover pie.
     Makes 8 to 10 servings

Orange Pecan Pie

Grasshopper Mint Pie

Prep Time: 15 minutes
Chill Time: 3 hours

> 1 (8-ounce) package cream cheese, softened
> ⅓ cup sugar
> 1 (8-ounce) tub frozen whipped topping, thawed
> 1 cup chopped KEEBLER® Fudge Shoppe® Grasshopper Cookies
> 3 drops green food coloring
> 1 (6-ounce) READY CRUST® Chocolate Pie Crust
>   Additional KEEBLER® Fudge Shoppe® Grasshopper Cookies, halved, for garnish

1. Mix cream cheese and sugar with electric mixer until well blended. Fold in whipped topping, chopped cookies and green food coloring. Spoon into crust.

2. Refrigerate 3 hours or overnight.

3. Garnish with cookie halves. Refrigerate leftovers.

Makes 8 servings

Peachy Blueberry Pie

> 1 Classic CRISCO® Double Crust (page 320)
> 4 cups peeled and thinly sliced fresh ripe peaches
> 1½ cups fresh blueberries washed and well drained
> 1 cup plus 2 tablespoons granulated sugar, divided
> 2 teaspoons vanilla
> 2 tablespoons cornstarch
> ¼ cup milk

1. Heat oven to 350°F. Combine peaches, blueberries, 1 cup sugar, vanilla and cornstarch in large bowl. Mix gently until cornstarch is dissolved and fruit is well coated. Pour into crust. Moisten pastry edge with water. Cover pie with top crust. Trim ½ inch beyond edge of pie plate. Fold top edge under bottom crust; flute. Cut slits in top of crust to allow steam to escape.

2. Bake at 350°F for about 35 minutes. Remove from oven, brush top with milk and sprinkle with remaining 2 tablespoons sugar. Return to oven and continue to bake for an additional 15 to 20 minutes or until peach-blueberry mixture bubbles and crust is golden. Let rest 10 minutes before serving.

Makes 1 (9-inch) pie (8 servings)

Grasshopper Mint Pie

Triple Berry Spring Pie

Prep Time: 20 minutes
Chill Time: 3 hours

    3 cups assorted berries
    1 prepared graham cracker crumb or
        shortbread crumb crust (6 ounces
        or 9 inches)
 1½ cups orange juice
    ½ cup sugar
    2 tablespoons cornstarch
    1 package (4-serving size) JELL-O® Brand
        Gelatin, any red flavor
      Thawed COOL WHIP® Whipped Topping,
        optional

ARRANGE berries in bottom of crust.

MIX juice, sugar and cornstarch in medium
saucepan over medium heat. Cook on medium heat,
stirring constantly, until mixture comes to boil; boil
1 minute. Remove from heat. Stir in gelatin until
completely dissolved. Cool to room temperature.
Pour over berries in crust.

REFRIGERATE 3 hours or until firm. Garnish
with Whipped topping, if desired. Store leftover
pie in refrigerator.   *Makes 8 servings*

Cream Cheese Brownie Pie

Prep Time: 30 minutes
Bake Time: 45 minutes

    ½ package (15 ounces) refrigerated pie crust
    1 package (8 ounces) PHILADELPHIA®
        Cream Cheese, softened
    ¼ cup sugar
    3 eggs, divided
    6 squares BAKER'S® Semi-Sweet Baking
        Chocolate
    ½ cup (1 stick) butter *or* margarine
    ⅔ cup sugar
    1 teaspoon vanilla
    1 cup flour
    2 squares BAKER'S® Semi-Sweet Baking
        Chocolate, melted (optional)

HEAT oven to 350°F. Prepare crust as directed on
package, using 9-inch pie plate. Mix cream cheese,
¼ cup sugar and 1 egg in medium bowl until well
blended; set aside.

MICROWAVE chocolate and butter in large
microwavable bowl on HIGH 2 minutes or until
butter is melted. Stir until chocolate is completely
melted.

STIR ⅔ cup sugar into chocolate mixture until well
blended. Mix in 2 eggs and vanilla. Stir in flour until
well blended. Spread half of the brownie batter into
prepared crust. Carefully spread cream cheese
mixture over top. Top with remaining brownie
batter.

BAKE 45 minutes or until toothpick inserted
in center comes out with fudgy crumbs. Cool
completely on wire rack. Drizzle with melted
chocolate, if desired.   *Makes 10 servings*

Triple Berry Spring Pie

Easy Peanut Butter Chip Pie

1 package (3 ounces) cream cheese, softened
1 teaspoon lemon juice
1⅔ cups (10-ounce package) REESE'S® Peanut Butter Chips, divided
⅔ cup sweetened condensed milk (not evaporated milk)
1 cup (½ pint) cold whipping cream, divided
1 packaged chocolate or graham cracker crumb crust (6 ounces)
1 tablespoon powdered sugar
1 teaspoon vanilla extract

1. Beat cream cheese and lemon juice in medium bowl until fluffy, about 2 minutes; set aside.

2. Place 1 cup peanut butter chips and sweetened condensed milk in medium microwave-safe bowl. Microwave at HIGH (100%) 45 seconds; stir. If necessary, microwave an additional 15 seconds at a time, stirring after each heating, until chips are melted and mixture is smooth when stirred.

3. Add warm peanut butter mixture to cream cheese mixture. Beat on medium speed until blended, about 1 minute. Beat ½ cup whipping cream in small bowl until stiff; fold into peanut butter mixture. Pour into crust. Cover; refrigerate several hours or overnight until firm.

4. Just before serving, combine remaining ½ cup whipping cream, powdered sugar and vanilla in small bowl. Beat until stiff; spread over filling. Garnish with remaining peanut butter chips. Cover; refrigerate leftover pie. *Makes 6 to 8 servings*

Classic Crisco® Double Crust

2 cups all-purpose flour
1 teaspoon salt
¾ CRISCO® Stick or ¾ cup CRISCO® all-vegetable shortening
5 tablespoons cold water (or more as needed)

1. Spoon flour into measuring cup and level. Combine flour and salt in medium bowl.

2. Cut in ¾ cup shortening using pastry blender or 2 knives until all flour is blended to form pea-size chunks.

3. Sprinkle with water, 1 tablespoon at a time. Toss lightly with fork until dough forms a ball. Divide dough in half.

4. Press dough between hands to form 5- to 6-inch "pancake." Flour rolling surface and rolling pin lightly. Roll both halves of dough into circle. Trim one circle of dough 1 inch larger than upside-down pie plate. Carefully remove trimmed dough. Set aside to reroll and use for pastry cutout garnish, if desired.

5. Fold dough into quarters. Unfold and press into pie plate. Trim edge even with plate. Add desired filling to unbaked crust. Moisten pastry edge with water. Lift top crust onto filled pie. Trim ½ inch beyond edge of pie plate. Fold top edge under bottom crust. Flute. Cut slits in top crust to allow steam to escape. Follow baking directions given for that recipe. *Makes 1 (9-inch) double crust*

Easy Peanut Butter Chip Pie

Apple-Raisin Cobbler Pie

Prep Time: 10 minutes
Bake Time: 35 minutes

  2 (20-ounce) cans apple pie filling
  1 cup raisins
  ¼ teaspoon ground nutmeg
  1 (6-ounce) READY CRUST® Shortbread
     Pie Crust
  ⅓ cup all-purpose flour
  ¼ cup packed brown sugar
  3 tablespoons butter or margarine, melted
  ¾ cup chopped walnuts

1. Preheat oven to 375°F.

2. Combine pie filling, raisins and nutmeg in large
bowl. Spoon into crust. Combine flour and sugar
in small bowl; stir in butter until crumbly. Stir in
walnuts; sprinkle over filling.

3. Bake 35 to 45 minutes or until topping is golden.
Makes 8 servings

Sweet Potato Pecan Pie

  1 pound sweet potatoes or yams,
     cooked and peeled
  ¼ cup (½ stick) butter or margarine,
     softened
  1 (14-ounce) can EAGLE® BRAND
     Sweetened Condensed Milk
     (NOT evaporated milk)
  1 egg
  1 teaspoon grated orange peel
  1 teaspoon ground cinnamon
  1 teaspoon vanilla extract
  ½ teaspoon ground nutmeg
  ¼ teaspoon salt
  1 (6-ounce) graham cracker crumb
     pie crust
  Pecan Topping (recipe follows)

1. Preheat oven to 425°F. In large mixing bowl,
beat hot sweet potatoes and butter until smooth.
Add Eagle Brand and remaining ingredients except
crust and Pecan Topping; mix well. Pour into crust.

2. Bake 20 minutes. Meanwhile, prepare Pecan
Topping.

3. Remove pie from oven; reduce oven temperature
to 350°F. Spoon Pecan Topping over pie.

4. Bake 25 minutes longer or until set. Cool. Serve
warm or at room temperature. Garnish, if desired.
Refrigerate leftovers. *Makes 1 pie*

Pecan Topping: In small mixing bowl, beat 1 egg,
2 tablespoons firmly packed light brown sugar,
2 tablespoons dark corn syrup, 1 tablespoon melted
butter and ½ teaspoon maple flavoring. Stir in 1 cup
chopped pecans.

Apple-Raisin Cobbler Pie

Rustic Apple Croustade

1⅓ cups all-purpose flour
¼ teaspoon salt
2 tablespoons margarine or butter
2 tablespoons vegetable shortening
4 to 5 tablespoons ice water
⅓ cup packed light brown sugar
1 tablespoon cornstarch
1 teaspoon cinnamon, divided
3 large Jonathan or MacIntosh apples
  peeled, cored and thinly sliced (4 cups)
1 egg white, beaten
1 tablespoon granulated sugar

1. Combine flour and salt in small bowl. Cut in margarine and shortening with pastry blender or two knives until mixture resembles coarse crumbs. Mix in ice water, 1 tablespoon at a time, until mixture comes together and forms a soft dough. Wrap in plastic wrap; refrigerate 30 minutes.

2. Preheat oven to 375°F. Roll out pastry on floured surface to ⅛-inch thickness. Cut into 12-inch circle. Transfer pastry to nonstick jelly-roll pan.

3. Combine brown sugar, cornstarch and ¾ teaspoon cinnamon in medium bowl; mix well. Add apples; toss well. Spoon apple mixture into center of pastry, leaving 1½-inch border. Fold pastry over apples, folding edges in gently and pressing down lightly. Brush egg white over pastry. Combine remaining ¼ teaspoon cinnamon and granulated sugar in small bowl; sprinkle evenly over tart.

4. Bake 35 to 40 minutes or until apples are tender and crust is golden brown. Let stand 20 minutes before cutting into wedges. *Makes 8 servings*

Peanut Butter Magic Pie

Prep Time: 15 minutes
Chill Time: 4 hours

1 (8-ounce) package cream cheese, softened
¾ cup honey
1 (16-ounce) jar creamy or chunky peanut
  butter
1 (8-ounce) tub frozen non-dairy whipped
  topping, thawed
1 (6-ounce) READY CRUST® Chocolate
  Pie Crust
2 (1-ounce) squares semi-sweet baking
  chocolate
½ teaspoon shortening

1. Beat cream cheese and honey in medium bowl until well combined. Stir in peanut butter; mix well. Fold in whipped topping. Spoon into crust.

2. Heat chocolate and shortening in small saucepan over low heat until melted; drizzle over pie.

3. Chill 4 hours or overnight. Refrigerate leftovers.
Makes 8 servings

Rustic Apple Croustade

Chocolate, Chocolate, Chocolate!

Chocolate Peanut Butter Chip Cookies

Prep Time: 15 minutes
Bake Time: 6 to 8 minutes

8 (1-ounce) squares semi-sweet chocolate
3 tablespoons butter or margarine
1 (14-ounce) can EAGLE® BRAND Sweetened Condensed Milk
   (NOT evaporated milk)
2 cups biscuit baking mix
1 egg
1 teaspoon vanilla extract
1 cup (6 ounces) peanut butter-flavored chips

1. Preheat oven to 350°F. In large saucepan over low heat, melt chocolate and butter with Eagle Brand; remove from heat. Add biscuit mix, egg and vanilla; with mixer, beat until smooth and well blended.

2. Let mixture cool to room temperature. Stir in peanut butter chips. Shape into 1¼-inch balls. Place 2 inches apart on ungreased baking sheets. Bake 6 to 8 minutes or until tops are lightly crusty. Cool. Store tightly covered at room temperature.

Makes about 4 dozen cookies

Chocolate Peanut Butter Chip Cookies

Chocolate Fudge Pie

Prep Time: about 30 minutes
Bake Time: about 40 minutes

    ¼ cup CRISCO® all-vegetable shortening or
        ¼ CRISCO® Stick
    1 bar (4 ounces) sweet baking chocolate
    1 can (14 ounces) sweetened condensed
        milk
    2 eggs, beaten
    ½ cup all-purpose flour
    1 teaspoon vanilla
    ¼ teaspoon salt
    1 cup flaked coconut
    1 cup chopped pecans
    1 unbaked Classic CRISCO® Single Crust
        (recipe follows)
        Unsweetened whipped cream or ice
        cream

1. Heat oven to 350°F.

2. Melt ¼ cup shortening and chocolate in heavy saucepan over low heat. Remove from heat. Stir in sweetened condensed milk, eggs, flour, vanilla and salt; mix well. Stir in coconut and nuts. Pour into unbaked pie crust.

3. Bake at 350°F for 40 minutes or until wooden pick inserted into center comes out clean. Cool completely on cooling rack before cutting.

4. Serve with unsweetened whipped cream or ice cream, if desired. Refrigerate leftover pie.

Makes 1 (9-inch) pie (8 servings)

Classic Crisco® Single Crust

    1⅓ cups all-purpose flour
    ½ teaspoon salt
    ½ CRISCO® Stick or ½ cup CRISCO®
        all-vegetable Shortening
    3 tablespoons cold water

1. Spoon flour into measuring cup and level. Combine flour and salt in medium bowl.

2. Cut in ½ cup shortening using pastry blender or 2 knives until all flour is blended to form pea-size chunks.

3. Sprinkle with water, 1 tablespoon at a time. Toss lightly with fork until dough forms a ball.

4. Press dough between hands to form 5- to 6-inch "pancake." Flour rolling surface and rolling pin lightly. Roll dough into circle. Trim 1 inch larger than upside-down pie plate. Loosen dough carefully.

5. Fold dough into quarters. Unfold and press into pie plate. Fold edge under. Flute.

Makes 8- to 9-inch single crust

Chocolate Fudge Pie

Wellesley Fudge Cake

Prep Time: 30 minutes
Bake Time: 35 minutes

    4 squares BAKER'S® Unsweetened Baking
        Chocolate
 1¾ cups sugar, divided
    ½ cup water
 1⅔ cups flour
    1 teaspoon baking soda
    ¼ teaspoon salt
    ½ cup (1 stick) butter *or* margarine,
        softened
    3 eggs
    ¾ cup milk
    1 teaspoon vanilla
        Chocolate Fudge Frosting (recipe follows)

HEAT oven to 350°F. Grease and flour 2 (9-inch) round cake pans.

MICROWAVE chocolate, ½ cup of the sugar and water in large microwavable bowl on HIGH 2 minutes or until chocolate is almost melted. Stir until chocolate is completely melted. Cool to lukewarm.

MIX flour, baking soda and salt; set aside. Beat butter and remaining 1¼ cups sugar in large bowl with electric mixer on medium speed until light and fluffy. Add eggs, 1 at a time, beating well after each addition. Add flour mixture alternately with milk, beating after each addition until smooth. Stir in chocolate mixture and vanilla. Pour into prepared pans.

BAKE 30 to 35 minutes or until cake springs back when lightly touched. Cool cakes in pans 10 minutes; remove from pans. Cool completely on wire racks. Fill and frost with Chocolate Fudge Frosting. *Makes 12 to 16 servings*

Melting Chocolate on Top of Stove: Heat chocolate and water in heavy 1-quart saucepan on very low heat, stirring constantly until chocolate is melted and mixture is smooth. Add ½ cup sugar; cook and stir 2 minutes. Cool to lukewarm. Continue as directed above.

Chocolate Fudge Frosting

    4 squares BAKER'S® Unsweetened Baking
        Chocolate
    1 package (16 ounces) powdered sugar
        (about 4 cups)
    ½ cup (1 stick) butter *or* margarine,
        softened
    2 teaspoon vanilla
    ⅓ cup milk

MICROWAVE chocolate in small microwavable bowl on HIGH 2 minutes. Stir until chocolate is melted and smooth. Cool 5 minutes or to room temperature.

ADD sugar, butter and vanilla. Gradually beat in milk with electric mixer on low speed until well blended. If frosting becomes too thick, beat in additional milk by teaspoonfuls until of spreading consistency. *Makes 3 cups*

Super Chocolate Cookies

2 cups all-purpose flour
⅓ cup unsweetened cocoa powder
1 teaspoon baking soda
½ teaspoon salt
½ cup butter, softened
½ cup shortening
1⅓ cups packed brown sugar
2 eggs
2 teaspoons vanilla
1 cup candy-coated chocolate pieces
1 cup raisins
¾ cup salted peanuts, coarsely chopped

1. Preheat oven to 350°F. Combine flour, cocoa, baking soda and salt in medium bowl; set aside.

2. Beat butter, shortening and brown sugar in large bowl of electric mixer at medium speed until light and fluffy. Beat in eggs and vanilla until well blended. Gradually add flour mixture, beating at low speed until blended. Stir in candy pieces, raisins and peanuts.

3. Drop dough by ¼ cupfuls onto ungreased cookie sheets, spacing 3 inches apart. Flatten slightly with fingertips. Bake cookies 13 to 15 minutes or until almost set. Cool 2 minutes on cookie sheets. Transfer to wire racks. Cool completely.

Makes 18 to 20 (4-inch) cookies

Chocolate Marshmallow Thumbprints

¾ cup (1½ sticks) butter, softened
½ cup granulated sugar
1 large egg
1 teaspoon vanilla extract
1½ cups all-purpose flour
2 tablespoons unsweetened cocoa powder
¼ teaspoon salt
1¼ cups "M&M's"® Chocolate Mini Baking Bits, divided
¼ cup marshmallow cream
¼ cup vanilla frosting

Preheat oven to 350°F. Lightly grease cookie sheets; set aside. In large bowl cream butter and sugar until light and fluffy; beat in egg and vanilla. In medium bowl combine flour, cocoa powder and salt; add to creamed mixture. Stir in 1 cup "M&M's"® Chocolate Mini Baking Bits. Roll dough into 1-inch balls and place about 2 inches apart on prepared cookie sheets. Make indentation in center of each ball with thumb. Bake 10 minutes. Remove from oven and re-indent; bake 1 minute. Cool completely on wire racks. In small bowl combine marshmallow cream and frosting. Fill each indentation with about ½ teaspoon marshmallow mixture. Sprinkle with remaining ¼ cup "M&M's"® Chocolate Mini Baking Bits. Store between layers of waxed paper in tightly covered container. *Makes 3 dozen cookies*

Super Chocolate Cookies

Lots o' Chocolate Bread

⅔ cup packed light brown sugar
½ cup butter, softened
1½ cups miniature semi-sweet chocolate chips, divided
2 eggs
2½ cups all-purpose flour
1½ cups applesauce
1 teaspoon baking soda
1 teaspoon baking powder
½ teaspoon salt
1½ teaspoons vanilla
½ cup chocolate chips
1 tablespoon shortening (do not use butter, margarine, spread or oil)

Preheat oven to 350°F. Grease 5 (5½×3-inch) mini loaf pans. Beat brown sugar and butter in large bowl with electric mixer until creamy. Melt 1 cup miniature chocolate chips; cool slightly and add to sugar mixture with eggs. Add flour, applesauce, baking soda, baking powder, salt and vanilla; beat until well mixed. Stir in remaining ½ cup miniature chocolate chips. Spoon batter into prepared pans; bake 35 to 40 minutes or until center crack is dry to the touch. Cool 10 minutes before removing from pans.

Place ½ cup chocolate chips and shortening in small microwavable bowl. Microwave at HIGH 1 minute; stir. If neccesary, microwave at HIGH an additional 15 seconds at a time, stirring after each heating. Drizzle warm loaves with glaze. Cool completely.

Makes 5 mini loaves

Double Chocolate Dream Cookies

2¼ cups all-purpose flour
½ cup NESTLÉ® TOLL HOUSE® Baking Cocoa
1 teaspoon baking soda
½ teaspoon salt
1 cup (2 sticks) butter or margarine, softened
1 cup packed brown sugar
¾ cup granulated sugar
1 teaspoon vanilla extract
2 large eggs
2 cups (12-ounce package) NESTLÉ® TOLL HOUSE® Semi-Sweet Chocolate Morsels

PREHEAT oven to 375°F.

COMBINE flour, cocoa, baking soda and salt in small bowl. Beat butter, brown sugar, granulated sugar and vanilla extract in large mixer bowl until creamy. Beat in eggs for about 2 minutes or until light and fluffy. Gradually beat in flour mixture. Stir in morsels. Drop by rounded tablespoon onto ungreased baking sheets.

BAKE for 8 to 10 minutes or until cookies are puffed. Cool on baking sheets for 2 minutes; remove to wire racks to cool completely.

Makes about 4½ dozen cookies

Triple Chocolate Brownies

3 squares (1 ounce each) unsweetened
    chocolate, coarsely chopped
2 squares (1 ounce each) semisweet
    chocolate, coarsely chopped
½ cup butter
1 cup all-purpose flour
½ teaspoon salt
¼ teaspoon baking powder
1½ cups sugar
3 large eggs
1 teaspoon vanilla
¼ cup sour cream
½ cup milk chocolate chips
    Powdered sugar (optional)

Preheat oven to 350°F. Lightly grease 13×9-inch baking pan. Place unsweetened chocolate, semisweet chocolate and butter in medium microwavable bowl. Microwave at HIGH 2 minutes or until butter is melted; stir until chocolate is completely melted. Cool to room temperature.

Place flour, salt and baking powder in small bowl; stir to combine. Beat sugar, eggs and vanilla in large bowl with electric mixer at medium speed until slightly thickened. Beat in chocolate mixture until well combined. Add flour mixture; beat at low speed until blended. Add sour cream; beat at low speed until combined. Stir in milk chocolate chips. Spread mixture evenly into prepared pan.

Bake 20 to 25 minutes or until toothpick inserted into center comes out almost clean. (Do not overbake.) Cool completely in pan on wire rack. Cut into 2-inch squares; sprinkle with powdered sugar, if desired. Store tightly covered at room temperature or freeze up to 3 months.

Makes 2 dozen brownies

Chocolate Pecan Pie Bars

2 cups flour
2 cups sugar, divided
1 cup (2 sticks) butter *or* margarine,
    softened
¼ teaspoon salt
1½ cups corn syrup
6 squares BAKER'S® Semi-Sweet
    Baking Chocolate
4 eggs, slightly beaten
1½ teaspoons vanilla
2½ cups chopped pecans

HEAT oven to 350°F. Lightly grease sides of 15×10×1-inch baking pan.

BEAT flour, ½ cup of the sugar, butter and salt in large bowl with electric mixer on medium speed until mixture resembles coarse crumbs. Press firmly and evenly into prepared baking pan. Bake 20 minutes or until lightly browned.

MICROWAVE corn syrup and chocolate in large microwavable bowl on HIGH 2½ minutes or until chocolate is almost melted, stirring halfway through heating time. Stir until chocolate is completely melted. Mix in remaining 1½ cups sugar, eggs and vanilla until blended. Stir in pecans. Pour filling over hot crust; spread evenly.

BAKE 35 minutes or until filling is firm around edges and slightly soft in center. Cool completely in pan on wire rack. *Makes 48 bars*

Melting Chocolate on Top of Stove: Heat corn syrup and chocolate in heavy 3-quart saucepan on very low heat, stirring constantly until chocolate is just melted. Remove from heat. Continue as directed above.

Triple Chocolate Brownies

Double Chocolate Cranberry Chunkies

1¾ cups all-purpose flour
⅓ cup unsweetened cocoa powder
½ teaspoon baking powder
½ teaspoon salt
1 cup butter, softened
1 cup granulated sugar
½ cup packed brown sugar
1 egg
1 teaspoon vanilla
2 cups semisweet chocolate chunks
   or large chocolate chips
¾ cup dried cranberries or dried tart
   cherries
Additional granulated sugar

1. Preheat oven to 350°F.

2. Combine flour, cocoa, baking powder and salt in small bowl; set aside. Beat butter, 1 cup granulated sugar and brown sugar in large bowl of electric mixer at medium speed until light and fluffy. Beat in egg and vanilla until well blended. Gradually beat in flour mixture on low speed until blended. Stir in chocolate chunks and cranberries.

3. Drop dough by level ¼ cupfuls onto ungreased cookie sheets, spacing 3 inches apart. Flatten dough until 2 inches in diameter with bottom of glass that has been dipped in additional granulated sugar.

4. Bake 11 to 12 minutes or until cookies are set. Cool cookies 2 minutes on cookie sheets; transfer to wire racks. Cool completely.

Makes about 1 dozen (4-inch) cookies

Chocolate Peanut Butter Bars

Prep Time: 20 minutes
Bake Time: 20 minutes

1½ cups chocolate-covered graham cracker
   crumbs (about 17 crackers)
3 tablespoons butter *or* margarine, melted
1 package (8 ounces) PHILADELPHIA®
   Cream Cheese, softened
½ cup crunchy peanut butter
1 cup powdered sugar
2 squares BAKER'S® Semi-Sweet
   Baking Chocolate
1 teaspoon butter or margarine

MIX crumbs and 3 tablespoons melted butter. Press onto bottom of 9-inch square baking pan. Bake at 350°F for 20 minutes. Cool.

BEAT cream cheese, peanut butter and sugar with electric mixer on medium speed until well blended. Spoon over crust.

MICROWAVE chocolate with 1 teaspoon butter on HIGH 1 to 2 minutes or until chocolate begins to melt, stirring halfway through heating time. Stir until chocolate is completely melted. Drizzle over cream cheese mixture.

REFRIGERATE 6 hours or overnight. Cut into squares. Store in airtight container in refrigerator.

Makes 18 servings

Double Chocolate Cranberry Chunkies

Decadent Triple Layer Mud Pie

Prep Time: 10 minutes
Chill Time: 3 hours

- ¼ cup sweetened condensed milk
- 2 (1-ounce) squares semi-sweet baking chocolate, melted
- 1 (6-ounce) READY CRUST® Chocolate Pie Crust
- ¾ cup chopped pecans, toasted
- 2 cups cold milk
- 2 (4-serving-size) packages JELL-O® Chocolate Flavor Instant Pudding & Pie Filling
- 1 (8-ounce) tub COOL WHIP® Whipped Topping, thawed, divided

1. Combine sweetened condensed milk and chocolate in medium bowl; stir until smooth. Pour into crust. Press nuts evenly onto chocolate mixture in crust. Refrigerate 10 minutes.

2. Pour milk into large bowl. Add pudding mixes. Beat with wire whisk 2 minutes or until smooth. (Mixture will be thick.) Spread 1½ cups pudding over chocolate mixture in crust. Immediately stir half of whipped topping into remaining pudding. Spread over pudding in crust. Top with remaining whipped topping.

3. Refrigerate 3 hours or until set. Garnish as desired. Refrigerate leftovers.   *Makes 8 servings*

Chocolate Chip Chocolate Cookies

- ½ cup (1 stick) butter or margarine, softened
- 1 cup sugar
- 1 egg
- 1 teaspoon vanilla extract
- 1½ cups all-purpose flour
- ⅓ cup HERSHEY'S Cocoa
- ½ teaspoon baking soda
- ½ teaspoon salt
- ¼ cup milk
- 1 cup HERSHEY'S Semi-Sweet Chocolate Chips

1. Heat oven to 375°F.

2. Beat butter, sugar, egg and vanilla in large bowl until fluffy. Combine flour, cocoa, baking soda and salt; add alternately with milk to butter mixture, blending well. Stir in chocolate chips. Drop by rounded teaspoons onto ungreased cookie sheets.

3. Bake 8 to 10 minutes or until set. *Do not overbake.* Cool 1 minute. Remove from cookie sheets; cool completely on wire racks.

Makes about 3½ dozen cookies

Decadent Triple Layer Mud Pie

Dark Chocolate Dreams

16 ounces bittersweet chocolate candy bars
    or bittersweet chocolate chips
¼ cup butter
½ cup all-purpose flour
¾ teaspoon ground cinnamon
½ teaspoon baking powder
¼ teaspoon salt
1½ cups sugar
3 eggs
1 teaspoon vanilla
1 package (12 ounces) white chocolate chips
1 cup chopped pecans, lightly toasted

1. Preheat oven to 350°F. Grease cookie sheets.

2. Coarsely chop chocolate bars; place in microwavable bowl. Add butter. Microwave at HIGH 2 minutes; stir. Microwave 1 to 2 minutes, stirring after 1 minute, or until chocolate is melted. Cool to lukewarm.

3. Combine flour, cinnamon, baking powder and salt in small bowl; set aside.

4. Combine sugar, eggs and vanilla in large bowl of electric mixer. Beat at medium-high speed until very thick and mixture turns a pale color, about 6 minutes.

5. Reduce speed to low; slowly beat in chocolate mixture until well blended. Gradually beat in flour mixture until blended. Fold in white chocolate chips and pecans.

6. Drop batter by level ⅓ cupfuls onto prepared cookie sheets, spacing 3 inches apart. Place piece of plastic wrap over dough; flatten dough with fingertips to form 4-inch circles. Remove plastic wrap.

7. Bake 12 minutes or until just firm to the touch and surface begins to crack. *Do not overbake.* Cool cookies 2 minutes on cookie sheets; transfer to wire racks. Cool completely.

Makes 10 to 12 (5-inch) cookies

Note: Cookies may be baked on ungreased cookie sheets lined with parchment paper. Cool cookies 2 minutes on cookie sheets; slide parchment paper and cookies onto countertop. Cool completely.

Tip

Bittersweet chocolate is pure chocolate with some sugar added. It is available in specialty food shops and some supermarkets, packaged in 1-ounced squares. If unavailable, substitute half unsweetened chocolate and half semisweet chocolate.

Dark Chocolate Dreams

White Chocolate Brownie Drops

½ **Butter Flavor CRISCO® Stick or**
  ½ **cup Butter Flavor CRISCO®**
  all-vegetable shortening
½ **cup sugar**
2 **eggs**
1 **teaspoon vanilla**
1 **cup (6-ounce package) semi-sweet**
  chocolate chips, melted (see Tip)
1 **cup oats (quick or old-fashioned,**
  uncooked)
¾ **cup all-purpose flour**
1 **teaspoon baking powder**
½ **cup vanilla milk chips**

1. Heat oven to 350°F. Place sheets of foil on countertop for cooling cookies.

2. Combine ½ cup shortening, sugar, eggs and vanilla in large bowl. Beat at medium speed of electric mixer until well blended. Add melted chocolate chips.

3. Combine oats, flour and baking powder. Add gradually to creamed mixture at low speed. Beat just until blended. Stir in vanilla milk chips with spoon. Drop by rounded teaspoonfuls 2 inches apart onto ungreased baking sheet.

4. Bake at 350°F for 7 to 9 minutes or until cookies are almost set. (Centers will still be moist. *Do not overbake*.) Cool 2 minutes on baking sheet. Remove cookies to foil to cool completely.

Makes about 3 dozen cookies

Tip: For melting or drizzling, choose one of these easy methods. Start with chips and Butter Flavor Crisco (if called for), then place in a small microwave-safe measuring cup or bowl. Microwave at 50% (MEDIUM). Stir after 1 minute. Repeat until smooth. Or, place in chips and Butter Flavor Crisco in a small saucepan. Melt on rangetop over very low heat. Stir until smooth.

Cracked Chocolate Cookies

1½ cups firmly packed light brown sugar
⅔ CRISCO® Stick or ⅔ cup CRISCO®
    all-vegetable shortening
1 tablespoon water
1 teaspoon vanilla
2 eggs
1½ cups all-purpose flour
⅓ cup unsweetened cocoa powder
½ teaspoon salt
¼ teaspoon baking soda
2 cups (12 ounces) miniature semisweet
    chocolate chips
1 cup confectioners' sugar

1. Heat oven to 375°F. Place sheets of foil on countertop for cooling cookies.

2. Place brown sugar, ⅔ cup shortening, water and vanilla in large bowl. Beat at medium speed of electric mixer until well blended. Add eggs; beat well.

3. Combine flour, cocoa, salt and baking soda. Add to shortening mixture; beat at low speed just until blended. Stir in miniature chocolate chips.

4. Shape dough into 1¼-inch balls. Roll in confectioners' sugar. Place 2 inches apart on ungreased baking sheet.

5. Bake one baking sheet at a time at 375°F for 7 to 9 minutes or until cookies are set. *Do not overbake.* Cool 2 minutes on baking sheet. Remove cookies to foil to cool completely.

Makes about 4 dozen cookies

Double Chocolate Fantasy Bars

Prep Time: 15 minutes
Bake Time: 25 to 30 minutes

1 (18.25-ounce) package chocolate cake mix
¼ cup vegetable oil
1 egg
1 cup chopped nuts
1 (14-ounce) can EAGLE® BRAND
    Sweetened Condensed Milk
    (NOT evaporated milk)
1 (6-ounce) package semi-sweet chocolate
    chips
1 teaspoon vanilla extract
    Dash salt

1. Preheat oven to 350°F. Grease 13×9-inch baking pan. In large mixing bowl, combine cake mix, oil and egg; beat at medium speed until crumbly. Stir in nuts. Reserve 1½ cups crumb mixture. Press remaining crumb mixture firmly on bottom of prepared pan.

2. In small saucepan over medium heat, combine remaining ingredients. Cook and stir until chips melt.

3. Pour chocolate mixture evenly over prepared crust. Sprinkle reserved crumb mixture evenly over top. Bake 25 to 30 minutes or until set. Cool. Cut into bars. Store loosely covered at room temperature.

Makes 36 bars

Triple Chocolate Cake

¾ cup butter, softened
1½ cups sugar
1 egg
1 teaspoon vanilla
2 cups all-purpose flour
⅔ cup unsweetened cocoa powder
2 teaspoons baking soda
¼ teaspoon salt
1 cup buttermilk
¾ cup sour cream
Chocolate Ganache Filling (recipe follows)
Easy Chocolate Frosting (recipe follows)

Preheat oven to 350°F. Grease and flour two 9-inch round cake pans. Beat butter and sugar in large bowl with electric mixer at medium speed until light and fluffy. Beat in egg and vanilla until blended. Combine flour, cocoa, baking soda and salt in medium bowl. Add flour mixture to butter mixture alternately with buttermilk and sour cream, beginning and ending with flour mixture. Beat well after each addition. Divide batter evenly between prepared pans.

Bake 30 to 35 minutes or until wooden toothpick inserted in centers comes out clean. Cool in pans 10 minutes. Remove from pans to wire racks; cool completely. Cut each cake layer in half horizontally.

Meanwhile, prepare Chocolate Ganache Filling. Place one cake layer on serving plate. Spread with ⅓ of filling. Repeat layers two more times. Top with remaining cake layer. Prepare Easy Chocolate Frosting; spread over cake. Garnish as desired.

Makes 1 (9-inch) layer cake

Chocolate Ganache Filling: Heat ¾ cup heavy cream, 1 tablespoon butter and 1 tablespoon granulated sugar to a boil; stir until sugar is dissolved. Place 1½ cups semisweet chocolate chips in medium bowl; pour cream mixture over chocolate and let stand 5 minutes. Stir until smooth; let stand 15 minutes or until filling reaches desired consistency. (Filling will thicken as it cools.) Makes about 1½ cups.

Easy Chocolate Frosting: Beat ½ cup softened butter in large bowl with electric mixer at medium speed until creamy. Add 4 cups powdered sugar and ¾ cup cocoa alternately with ½ cup milk; beat until smooth. Stir in 1½ teaspoons vanilla. Makes about 3 cups.

Triple Chocolate Cake

Marvelous Cookie Bars

½ cup (1 stick) butter or margarine,
   softened
1 cup firmly packed light brown sugar
2 large eggs
1⅓ cups all-purpose flour
1 cup quick-cooking or old-fashioned oats,
   uncooked
⅓ cup unsweetened cocoa powder
1 teaspoon baking powder
½ teaspoon salt
¼ teaspoon baking soda
½ cup chopped walnuts, divided
1 cup "M&M's"® Semi-Sweet Chocolate
   Mini Baking Bits, divided
½ cup cherry preserves
¼ cup shredded coconut

Preheat oven to 350°F. Lightly grease 9×9×2-inch baking pan; set aside. In large bowl cream butter and sugar until light and fluffy; beat in eggs. In medium bowl combine flour, oats, cocoa powder, baking powder, salt and baking soda; blend into creamed mixture. Stir in ¼ cup nuts and ¾ cup "M&M's"® Semi-Sweet Chocolate Mini Baking Bits. Reserve 1 cup dough; spread remaining dough into prepared pan. Combine preserves, coconut and remaining ¼ cup nuts; spread evenly over dough to within ½ inch of edge. Drop reserved dough by rounded teaspoonfuls over preserves mixture; sprinkle with remaining ¼ cup "M&M's"® Semi-Sweet Chocolate Mini Baking Bits. Bake 25 to 30 minutes or until slightly firm near edges. Cool completely. Cut into bars. Store in tightly covered container.

Makes 16 bars

Chocolate Bursts

6 squares (1 ounce each) semisweet
   chocolate
½ cup (1 stick) I CAN'T BELIEVE IT'S
   NOT BUTTER!® Spread
¾ cup sugar
2 eggs
⅓ cup all-purpose flour
¼ cup unsweetened cocoa powder
1½ teaspoons vanilla extract
1 teaspoon baking powder
¼ teaspoon salt
2 cups coarsely chopped pecans or walnuts
1 cup semisweet chocolate chips

Preheat oven to 325°F. Grease baking sheets; set aside.

In medium microwave-safe bowl, heat chocolate squares and I Can't Believe It's Not Butter! Spread on HIGH (Full Power) 1 to 2 minutes or until chocolate is almost melted. Stir until completely melted.

In large bowl, with electric mixer, beat sugar and eggs until light and ribbony, about 2 minutes. Beat in chocolate mixture, flour, cocoa, vanilla, baking powder and salt, scraping side occasionally, until well blended. Stir in nuts and chocolate chips. Drop dough by rounded tablespoonfuls onto prepared sheets, about 2 inches apart.

Bake 15 minutes or until cookies are just set. On wire rack, let stand 2 minutes; remove from sheets and cool completely.

Makes about 3 dozen cookies

Marvelous Cookie Bars

Death By Chocolate Cookies

Prep Time: 15 minutes
Bake Time: 13 to 14 minutes

> 2 packages (8 squares each) BAKER'S®
>   Semi-Sweet Baking Chocolate, divided
> ¾ cup firmly packed brown sugar
> ¼ cup (½ stick) butter *or* margarine
> 2 eggs
> 1 teaspoon vanilla
> ½ cup flour
> ¼ teaspoon CALUMET® Baking Powder
> 2 cups chopped nuts (optional)

HEAT oven to 350°F. Coarsely chop 8 squares (1 package) of the chocolate; set aside.

MICROWAVE remaining 8 squares chocolate in large microwavable bowl on HIGH 2 minutes. Stir until chocolate is melted and smooth. Stir in sugar, butter, eggs and vanilla with wooden spoon until well blended. Stir in flour and baking powder. Stir in reserved chopped chocolate and nuts. Drop by scant ¼ cupfuls onto ungreased cookie sheets.

BAKE 13 to 14 minutes or until cookies are puffed and feel set to the touch. Cool on cookie sheet 1 minute. Remove to wire racks and cool completely.
Makes about 18 large cookies

Note: If omitting nuts, increase flour to ¾ cup to prevent spreading. Makes about 15 large cookies.

Everything-But-The-Kitchen-Sink Cookies:
Prepare as directed, substituting 2 cups total of any of the following for the nuts: raisins, toasted BAKER'S® ANGEL FLAKE® Coconut, dried cherries, chopped macadamia nuts, dried cranberries, toasted slivered almonds, dried chopped apricots, or dried mixed fruit bits.

Bar Cookies: Spread dough in greased, foil-lined 13×9-inch baking pan. Bake at 350°F for 22 to 24 minutes. Cool completely in pan on wire rack. Makes 2 dozen.

Smaller Cookies: Drop by heaping tablespoonfuls onto ungreased cookie sheets. Bake at 350°F for 12 to 13 minutes. Makes about 2½ dozen smaller cookies.

Make Ahead: After cookies are completely cooled, wrap in plastic wrap and place in an airtight plastic container or freezer zipper-style plastic bag. Freeze cookies up to 1 month. Bring cookies to room temperature before serving.

Freezing Cookie Dough: Freeze ¼ cupfuls of cookie dough on cookie sheet 1 hour. Transfer to airtight plastic container or freezer zipper-style plastic bag. Freeze dough up to 1 month. Bake frozen cookie dough on ungreased cookie sheet at 350°F for 20 to 23 minutes.

Death By Chocolate Cookies

Chocolate Bar Filled Chocolate Cupcakes

    Chocolate Bar Filling (recipe follows)
   3 cups all-purpose flour
   2 cups sugar
   ⅔ cup HERSHEY'S Cocoa
   2 teaspoons baking soda
   1 teaspoon salt
   2 cups water
   ⅔ cup vegetable oil
   2 tablespoons white vinegar
   2 teaspoons vanilla extract
   2 HERSHEY'S Milk Chocolate Bars
      (7 ounces *each*), broken into pieces

1. Prepare Chocolate Bar Filling.

2. Heat oven to 350°F. Line muffin cups (2½ inches in diameter) with paper bake cups.

3. Stir together flour, sugar, cocoa, baking soda and salt in large bowl. Add water, oil, vinegar and vanilla; beat on medium speed of mixer 2 minutes. Fill muffin cups ⅔ full with batter. Spoon 1 level tablespoon prepared filling into center of each cupcake.

4. Bake 20 to 25 minutes or until wooden pick inserted in cake portion comes out clean. Remove from pans to wire racks. Cool completely. Top each cupcake with chocolate bar piece.

Makes about 2½ dozen cupcakes

Chocolate Bar Filling

   1 package (8 ounces) cream cheese,
      softened
   ⅓ cup sugar
   1 egg
   ⅛ teaspoon salt
   1 HERSHEY'S Milk Chocolate Bar
      (7 ounces), cut into ¼-inch pieces

1. Beat cream cheese, sugar, egg and salt in small bowl until smooth and creamy. Stir in chocolate bar pieces.

Chocolate Streusel Bars

Prep Time: 15 minutes
Bake Time: 40 minutes

1¾ cups all-purpose flour
1½ cups powdered sugar
½ cup unsweetened cocoa
1 cup (2 sticks) cold butter or margarine
1 (8-ounce) package cream cheese, softened
1 (14-ounce) can EAGLE® BRAND
   Sweetened Condensed Milk
   (NOT evaporated milk)
1 egg
2 teaspoons vanilla extract
½ cup chopped walnuts

1. Preheat oven to 350°F. In large mixing bowl, combine flour, sugar and cocoa; cut in butter until crumbly (mixture will be dry). Reserve 2 cups crumb mixture. Press remaining crumb mixture firmly on bottom of ungreased 13×9-inch baking pan. Bake 15 minutes.

2. Meanwhile, in large mixing bowl, beat cream cheese until fluffy. Gradually beat in Eagle Brand until smooth. Add egg and vanilla; mix well. Pour evenly over baked crust.

3. Combine reserved crumb mixture and walnuts; sprinkle evenly over cheese mixture. Bake 25 minutes or until bubbly. Cool. Chill. Cut into bars. Store covered in refrigerator.

Makes 24 to 36 bars

Devil's Food Fudge Cookies

1 package DUNCAN HINES® Moist Deluxe®
   Devil's Food Cake Mix
2 eggs
½ cup vegetable oil
1 cup semisweet chocolate chips
½ cup chopped walnuts

1. Preheat oven to 350°F. Grease baking sheets.

2. Combine cake mix, eggs and oil in large bowl. Stir until thoroughly blended. Stir in chocolate chips and walnuts. (Mixture will be stiff.) Shape dough into 36 (1¼-inch) balls. Place 2 inches apart on prepared baking sheets.

3. Bake at 350°F for 10 to 11 minutes. (Cookies will look moist.) *Do not overbake.* Cool 2 minutes on baking sheets. Remove to cooling racks. Cool completely. Store in airtight container.

Makes 3 dozen cookies

Tip: For a delicious flavor treat, substitute peanut butter chips for the chocolate chips and chopped peanuts for the chopped walnuts.

Easy Mini Kisses Choco-Cherry Pie

1 baked (9-inch) pie crust, cooled
1¾ cups (10-ounce package) HERSHEY'S MINI KISSES™ Semi-Sweet or Milk Chocolates, divided
1½ cups miniature marshmallows
⅓ cup milk
1 cup (½ pint) cold whipping cream
1 can (21 ounces) cherry pie filling, chilled
Whipped topping

1. Place 1 cup Mini Kisses™, marshmallows and milk in medium microwave-safe bowl. Microwave at HIGH (100%) 1½ to 2 minutes or until chocolate is softened and mixture is melted and smooth when stirred; cool completely.

2. Beat whipping cream in small bowl until stiff; fold into chocolate mixture. Spoon into prepared crust. Cover; refrigerate 4 hours or until firm.

3. Garnish top of pie with cherry pie filling, whipped topping and remaining Mini Kisses™ just before serving. Refrigerate leftover pie.

Makes about 8 servings

Double Chocolate Oat Cookies

1 package (12 ounces) semisweet chocolate pieces, divided (about 2 cups)
½ cup (1 stick) margarine or butter, softened
½ cup granulated sugar
1 egg
¼ teaspoon vanilla
¾ cup all-purpose flour
¾ cup QUAKER® Oats (quick or old fashioned, uncooked)
1 teaspoon baking powder
¼ teaspoon baking soda
¼ teaspoon salt (optional)

Preheat oven to 375°F. Melt 1 cup chocolate pieces in small saucepan; set aside. Beat margarine and sugar until fluffy; add melted chocolate, egg and vanilla. Add combined flour, oats, baking powder, baking soda and salt; mix well. Stir in remaining chocolate pieces. Drop by rounded tablespoonfuls onto *ungreased* cookie sheets. Bake 8 to 10 minutes. Cool 1 minute on cookie sheets; remove to wire rack.

Makes about 3 dozen cookies

Easy Mini Kisses Choco-Cherry Pie

White Chocolate Chunk & Macadamia Nut Brownie Cookies

1½ cups firmly packed light brown sugar
⅔ CRISCO® Stick or ⅔ cup CRISCO®
    all-vegetable shortening
1 tablespoon water
1 teaspoon vanilla
2 eggs
1½ cups all-purpose flour
⅓ cup unsweetened cocoa powder
½ teaspoon salt
¼ teaspoon baking soda
1 cup white chocolate chunks or chips
1 cup coarsely chopped macadamia nuts

1. Heat oven to 375°F. Place sheets of foil on countertop for cooling cookies.

2. Place brown sugar, ⅔ cup shortening, water and vanilla in large bowl. Beat at medium speed of electric mixer until well blended. Add eggs; beat well.

3. Combine flour, cocoa, salt and baking soda. Add to shortening mixture; beat at low speed just until blended. Stir in white chocolate chunks and macadamia nuts.

4. Drop dough by rounded measuring tablespoonfuls 2 inches apart onto ungreased baking sheet.

5. Bake one baking sheet at a time at 375°F for 7 to 9 minutes or until cookies are set. *Do not overbake.* Cool 2 minutes on baking sheet. Remove cookies to foil to cool completely.
Makes about 3 dozen cookies

Mini Morsel Meringue Cookies

Prep Time: 15 minutes
Cook Time: 20 minutes

4 large egg whites
½ teaspoon salt
½ teaspoon cream of tartar
1 cup granulated sugar
2 cups (12-ounce package) NESTLÉ®
    TOLL HOUSE® Semi-Sweet
    Chocolate Mini Morsels

PREHEAT oven to 300°F. Grease baking sheets.

BEAT egg whites, salt and cream of tartar in small mixer bowl until soft peaks form. Gradually add sugar; beat until stiff peaks form. Gently fold morsels, ⅓ cup at a time. Drop by level tablespoon onto prepared baking sheets.

BAKE for 20 to 25 minutes or until meringues are dry and crisp. Cool on baking sheets for 2 minutes; remove to wire racks to cool completely. Store in airtight containers.   *Makes about 5 dozen cookies*

White Chocolate Chunk & Macadamia Nut Brownie Cookies

Fudge-Filled Bars

Prep Time: 20 minutes
Bake Time: 25 to 30 minutes

- 1 (14-ounce) can EAGLE® BRAND Sweetened Condensed Milk (NOT evaporated milk)
- 1 (12-ounce) package semi-sweet chocolate chips
- 2 tablespoons butter or margarine
- 2 teaspoons vanilla extract
- 2 (18-ounce) packages refrigerated cookie dough (oatmeal-chocolate chip, chocolate chip or sugar cookie dough)

1. Preheat oven to 350°F. In heavy saucepan over medium heat, combine Eagle Brand, chips and butter; heat until chips melt, stirring often. Remove from heat; stir in vanilla. Cool 15 minutes.

2. Using floured hands, press 1½ packages of cookie dough into ungreased 15×10×1-inch baking pan. Pour cooled chocolate mixture evenly over dough. Crumble remaining dough over chocolate mixture.

3. Bake 25 to 30 minutes. Cool. Cut into bars. Store covered at room temperature.   *Makes 48 bars*

Helpful Hint: If you want to trim the fat in any Eagle Brand recipe, just use Eagle® Brand Fat Free or Low Fat Sweetened Condensed Milk instead of the original Eagle Brand.

Chocolate Snowball Cookies

- 1 cup (2 sticks) butter or margarine, softened
- ¾ cup packed light brown sugar
- 1 egg
- 1 teaspoon vanilla extract
- 2 cups all-purpose flour
- ½ cup HERSHEY'S Dutch Processed Cocoa or HERSHEY'S Cocoa
- 1 teaspoon baking powder
- ¼ teaspoon baking soda
- 3 tablespoons milk
- ¾ cup finely chopped macadamia nuts or almonds
- ¾ cup SKOR® English Toffee Bits
  Powdered sugar

1. Beat butter, brown sugar, egg and vanilla in large bowl until blended. Stir together flour, cocoa, baking powder and baking soda; add with milk to butter mixture until well blended. Stir in nuts and toffee.

2. Refrigerate until firm enough to handle, at least 2 hours. Heat oven to 350°F. Shape dough into 1-inch balls; place 2 inches apart on ungreased cookie sheet.

3. Bake 8 to 10 minutes or until set. Remove from cookie sheet to wire rack. Cool completely; roll in powdered sugar.   *Makes about 4 dozen cookies*

Fudge-Filled Bars

Double Chocolate Brownie Bars

½ cup (1 stick) butter or margarine
2 cups (12-ounce package) HERSHEY'S Semi-Sweet Chocolate Chips, divided
1½ cups sugar
1¼ cups all-purpose flour
3 eggs
1 teaspoon vanilla extract
½ teaspoon baking powder
½ teaspoon salt
1 cup coarsely chopped walnuts

1. Heat oven to 350°F. Grease 13×9×2-inch baking pan.

2. Place butter and 1 cup chocolate chips in large microwave-safe bowl. Microwave at HIGH (100%) 1 to 1½ minutes or until chips are melted when stirred. Add sugar, flour, eggs, vanilla, baking powder and salt; stir with spoon until smooth. Stir in remaining 1 cup chips. Spread batter into prepared pan; sprinkle walnuts over top.

3. Bake 30 minutes or until center is set. Cool completely in pan on wire rack. Cut into bars. Store tightly covered.   *Makes about 36 brownies*

Variation: Cut brownies into 3×3¼-inch squares. Serve topped with scoop of ice cream, fruit and Hershey's Syrup.

Chocolate-Lovers' Angel Food Cake

1½ cups granulated sugar, divided
¾ cup sifted cake flour
⅓ cup unsweetened cocoa powder
¼ teaspoon salt
12 egg whites
1½ teaspoons cream of tartar
1½ teaspoons vanilla
Powdered sugar (optional)

1. Preheat oven to 375°F. Sift ¾ cup granulated sugar with flour, cocoa and salt two times; set aside.

2. Beat egg whites in large bowl at medium speed with electric mixer until foamy. Add cream of tartar; beat at high speed until soft peaks form. Gradually add remaining ¾ cup granulated sugar, 2 tablespoons at a time, beating until stiff peaks form. Blend in vanilla.

3. Sift about ¼ of the cocoa mixture over egg white mixture. Fold cocoa mixture into batter. Repeat with remaining cocoa mixture. Pour into ungreased 10-inch tube pan.

4. Bake 35 to 40 minutes or until cake springs back when lightly touched. Turn pan upside-down and allow cake to cool completely before removing from pan.

5. Turn cake onto cake plate. Dust lightly with powdered sugar, if desired.

Makes one 10-inch tube cake

German Chocolate Oatmeal Cookies

¾ Butter Flavor CRISCO® Stick or ¾ cup
   Butter Flavor CRISCO® all-vegetable
   shortening plus additional for greasing
1 cup firmly packed dark brown sugar
½ cup granulated sugar
2 eggs
2 packages (4 ounces each) German
   chocolate, melted and cooled
1 tablespoon water
1¼ cups all-purpose flour
½ teaspoon baking soda
½ teaspoon salt
3 cups quick oats (not instant or
   old-fashioned)
1 cup coarsely chopped pecans
1 cup flake coconut

1. Heat oven to 375°F. Grease baking sheet with shortening. Place sheets of foil on countertop for cooling cookies.

2. Combine ¾ cup shortening, brown sugar, granulated sugar, eggs, chocolate and water in large bowl. Beat at medium speed of electric mixer until well blended.

3. Combine flour, baking soda and salt. Mix into creamed mixture at low speed until blended. Stir in oats, nuts and coconut with spoon.

4. Drop rounded tablespoonfuls of dough 2 inches apart onto prepared baking sheet.

5. Bake at 375°F for 10 minutes, or until bottoms are browned, but tops are slightly soft. Cool 2 minutes on baking sheet. Remove cookies to foil to cool completely.   *Makes about 4 dozen cookies*

Cocoa Kiss Cookies

1 cup (2 sticks) butter or margarine,
   softened
⅔ cup sugar
1 teaspoon vanilla extract
1⅔ cups all-purpose flour
¼ cup HERSHEY'S Cocoa
1 cup finely chopped pecans
   54 HERSHEY'S KISSES® Chocolates
   Powdered sugar

1. Beat butter, sugar and vanilla in large bowl until creamy. Stir together flour and cocoa; gradually add to butter mixture, beating until well blended. Add pecans; beat until well blended. Refrigerate dough about 1 hour or until firm enough to handle.

2. Heat oven to 375°F. Remove wrappers from chocolate pieces. Mold scant tablespoon of dough around each chocolate piece, covering completely. Shape into balls. Place on ungreased cookie sheet.

3. Bake 10 to 12 minutes or until almost set. Cool slightly, about 1 minute; remove from cookie sheet to wire rack. Cool completely. Roll in powdered sugar. Roll in sugar again just before serving, if desired.   *Makes about 4½ dozen cookies*

Chocolate White Chocolate Chunk Cookies

Prep Time: 15 minutes
Bake Time: 11 to 12 minutes

    2 cups flour
    2 teaspoons CALUMET® Baking Powder
    ¼ teaspoon salt
    ¾ cup (1½ sticks) butter *or* margarine,
        softened
  1½ cups firmly packed brown sugar
    2 eggs
    1 teaspoon vanilla
    4 squares BAKER'S® Unsweetened Baking
        Chocolate, melted, cooled slightly
    1 package (12 ounces) BAKER'S® White
        Chocolate Chunks
    1 cup chopped nuts (optional)

HEAT oven to 350°F.

MIX flour, baking powder and salt in medium bowl; set aside.

BEAT butter and sugar in large bowl with electric mixer on medium speed until light and fluffy. Add eggs and vanilla; beat well. Stir in melted chocolate. Gradually beat in flour mixture. Stir in chocolate chunks and nuts. Drop by heaping tablespoonfuls onto ungreased cookie sheets.

BAKE 11 to 12 minutes or until cookies feel set to the touch. Cool on cookie sheets 1 minute. Remove to wire racks and cool completely.

Makes about 3½ dozen

Storage Know-How: Store in tightly covered container up to 1 week.

Make-Ahead: After cookies are completely cooled, wrap in plastic wrap and place in an airtight plastic container or zipper-style plastic freezer bag. Cookies can be frozen for up to 1 month. Bring cookies to room temperature before serving.

Tip

To melt chocolate squares in the microwave, place unwrapped chocolate in a microwave-safe bowl. For one square of chocolate, microwave on HIGH 1 to 2 minutes or until almost melted, stirring after each minute. Remove from the microwave and stir until completely melted. Add 10 seconds for each additional square of chocolate.

Chocolate White Chocolate Chunk Cookies

Philadelphia® 3-Step® Chocolate Lover's Cheesecake

Prep Time: 10 minutes
Bake Time: 40 minutes

> 2 packages (8 ounces each)
>   PHILADELPHIA® Cream Cheese,
>   softened
> ½ cup sugar
> ½ teaspoon vanilla
> 2 eggs
> 4 squares BAKER'S® Semi-Sweet
>   Chocolate, melted, slightly cooled
> 1 OREO® Pie Crust (6 ounces)

BEAT cream cheese, sugar and vanilla with electric mixer on medium speed until well blended. Add eggs, 1 at a time, mixing on low speed after each addition just until blended. Stir in melted chocolate.

POUR into crust.

BAKE at 350°F for 35 to 40 minutes or until center is almost set. Cool. Refrigerate 3 hours or overnight.
Makes 8 servings

Mocha: Blend 3 tablespoons coffee-flavored liqueur or black coffee into batter.

Chocolate Sweetheart Pie

Prep Time: 15 minutes
Bake Time: 45 minutes

> 1 package (8 squares) BAKER'S®
>   Semi-Sweet Baking Chocolate,
>   divided
> ⅔ cup corn syrup
> 1 cup whipping (heavy) cream, divided
> 3 eggs
> 1 unbaked pie shell (9 inch)
> 2 tablespoons sugar
> ½ teaspoon vanilla
> 1 pint strawberries, sliced

HEAT oven to 350°F.

MICROWAVE 6 squares of the chocolate in large microwavable bowl on HIGH 2 minutes until almost melted, stirring halfway through heating time. Stir until completely melted.

STIR corn syrup and ½ cup of the cream into chocolate until well blended. Add eggs, 1 at a time. Pour into pie shell.

BAKE 45 minutes or until knife inserted 1 inch from center comes out clean. Cool on rack. (Center of pie will sink after cooling.)

WHIP remaining ½ cup cream. Add sugar and vanilla; beat until fluffy and fully whipped. Fill center of cooled pie. Garnish with strawberries. Melt remaining chocolate and drizzle over berries.
Makes 8 servings

Variation: Prepare as directed, substituting 1 cup thawed COOL WHIP® Whipped Topping for ½ cup of cream whipped. Omit sugar and vanilla.

Philadelphia® 3-Step® Chocolate Lover's Cheesecake

Brownie Turtle Cookies

2 squares (1 ounce each) unsweetened
    baking chocolate
⅓ cup solid vegetable shortening
1 cup granulated sugar
½ teaspoon vanilla extract
2 large eggs
1¼ cups all-purpose flour
½ teaspoon baking powder
½ teaspoon salt
1 cup "M&M's"® Milk Chocolate Mini
    Baking Bits, divided
1 cup pecan halves
⅓ cup caramel ice cream topping
⅓ cup shredded coconut
⅓ cup finely chopped pecans

Preheat oven to 350°F. Lightly grease cookie sheets; set aside. Heat chocolate and shortening in 2-quart saucepan over low heat, stirring constantly until melted; remove from heat. Mix in sugar, vanilla and eggs. Blend in flour, baking powder and salt. Stir in ⅔ cup "M&M's"® Milk Chocolate Mini Baking Bits. For each cookie, arrange 3 pecan halves, with ends almost touching at center, on prepared cookie sheets. Drop dough by rounded teaspoonfuls onto center of each group of pecans; mound the dough slightly. Bake 8 to 10 minutes just until set. *Do not overbake.* Cool completely on wire racks. In small bowl combine ice cream topping, coconut and chopped nuts; top each cookie with about 1½ teaspoons mixture. Press remaining ⅓ cup "M&M's"® Milk Chocolate Mini Baking Bits into topping.   *Makes about 2½ dozen cookies*

Fudgy Chip Bars

50 OREO® Chocolate Sandwich Cookies,
    coarsely crushed
1 cup flaked coconut
1 cup semisweet chocolate chips
¼ cup margarine or butter, melted
1 (14-ounce) can sweetened condensed milk
1 teaspoon vanilla extract

1. Combine cookie crumbs, coconut and chocolate chips in bowl. Stir in margarine or butter, condensed milk and vanilla extract. Spread into greased 9×9×2-inch baking pan.

2. Bake at 375°F for 30 minutes or until done. Cool and cut into bars.   *Makes 2 dozen bars*

Brownie Turtle Cookies

Chocolate-Coconut-Toffee Delights

½ cup all-purpose flour
¼ teaspoon baking powder
¼ teaspoon salt
1 package (12 ounces) semisweet
   chocolate chips, divided
¼ cup butter, cut into small pieces
¾ cup packed light brown sugar
2 eggs, beaten
1 teaspoon vanilla
1½ cups flaked coconut
1 cup toffee baking pieces

1. Preheat oven to 350°F. Line cookie sheets with parchment paper.

2. Combine flour, baking powder and salt in small bowl; set aside. Place 1 cup chocolate chips in large microwavable bowl. Microwave at HIGH 1 minute; stir. Microwave 30 to 60 seconds more or until chips are melted; stir well.

3. Add butter to bowl; stir until melted. Beat in brown sugar, eggs and vanilla until well blended. Beat in flour mixture until blended. Stir in coconut, toffee pieces and remaining 1 cup chocolate chips.

4. Drop dough by heaping ⅓ cupfuls onto prepared cookie sheets, spacing 3 inches apart. Flatten with rubber spatula into 3½-inch circles. Bake 15 to 17 minutes or until edges are just firm to the touch. Cool cookies on cookie sheets 2 minutes; slide parchment paper and cookies onto countertop. Cool completely.   *Makes 1 dozen (5-inch) cookies*

Philadelphia® 3-Step® Triple Chocolate Layer Cheesecake

Prep Time: 10 minutes
Bake Time: 40 minutes

2 packages (8 ounces each)
   PHILADELPHIA® Cream Cheese,
   softened
½ cup sugar
½ teaspoon vanilla
2 eggs
3 squares BAKER'S® Semi-Sweet Baking
   Chocolate, melted, slightly cooled
4 squares BAKER'S® Premium White
   Baking Chocolate, melted, slightly
   cooled
1 OREO Pie Crust (6 ounces)

BEAT cream cheese, sugar and vanilla with electric mixer on medium speed until well blended. Add eggs, 1 at a time, mixing on low speed after each addition just until blended. Stir melted dark chocolate into 1 cup of the batter. Stir melted white chocolate into remaining plain batter.

POUR dark chocolate batter into crust. Top with white chocolate batter.

BAKE at 350°F for 35 to 40 minutes or until center is almost set. Cool. Refrigerate 3 hours or overnight.
Makes 8 servings

Chocolate-Coconut-Toffee Delights

Double Chocolate Bundt Cake

1 package (about 18 ounces) chocolate cake
  mix
1 package (4-serving size) instant chocolate
  pudding mix
4 eggs, beaten
¾ cup water
¾ cup sour cream
½ cup oil
6 ounces (1 cup) semisweet chocolate chips
  Powdered sugar

1. Preheat oven to 350°F. Spray 10-inch Bundt or
tube pan with nonstick cooking spray.

2. Beat cake mix, pudding mix, eggs, water, sour
cream and oil in large bowl with electric mixer at
medium speed until ingredients are blended. Stir
in chocolate chips; pour into prepared pan.

3. Bake 55 to 60 minutes or until cake springs
back when lightly touched. Cool 1 hour in pan
on wire rack. Invert cake onto serving plate; cool
completely. Sprinkle with powdered sugar before
serving. *Makes 10 to 12 servings*

Toffee Bars

1 cup quick-cooking oats
½ cup all-purpose flour
½ cup firmly packed light brown sugar
½ cup finely chopped walnuts
½ cup (1 stick) butter or margarine, melted
  and divided
¼ teaspoon baking soda
1 (14-ounce) can EAGLE® BRAND
  Sweetened Condensed Milk
  (NOT evaporated milk)
2 teaspoons vanilla extract
2 cups (12 ounces) semi-sweet chocolate
  chips
  Additional chopped walnuts, if desired

1. Preheat oven to 350°F. Grease 13×9-inch baking
pan. In large mixing bowl, combine oats, flour,
brown sugar, walnuts, 6 tablespoons butter and
baking soda. Press firmly on bottom of prepared
pan. Bake 10 to 15 minutes or until lightly browned.

2. Meanwhile, in medium saucepan over medium
heat, combine remaining 2 tablespoons butter and
Eagle Brand. Cook and stir until mixture thickens
slightly, about 15 minutes. Remove from heat; stir
in vanilla. Pour evenly over baked crust.

3. Bake 10 to 15 minutes or until golden brown.

4. Remove from oven; immediately sprinkle chips
on top. Let stand 1 minute; spread chips while still
warm. Garnish with additional walnuts, if desired;
press down firmly. Cool completely. Cut into bars.
Store tightly covered at room temperature.
Makes 3 dozen bars

Double Chocolate Bundt Cake

Acknowledgments

The publisher would like to thank the companies and organizations listed below for the use of their recipes and photographs in this publication.

Arm & Hammer Division, Church & Dwight Co., Inc.

Blue Diamond Growers®

Cherry Marketing Institute

CHIPS AHOY!® Chocolate Chip Cookies

ConAgra Foods®

Dole Food Company, Inc.

Domino® Foods, Inc.

Duncan Hines® and Moist Deluxe® are registered trademarks of Aurora Foods Inc.

Eagle® Brand

Egg Beaters®

Equal® sweetener

Filippo Berio® Olive Oil

Grandma's® is a registered trademark of Mott's, Inc.

Hershey Foods Corporation

HONEY MAID® Honey Grahams

Keebler® Company

Kellogg Company

Kraft Foods Holdings

© Mars, Incorporated 2003

McIlhenny Company
(TABASCO® brand Pepper Sauce)

Mott's® is a registered trademark of Mott's, Inc.

Nabisco Biscuit and Snack Division

National Honey Board

Nestlé USA

Newman's Own, Inc.®

NILLA® Wafers

North Dakota Wheat Commission

OREO® Chocolate Sandwich Cookies

PLANTERS® Nuts

The Quaker® Oatmeal Kitchens

Reynolds Consumer Products, A Business of Alcoa Inc.

The J.M. Smucker Company

The Sugar Association, Inc.

Property of © 2003 Sunkist Growers, Inc.
All rights reserved

Texas Peanut Producers Board

Unilever Bestfoods North America

Washington Apple Commission

Index

METRIC CONVERSION CHART

VOLUME MEASUREMENTS (dry)

1/8 teaspoon = 0.5 mL
1/4 teaspoon = 1 mL
1/2 teaspoon = 2 mL
3/4 teaspoon = 4 mL
1 teaspoon = 5 mL
1 tablespoon = 15 mL
2 tablespoons = 30 mL
1/4 cup = 60 mL
1/3 cup = 75 mL
1/2 cup = 125 mL
2/3 cup = 150 mL
3/4 cup = 175 mL
1 cup = 250 mL
2 cups = 1 pint = 500 mL
3 cups = 750 mL
4 cups = 1 quart = 1 L

VOLUME MEASUREMENTS (fluid)

1 fluid ounce (2 tablespoons) = 30 mL
4 fluid ounces (1/2 cup) = 125 mL
8 fluid ounces (1 cup) = 250 mL
12 fluid ounces (1 1/2 cups) = 375 mL
16 fluid ounces (2 cups) = 500 mL

WEIGHTS (mass)

1/2 ounce = 15 g
1 ounce = 30 g
3 ounces = 90 g
4 ounces = 120 g
8 ounces = 225 g
10 ounces = 285 g
12 ounces = 360 g
16 ounces = 1 pound = 450 g

DIMENSIONS

1/16 inch = 2 mm
1/8 inch = 3 mm
1/4 inch = 6 mm
1/2 inch = 1.5 cm
3/4 inch = 2 cm
1 inch = 2.5 cm

OVEN TEMPERATURES

250°F = 120°C
275°F = 140°C
300°F = 150°C
325°F = 160°C
350°F = 180°C
375°F = 190°C
400°F = 200°C
425°F = 220°C
450°F = 230°C

BAKING PAN SIZES

Utensil	Size in Inches/Quarts	Metric Volume	Size in Centimeters
Baking or Cake Pan (square or rectangular)	8×8×2	2 L	20×20×5
	9×9×2	2.5 L	23×23×5
	12×8×2	3 L	30×20×5
	13×9×2	3.5 L	33×23×5
Loaf Pan	8×4×3	1.5 L	20×10×7
	9×5×3	2 L	23×13×7
Round Layer Cake Pan	8×1½	1.2 L	20×4
	9×1½	1.5 L	23×4
Pie Plate	8×1¼	750 mL	20×3
	9×1¼	1 L	23×3
Baking Dish or Casserole	1 quart	1 L	—
	1½ quart	1.5 L	—
	2 quart	2 L	—